AUTHORITY AND B

List of Figures and Tables

Figures

Tables

Preface

How does a relatively poor developing country, burgeoning with one-fifth of the world's total population, attend to the social needs and social well-being of its one billion-plus citizens? And, as we are speaking of the People's Republic of China (PRC), we must hasten to ask how its social policies and social programmes are influenced by two additional factors:

(a) The PRC is a nation founded on revolutionary principles, with current leadership bent on defending a discredited state socialist ideology while at the same time introducing capitalist practices; and

(b) It is a society with a long cultural heritage embracing social traditions that must be adapted to the demands of a modernising industrial state.

For three decades following its establishment in 1949, the PRC became a society closed to but a few outsiders. It was a period when the country's social, political and economic development could be equated with the policies of the then Chairman Mao Zedong. At the time of his failing health and subsequent death in September of 1976, a power struggle ensued for leadership. As we now know, Mao's ambitious wife, Jiang Qing and the "Gang of Four" were put down, and an enigmatic Hua Guofeng took over. But Hua's time at the top was very brief and in the manoeuvring for power, Deng Xiaoping emerged in late 1978 as the "paramount leader".

The 1980s has been called a period of "Deng Xiaoping's Reforms".[1] Others go even further to describe it as "Deng's Revolution",[2] or the "Second Revolution"[3] in China after the first one under Mao's leadership. However, whereas Mao had pushed class struggle and political movement along with a strategy of self-reliance that isolated China, Deng's priorities shifted to economic development and reform together with the acknowledgement that outside assistance would be required to help modernise the country's social and economic institutions.

Although plagued by continuing political cleavages and obscure economic direction, Deng's reforms introduced the concept of "market" into a structure based on centralised planning and resource allocation. The "socialist market economy" which emerged in the 1980s began to take on the characteristics of a pluralistic economy, with the individual family as the production unit in rural areas, and elsewhere, a mixture of enterprises organised under state, collective, and private ownership. As well, an "open door" policy brought joint ventures with foreign investors. And, seeping into the whole works have come such ideological contradictions (for an espoused socialist state) as individual responsibility, profit-making, materialistic reward, and open competition. Inevitably, these profound changes have had a major impact on the social condition of the Chinese people.

This book is about social welfare and social services in the PRC. Its focus may have been different had developments in recent history taken a different course. A North American model of professional training in social work and social welfare had appeared briefly in China during the early decades of this century.[4] However, such an approach did not take root. Social work programmes, along with most social science studies (considered as "bourgeois" sciences), disappeared from university curricula shortly after the establishment of the PRC. Reconstituted social science departments re-emerged in the early 1980s but there has been delay in reinstating social work and social welfare studies because these were considered unnecessary as well as undesirable due to perceived contradictions between social values in a socialist China and a capitalist West.

With renewed interest in the PRC in social welfare and social work training, the authors helped to launch, in 1986, a special three-year course of studies in a Chinese university that examined Western concepts and their potential application in the PRC.[5] Concomitantly, students from Hong Kong engaged in a series of research and fieldwork studies in the southern Chinese province of Guangdong, while study visits coming the other way to Hong Kong were arranged for cadres employed in various Mainland universities, training institutes, and organisations with welfare responsibilities.[6] Our activities inevitably brought us into meetings and consultations with PRC officials in the respective Ministries of Civil Affairs, Labour, and Personnel, which all deal with matters related to social welfare; and with officials in the State Education Commission which is responsible for the "Key Point" universities and colleges throughout the country that come under the jurisdiction of the central government. As we have reported elsewhere, these experiences led us to the conclusion that social welfare and social work approaches developed in the West cannot be simply applied in the PRC. Nevertheless, there are important elements in a Western-style social work curriculum that do appear to have relevance.[7]

As part of the general thrust to modernise social and economic institutions in the PRC, Chinese academics and officials involved particularly in social welfare matters have shown a great desire to establish a dialogue with foreign counterparts in order to learn from experiences in the West. For this to be effective, however, it is essential that interested outsiders have a better understanding of developments in the PRC. To provide a comprehensive account of social welfare and social services in China, and to highlight the achievements and difficulties is the primary objective of this book.

Social development and social welfare in China are subjects that have received relatively little attention from sinologists in the West. Over the years, English-language texts on China have tended to focus on the society's long history as a civilisation and culture; or on the political events related to the establishment of China as a major Communist regime; or more recently, on Chinese economic development, and on issues of human rights.

Accounts of social welfare in China published in the English language are therefore not abundant. Where important works have appeared, they are now out-dated. For example, Dixon's description of the Chinese welfare system covers a period up to 1979, and could not foresee the rapid changes wrought by economic reform in the 1980s.[8]

Some recent publications have appeared that focus on specific areas of social life and social provision. Several concentrate, for example, on issues of economic and social security provisions.[9] Others are concerned with problems particular to areas such as mental health[10]; the elderly[11]; status of women[12]; family and marriage[13]; youth[14]; inequalities[15]; neighbourhood welfare[16]; welfare values[17]; and social life.[18]

Diametrically opposing views of social welfare in the PRC are also found among the writings of outside observers. Some came away with romantic notions, portraying the PRC as "an ideal welfare society" based on such moral values as serving the people, self-help, self-reliance, and mutual help.[19] Other observers, however, were just as convinced that the Chinese social policy is regressive, or is mainly an instrument of social control.[20]

Such contradictory views are perhaps not surprising given the tendency among Westerners to envision China at times as a celestial place, and at other times as a nation of robots controlled by an autocratic ruler. A major problem in the understanding of Chinese social welfare has been a lack of basic information about the existing system of social provisions and

services, and about the societal forces that have, on the one hand, influenced social welfare development in recent decades and have, on the
other hand, created problems and contradictions that now confront the
current Chinese leadership.

To the Chinese Communist Party (CCP), social welfare is an instrument to promote economic productivity, to maintain social stability, and to
enhance the legitimacy of the Communist regime. Consequently, social
welfare in China does not have clear boundaries. Perhaps this is one reason
why there is no ministry or department under this name to be found at any
level of government. Because it is so intricately interwoven with political
and economic activities, it is difficult to fully understand the operation of
the social welfare system without an appreciation of the political-economic
systems, and vice versa.

An understanding of contemporary social welfare in the PRC must also
take into account recent developments initiated under the name of modernisation. Among the changes, rural communes established under Mao
Zedong have been replaced by a Household Responsibility System, and
priority given to the urbanisation of rural areas (intended in large part to
prevent peasants from flooding to the cities). A "socialist market economy"
now encourages some people to become wealthy. Although these changes
have brought about a general improvement in the social well-being of the
Chinese people, they have also created or intensified social inequalities
among various population groups.

Along with these profound changes, there has emerged the question of
the "Chineseness" of a modern industrialised state. To put it another way,
can China become a modern industrial state without abandoning a long and
proud cultural heritage? This is a central issue in recent debates among
Chinese intellectuals on the subject of "neo-authoritarianism", a doctrine
that incorporates a vision of a modern industrial economy operating in a
society headed by a strong central government. In the eyes of the "Big
Dragon", this vision is reinforced by the economic successes of the four
"Little Dragons" (Hong Kong, Taiwan, Singapore, and South Korea), perceived as societies imbued with Confucian values and governed by strong
authoritarian regimes.

Three themes, then, permeate the content of this book on Chinese
social welfare and social services. One is the continuing effect of social
structures established by a state socialist regime which by and large are still
in place; a second is the impact of new economic developments which are
unevenly distributed geographically and socially; and a third involves the

role of cultural traditions concerning norms of social conduct and the proper relationship between the state and its subjects.

A word needs to be said about the sources of data for this book. Information provided by Chinese officials is often coloured by political propaganda. This was particularly the case during the period of Mao's regime. Research studies by outsiders often had to rely on fieldwork carried out in Hong Kong, and interviews with persons coming out from China.[21] The situation has improved markedly over the past decade, especially after the reinstatement of social sciences in Chinese universities. There is now a growing number of studies both nationally and locally on social problems and social welfare provisions. National surveys on the well-being of urban families (1984), elderly persons (1987), the disabled (1987), and women (1990) are some outstanding examples. The findings from these studies are published in academic journals and books available to outsiders. Moreover, there is the beginning of cooperative research between Chinese and Western academics, albeit on matters that are considered to be less politically sensitive.

We have drawn on a number of sources of data for this book. These include Chinese-language publications from government annual reports, Communist Party organ newspapers and magazines, Chinese academic journals, monographs and books, along with English-language publications. (All of our reference titles are given in English. But for Chinese publications, Chinese characters are provided in the Selected Bibliography.) We have also had the good fortune of having access to fresh data produced by the research efforts of university academics and students located in Hong Kong.

The content of this book will be of specific interest to students of social welfare and social services in the PRC. Furthermore, persons with a general interest in China will also find this book useful in filling in aspects of Chinese social life and social problems that are often neglected in China studies. It is our hope that this book will contribute to a better understanding of a society that is significant not only because of its sheer size but also because the social policies of a modernising and industrialising China will have an important impact far beyond its immediate borders.

Notes

1. J. K. Fairbank, *China: A New History* (Cambridge, Mass: Belknap Press of Harvard University Press, 1992), p. 406.

2. H. E. Salisbury, *The New Emperors: China in the Era of Mao and Deng* (Boston: Little, Brown, 1992), p. 392.
3. Z. Q. Shi, "The Two Great Revolutions in the History of China", in *Supplementary Readings on the 14th Party Congress Report*, edited by the People's Publishers (Beijing: People's Publishers, 1992), pp. 51–67.
4. J. Q. Lei and S. Z. Shui, "Thirty Years' Social Service in Yanjing University", in *Status-quo, Challenge and Prospect — Collected Works of the Seminar of the Asia Pacific Association of Social Work Education*, edited by the Asia Pacific Association of Social Work Education and Sociology Department of Peking University of China (Beijing: Peking University Press, 1991), pp. 10–16.
5. R. Nann and J. Leung, *Introducing Social Work and Social Work Education in the PRC* (Hong Kong: Department of Social Work and Social Administration, University of Hong Kong, 1990).
6. V. Pearson and J. Leung (eds.), *Welfare in China: A Collection of Vignettes 1986–1989*, Monograph Series, Social Welfare in China No. 2 (Hong Kong: Department of Social Work and Social Administration, University of Hong Kong, 1992).
7. See J. Leung, "Development of Social Work Education in China: Issues and Prospects", *Asia Pacific Journal of Social Work*, 4.2 (July 1994), pp. 83–95.
8. J. Dixon, *The Chinese Welfare System 1949–1979* (New York: Praeger Publishers, 1981).
9. J. Dixon, op. cit.; J. Dixon, "China", *Social Welfare in Asia*, edited by J. Dixon (London: Croom Helm Ltd., 1985), pp. 21–65; N. Chow, *The Administration and Financing of Social Security in China* (Hong Kong: Centre of Asian Studies, University of Hong Kong, 1988); "Modernization and Social Security Reforms in China", *Asian Perspective*, 13.2 (Fall–Winter 1989), pp. 55–68; D. Davis, "Unequal Chances, Unequal Outcomes: Pension Reform and Urban Inequality", *The China Quarterly*, 114 (June 1988), pp. 223–43; "Chinese Social Welfare: Policies and Outcomes", *The China Quarterly*, 119 (September 1989), pp. 577–97; E. Ahmad and A. Hussain, "Social Security in China: A Historical Perspective", in *Social Security in Developing Countries*, edited by E. Ahmad, J. Dreze, J. Hills and A. Sen (Oxford: Clarendon Press, 1990), pp. 247–304; C. Chan, "Inequalities in the Provisions of Social and Occupational Welfare in Urban China", *Hong Kong Journal of Social Work*, xxiv (1990), pp. 1–10; J. Leung, "Social Welfare Provisions in Rural China: Mutual-help or Self-protection?" *Hong Kong Journal of Social Work*, 24 (1991), pp. 11–24; J. Kallgren, *Strategies for Support of the Rural Elderly in China: A Research and Policy Agenda*, Seminar Series No. 3 (Hong Kong: Institute of Asia-Pacific Studies, The Chinese University of Hong Kong, 1992); J. Leung, *The Transformation of Occupational Welfare in the PRC: From a Political Asset to an Economic Burden* (Hong Kong: Department

of Social Work and Social Administration, University of Hong Kong, 1992); C. Chan and N. Chow, *More Welfare After Economic Reform? Welfare Development in the PRC* (Hong Kong: Centre of Urban Planning and Environmental Management, University of Hong Kong, 1993); N. Chow, *Social Security Reform in China: An Attempt to Build up a Socialist Social Security System with Chinese Characteristics*, Monograph Series, Social Welfare in China No. 4 (Hong Kong: Department of Social Work and Social Administration, University of Hong Kong, 1994).

10. T. Y. Lin and L. Eisenberg (eds.), *Mental Health for One Billion People* (Vancouver: University of British Columbia, 1985); W. S. Tseng and D. Wu (eds.), *Chinese Culture and Mental Health* (London: Academic Press, 1985); V. Pearson, "Making a Virtue of Necessity: Hospital as Community Care for the Mentally Ill in China", *International Social Work*, 32 (1989), pp. 163–78; "The Community and Culture: A Chinese Model of Community Care of the Mentally Ill", *The International Journal of Social Psychiatry*, 38.3 (1992), pp. 163–78.

11. A. E. Sher, *Aging in Post Mao China* (Boulder, Col.: Westview Press, 1984); P. Olsen, "A Model of Elderly Care in PRC", *International Aging and Human Development*, 24.4 (1987), pp. 279–300; A. Sankar, "Gerontological Research in China: The Role of Anthropological Inquiry", *Journal of Cross-Cultural Gerontology*, 4 (1989), pp. 199–224; D. Davis-Friedmann, *Long Lives: Chinese Elderly and the Communist Revolution* (Stanford: Stanford University Press, 1991); N. Chow, "Does Filial Piety Exist Under Chinese Communism", *Journal of Aging and Social Policy*, 3.1 (1991), pp. 209–25; M. Tracy, *Social Policies for the Elderly in the Third World* (New York: Greenwood Press, 1991), pp. 39–59; P. Kwong and G. X. Cai, "Ageing in China: Trends, Problems and Strategies", in *Ageing in East and South-East Asia*, edited by D. Phillips (London: Edward Arnold, 1992), pp. 105–27; C. Y. Zhu and Q. Xu, "Family Care of the Elderly in China: Changes and Problems", in *Family Care of the Elderly, Social and Cultural Changes*, edited by J. Kosberg (Newbury Park: Sage Publications, 1992), pp. 67–81.

12. E. Croll, *Chinese Women Since Mao* (London: Zed Books, 1983); *Women and Rural Development in China* (International Labour Office, 1985); M. Wolf, *Revolution Postponed: Women in Contemporary China* (Stanford: University of Stanford Press, 1985); E. Honig, and G. Hershatter, *Personal Voices: Chinese Women in the 1980's* (Stanford, Cal.: Stanford University Press, 1988).

13. E. Croll, *The Politics of Marriages in Contemporary China* (London: Cambridge University Press, 1981); *China's One-child Family Policy* (London: Macmillan, 1985); J. Stacey, *Patriarchy and Socialist Revolution in China* (Berkeley: University of California Press, 1983); J. Leung, *Family Mediation with Chinese Characteristics: A Hybrid of Formal and Informal Service in*

China, Monograph Series, Social Welfare in China No. 1 (Hong Kong: Department of Social Work and Social Administration, University of Hong Kong, 1991); M. Whyte, *From Arranged Marriages to Love Matches in Urban China*, University Seminar Series No. 5 (Hong Kong Institute of Asia-Pacific Studies, The Chinese University of Hong Kong, 1992); D. Davis (ed.), *Chinese Families in the Post-Mao Era* (Berkeley: University of California Press, 1993).

14. A. Liu, "Opinions and Attitudes of Youth in the PRC", *Asian Survey*, 24.9 (1984), pp. 975–95; I. Epstein, *Juvenile Delinquency and Reformatory Education in Chinese Society* (Berkeley: University of California Press, 1984); B. Hooper, "The Youth Problem: Deviations from the Socialist Road", in *China: Dilemmas of Modernisation*, edited by G. Young (London: Croom Helm, 1985), pp. 189–236; S. Rosen, "Prosperity, Privatisation, and China's Youth", *Problems of Communism* (March/April 1985), pp. 1–20; "The Impact of Reform Policies on Youth Attitudes", in *Chinese Society on the Eve of Tiananmen*, edited by D. Davis and E. Vogel (Cambridge, Mass.: Harvard University Press, 1990), pp. 283–305; "Youth and Social Change in the PRC", in *Two Societies in Opposition: The Republic of China and the People's Republic of China After Forty Years*, edited by R. Myers, (Stanford, Cal.: Hoover Institution Press, 1991), pp. 288–315; N. P. Ngai, "Youth Work in China: A Case Study", *Social Work*, 39.1 (January 1994), pp. 90–96.

15. M. Selden, *The Political Economy of Chinese Development* (Armonk, N.Y.: M. E. Sharpe, 1988), pp. 137–60; M. Whyte, "The Politics of Life Chances in the People's Republic of China", in *Power and Policy in the PRC*, edited by Y. M. Shaw (Boulders, Col.: Westview Press, 1985), pp. 244–65; "Social Trends in China: The Triumph of Inequality?" in *Modernizing China*, edited by A. D. Barnett and R. Clough (Boulders, Col.: Westview, 1986), pp. 103–24.

16. B. H. Mok, "Grassroots Organising in China: The Residents' Committee as a Linking Mechanism", *Community Development Journal*, 23.3 (July 1988), pp. 164–69; E. L. Ko, "Mobilization of Community Energy in China — A Case Illustration: Wah Nam Sai Street", *Community Development Journal*, 23.3 (July 1988), pp. 170–75; J. Leung, "The Community-based Welfare System in China", *Community Development Journal*, 25.3 (July 1990), pp. 196–205; C. Chan, *The Myth of Neighbourhood Mutual Help* (Hong Kong: Hong Kong University Press, 1993).

17. B. H. Mok, "In the Service of Socialism: Social Welfare in China", *Social Work* (July/August 1983), pp. 269–72; N. Chow, "Western and Chinese Ideas of Social Welfare", *International Social Work*, 30 (1987), pp. 31–41; J. Leung, "Authoritarianism in Chinese Societies: Implications for Social Work", in *Conference on Social Work Education in Chinese Societies: Existing Patterns and Future Development*, edited by Asia and Pacific Association for Social

Work Education (Asian and Pacific Association for Social Work Education, 1994), pp. 30–36.

18. W. Parish and M. Whyte, *Urban Life in Contemporary China* (Chicago: University of Chicago Press, 1984); D. Davis and E. Vogel (eds.), *Chinese Society on the Eve of Tiananmen* (Cambrdige: Harvard University Press, 1990); A. Watson (ed.), *Economic Reform and Social Change in China* (London: Routledge, 1992).

19. J. Horn, *Away with All Pests* (New York: Monthly Review Press, 1969); I. Ascher, *China's Social Policy* (London: Anglo-Chinese Educational Institute, 1972); R. Sidel, *Women and Child Care in China* (New York: Hill and Wong, 1972); *Families of Fengsheng: Urban Life in China* (Hammondsworth, Middlesex: Penguin Books, 1974); V. Sidel and R. Sidel, *Serve the People* (New York: Josiah Macy Jr. Foundation, 1973); M. H. Bacon, "Social Work in China", *Social Work*, 20.1 (January 1975), pp. 68–69.

20. B. Deacon, *Social Policy and Socialism: The Struggle for Socialist Relations of Welfare* (London: Pluto Press, 1983); N. R. Lardy, *Agriculture in China's Modern Economic Development* (Cambridge: Cambridge University Press, 1983); L. Travers, "Agriculture in China's Modern Economic Development", *The China Quarterly*, 98 (June 1984), pp. 241–59; A. Liu, *How China Is Ruled* (Englewood Cliff: N.J.: Prentice Hall, 1986).

21. For examples, see L. Pye, *The Dynamics of Chinese Politics* (Cambridge, Mass.: Oelgeschlager, Gunn and Hain Publishers, 1981); M. K. Whyte, *Small Groups and Political Rituals in China* (Berkeley, Cal.: University of California Press, 1974); W. Parish and M. Whyte, *Village and Family in Contemporary China* (Chicago: University of Chicago Press, 1978); W. Parish and M. Whyte, *Urban Life in Contemporary China* (Chicago: University of Chicago Press, 1984).

Introduction:
Approaches to Understanding Chinese
Social Welfare

The term "social welfare" does not appear in traditional Chinese literature. Ancient writings speak of "relief" (*jiuji*); or "civil affairs" (*minzheng*) which refer to assistance provided for the well-being of civilians in such wide-ranging matters as natural disasters, help in building irrigation works, care for the elderly, and control over the price of essential commodities such as grain, salt, and precious metals. Nowadays, governmental publications in the People's Republic of China (PRC)[1] use the term *shehui fuli*. Literally, *shehui* means "society"; *fuli* refers to "happiness" or an equivalent to "benefits". Social welfare, therefore, may be loosely translated in Chinese to mean "happiness and benefits provided by society".

In modern nations, social welfare is seen to perform three important functions: to meet the basic needs of disadvantaged citizens through the provision of a "safety net"; to reduce inequality resulting from extreme disparities between the rich and the poor; and, as a further benefit arising from these functions, to serve as a mechanism for social integration.[2] Social programmes have evolved and expanded over the years to include a range of provisions in cash, in kind, or in services administered under such auspices as health, education, housing, income maintenance, and personal social services. As governments took on an increasingly significant role, the study of social welfare among social scientists in the West came to focus on the concept of the welfare state.

Much has been written about the welfare state, both *pro* and *con*, depending upon the writer's political ideology, but in recent years, the concept itself has come under re-examination. This has occurred for a number of reasons. Undoubtedly, one has been a reaction to cutbacks and retrenchments in social programmes as a consequence of economic downturns and huge government deficits among Western societies in the 1980s and the 1990s. Another motivation has come from the election during this same period of governments that seem set on dismantling state welfare.

Yet a further reason may be a greater measure of analytical sophistication in the scientific study of social welfare.

Recent literature in the field is contemplating such notions as the "privatisation" of social welfare;[3] and the development of a "mixed economy" model in which the responsibility for social welfare is shared between and among individuals, private sponsors, and the government.[4] As Walker observed:

> There is a discernable general shift from state dominated provision towards more mixed and pluralistic forms, and change in the dominant ideology of welfare in some countries in which social rationales are displaced, to some extent, by market ones.[5]

In some constituencies, social welfare has even come to include profit-making enterprises.[6] Even though there is a general convergence towards welfare pluralism among industrialised nations, their institutional characteristics or models of pluralism can still be markedly different.[7]

Among Chinese intellectuals, social welfare is not a well-developed subject of study. Indeed, social sciences in general were not partitioned off as separate disciplines in traditional Chinese literature, despite the fact (or perhaps because of the fact) that social behaviour, and especially norms of social conduct, were of central concern to classical schools of thought such as Confucianism, Taoism, and Buddhism.

In the PRC, the scientific study of social welfare has also been delayed because embryonic social science disciplines were suspended for almost thirty years in the university curriculum, and because social welfare is so interwoven with the political economy in Communist China. There are no clear boundaries demarcating social welfare in the PRC. No government department carries such a title, and it is rare to find such a designation among organisations in the community at large.

A term corresponding to "social security" (*shehui baozhang*) is often used today in the PRC to refer to measures of social protection and social provision. A former Head of the Ministry of Civil Affairs (MCA), which includes among its responsibilities functions associated with social welfare departments in Western governments, has defined social security to include four programmes:[8]

    (a) Social insurance: occupational and state social security programmes covering the loss of income in contingencies, such as old age, unemployment, maternity and injury.

    (b) Social welfare: collective welfare provided by work units to their employees and by the state to citizens on the promotion of material and spiritual civilisation. In addition, community services and the work of civil affairs in such areas as welfare factories and welfare institutions for the elderly and disabled are included.

(c) Social relief: relief services for the destitute, the poor and victims of natural disasters.

(d) Preferential treatment: relief services for disabled members of the armed forces, and pensions for families of martyrs.

In addition to the provisions and services covered under the label of social security, the PRC has developed a system of state subsidies for essential commodities and public services. Subsidies can take the form of cash allowances to help cover the costs of such items as food, fuel, and transportation. In addition, there are the "hidden subsidies"; so called because they do not involve direct transfer payments. Rather, they arise from state control of both production and consumption, which in turn allows for the centralised collection and allocation of resources. As both a "buyer" and a "seller" of essential goods and services, the government is able to manipulate prices so as to provide what amounts to subsidies in areas where these are deemed necessary.

For employees in State-owned enterprises (SOE), it is estimated that in the year 1992, cash benefits from visible subsidies made up some 23.8 per cent of the worker's income.[9] This proportion would of course be significantly higher if "invisible subsidies" are included but these benefits to individuals would be hard to measure in terms of dollars.

Statements by Chinese leaders on social welfare may refer to two different conceptions of welfare. One refers broadly to social policies and social benefits which promote the general well-being of people such as, for example, a policy of full employment and price control. The other conception refers more narrowly to ameliorative measures for persons seen as not economically productive, such as relief for those who have no job, no family, and no income. These two conceptions correspond generally to what the American social scientist, Nathan Glazer has termed "Welfare I" and "Welfare II". Presumably, the more that can be accomplished under Type I Welfare to promote the general well-being of society, the less the need for Type II Welfare.[10]

The PRC is today undergoing rapid change. This is occurring at a juncture when policies of reform and modernisation have not as yet been institutionalised and the basic structure of a socialist regime remains in place. An understanding of social welfare in China at this time must take into account the existing provisions and subsidies (which may be subsumed under Type I Welfare) as well as programmes and services of an ameliorative nature (i.e., Type II Welfare). This is the perspective taken in this book.

China As a State Socialist Society

Since the PRC espouses a state socialist ideology, it is appropriate to analyse its social welfare development according to Marxist concepts and from the experiences of other socialist countries. Socialist theory gives high priority to economic development as the means to transform the whole society. Therefore, social development is part of general economic progress. Faster economic growth is believed to ultimately entail a more favourable social development.[11]

Most state socialist countries are regarded as transitional societies on the road to communism which will be reached at some unspecified future time. They are also called Leninist regimes, as it was Lenin who worked out a system of rule by communist revolutionaries after they had taken power. In fact, until their collapse, most state socialist countries had followed the Soviet Union as their model of nation building and national development.[12] They shared similarities not only in their totalitarian political system based on one party rule and the command economy based on central planning, but also in social policy committed to an egalitarian ideology.

Generally speaking, it is expected that a socialist country is characterised by a centrally planned, egalitarian, and universal social policy. Accordingly, the state assumes an overriding responsibility for social provision, with benefits distributed primarily on the basis of need, rather than on an ability to pay. Ideally, under a socialist social policy, the users of social services are "not merely citizens entitled to a basic minimum of civilised existence under the auspices of the state but rather members of a socialist community whose needs are to be met to the fullest possible."[13] The welfare system is considered as a social contract between the socialist regime and its people. The latter accept the regime, and in return the government vows to provide a comprehensive welfare system.[14]

As noted by the Hungarian policy analyst, Ferge, the crucial underpinning of a socialist social security system is the replacement of a work-income connection with a needs-responsibility obligation:

> Social policy under socialist conditions is called to assert the principle of the un-
> conditional right to survive of every individual, independently of the individual's
> contribution or achievement ... the direct connection between production and

distribution, between performance and reward, between what one gives and what one takes is severed.[15]

Compared with advanced capitalist societies, socialist countries, despite lower levels of economic development, did apparently show greater commitment to promote Type I social welfare by directly or indirectly subsidising the provision of basic social needs such as food, health care, education, cultural services, housing and transport. There also seemed to be a commitment to devote more resources to the poor to reduce inequalities and promote national solidarity.[16] However, other studies indicated the existence of inequalities even in socialist countries.[17] As Deacon and Szalai criticised the social policy in Hungary before the collapse of communism:

> What social policy today gives its subjects are the many irritating, humiliating and painful experiences of unfairness, defencelessness and chronic shortage. Social policy has come to be associated with widely unsatisfied needs, of unacceptable bureaucratic regulations, of haphazard provision of services at more and more unacceptable levels.[18]

The collapse of communism in Eastern Europe and the disintegration of the former Soviet Union in the late 1980s have posed a serious challenge to the relevance of socialist welfare. Market-oriented economic reforms in the former socialist regimes have brought into the social welfare sector such developments as cost accounting, fee charging, removal of state subsidies, and privatisation. But even prior to the 1980s, one of the limitations in applying a state socialist theory of development to the PRC is the fact that, just as differing types of social welfare systems exist among capitalist societies, differing developments could be found among state socialist societies.[19] Within the Eastern European countries, for example, there is no uniform pattern of social policy and programmes. They vary significantly according to individual historical conditions, level of economic development and demographic structure.[20]

Within the PRC itself, recent developments reveal that a state socialist ideology has failed to bring about an egalitarian society with the economic achievements promised by Marx. Indeed, Deng Xiaoping's reforms and the movement to introduce a "socialist market economy" make it clear that the Chinese leadership is abandoning the Leninist model of state ownership and central planning, and is moving to introduce a free-market economy. However, legacies of a classical state socialism remain such as, a strong autocratic government, "top-down" reforms, a structure of collectivities, and to some extent, egalitarian ideals. The ideas of reform and modernisation however, are now predominant which suggest, for our purposes, another possible line of enquiry.

China As a Modernising Nation

There is general agreement that China is a developing country and, since the so-called "Deng's Revolution" adopted in the late 1970s, it is a country that is committed to modernisation and industrialisation. It would appear, therefore, that theories of industrialisation and modernisation might provide a useful paradigm for the purpose of understanding Chinese social welfare.

Modernisation theories are primarily based on an economic perspective popular in the 1950s and 1960s when reconstruction following the Second World War stressed capital-intensive industrialisation, the rapid commercialisation of agriculture, heavy infrastructural investments and the transformation of traditional values as the appropriate strategy for achieving self-sustaining economic growth, especially in "Third-world" or developing countries.[21] This approach brushes aside the role of political ideology and posits instead a direct relationship between social welfare and the level of industrialisation and technological development achieved by a country. Statutory social service provisions emerge in response to the social problems created by industrialisation and the disintegration of traditional forms of support. Social provision, and the emergence of welfare states is the eventual and inevitable consequence.

The application of this approach to an international level, and especially its application to developing countries, has produced what some have called a "convergence theory."[22] A term derived from biology, convergence refers to organisms without obvious relations which, in the process of adapting to similar environmental conditions, will gradually move towards similarity in characteristics and functions. The application of this theory to societal development is spelled out by Wilensky, one of the main proponents of "convergence":

> Economic growth and its demographic and bureaucratic outcomes are the root cause of the general emergence of the welfare state.... Such heavy brittle categories as "socialist" versus "capitalist" economics, "collectivist" versus "individualistic" ideologies, or even "democratic" versus "totalitarian" political systems ... are useless in explaining the origins and general development of the welfare state.[23]

Under the paradigm of "the end of ideology", writers such as Bell, Galbraith, Kerr et al., and Lipset, strongly supported the role of technological and industrial development in the transformation of societies towards a better world, marked by the abolition of conflict and deprivation, the destruction of totalitarianism, and the domination of welfare ideologies over the quest for profit.[24] Despite the existence of diversified forms of welfare in advanced capitalistic societies, unity is regarded as the dominant theme. Therefore, all modern societies would face similar problems, and the solutions and responses are determined by the level of industrialisation, economic affluence, and demographic factors rather than by ideological or cultural elements.

The theory strongly implies that social and economic progress in developing countries should be modelled after Western capitalist societies in North America and Western Europe. Any changes moving in this direction would then be considered as "normal" and "modernised". This raises a major problem in attempting to apply the convergence approach to a developing country in other parts of the world. Western definitions of social development and social problems more often than not reflect value assumptions that are not shared by a society such as China. Furthermore, a unitary theory that restricts societal development to economic technology would fly in the fact of recent research findings that illuminate some basic differences in social welfare development among Western capitalist states. Esping-Andersen, for example, identified three types of welfare state regimes ("social-democratic" exemplified by Scandinavian countries, "corporatist conservative" involving Continental European nations such as Germany, France and Italy, and "liberal" regimes involving the United States and nations with Anglo-saxon backgrounds).[25] The reasons for their differences are attributed to a combination of factors including ideology, political power, and a nation's particular historical legacy.

Undoubtedly, industrialisation and modernisation in China have brought benefits and problems similar to those of other nations at a comparable level of development. However, modernisation theories do not take into account some unique aspects of social development in a society still under the strong influence of cultural traditions.

China As a Chinese Society

A recent publication by Wang Gungwu is entitled, *The Chineseness of China*.[26] This curious phrase is not meant to be simply an aphorism. Rather, it refers in part to a capacity to absorb foreign ideas and to transform them into something distinctively Chinese. This phenomenon is a familiar one to sinologists. We would use, as one example, Spence's observations of Western experts who were employed as advisors in China from the 1620s to the 1950s:

> Despite the range of their expertise — among (them) were astronomers, soldiers and doctors, administrators, translators, engineers and even one professional revolutionary organizer — and despite the more than three centuries that their works span, their cumulative lives have a curious continuity. They experienced excitement and danger, entertained similar hopes, learnt to bear with similar frustrations, and operated with a combination of integrity and deviousness. They bared their own souls and mirrored their own societies in their actions, yet in doing so they highlighted fundamental Chinese values.[27]

Identity is a large part of it. In analysing political development in the PRC, Ogden found that on occasions when socialist values clashed with Chinese values, it was the former that gave way:

> In fact, the leadership seems far more willing to sacrifice socialist values than Chinese cultural values in the pursuit of development. If we pose the question of what is the most crucial element in a Chinese person's identity, what is a Chinese person most afraid of losing, it would be his or her Chineseness. "I am a Marxist" has a hollow ring. "I am a modern person" defies reality. But "I am a Chinese" speaks to a fundamental identity.[28]

China is acknowledged as a society with a long and unbroken continuity. Described as "a very past-conscious society",[29] it is important to ask what China is changing from as much as what it is changing to. In its current struggles over problems of modernisation, one might even conclude that it is a country with too much history. But this would be cynical as a long heritage cannot be equated with changelessness; indeed, endless volumes can be written about transitions and transformations that have occurred in a civilisation that goes back over three thousand years or so. Throughout these changes, there has persisted some fundamental values that contribute to the continuity of a part of the world that we can legitimately refer to as "the Chinese society". However, cultural traditions alone cannot explain its course of development in modern times. These same traditions were present when a Nationalist Government came to power under Chiang Kai-shek after the collapse of the Imperial Qing dynasty. And Chiang's regime, as we know, failed to bring about the unification and modernisation of the country, and gave way to a communist government.

Organisation of the Book

In the first three chapters we discuss the factors that have influenced social welfare development in China. They are, respectively: historical legacies of a culture that goes back thousands of years; Marxist-Leninist thought that came to China with the establishment of the PRC in 1949; and economic reforms since 1978 that are aimed at modernisation of China's institutions.

In Chapters 4 through 7 we examine the main elements of China's social welfare system, namely: employment-based welfare in state-owned enterprises, neighbourhood-based welfare in the cities, locality-based welfare in the rural areas, and the role of the government's Ministry of Civil Affairs which administers public welfare as one of its primary functions.

In Chapter 8 we discuss the benefits of economic reform in terms of social development and the general improvement of living standards in present-day China. We also identify systemic problems that have appeared as the PRC attempts to move from a state-controlled economy to a market-oriented system.

Chapter 9 looks at the impact of economic reform on the Chinese people, identifying disadvantaged groups who have not benefitted from economic reform.

In the concluding chapter, we summarise the major changes in social welfare strategies from the early days of Chinese Communist rule to the present day, and look at current attempts at social welfare reform. As the Chinese leaders grope for models to guide their economic and social development, there is a discernable shift away from Western influences to a fascination with the economic and developmental success of other Asian societies with Confucian backgrounds.

Notes

1. The official meaning of the PRC consists of the Mainland, Taiwan, Hong Kong, and Macau. In this book, the term "PRC" is used inter-changeably with the term "China", and refers to the Mainland.
2. N. Gilbert and B. Gilbert, *The Enabling State: Modern Welfare Capitalism in America* (New York: Oxford University Press, 1989), pp. 5–6.
3. See J. Le Grand and R. Robinson (eds.), *Privatization and the Welfare State* (London: George, Allen and Unwin, 1984); E. Papadakis and P. Taylor-Gooby, *The Private Provision of Public Welfare* (Sussex: Wheatsheaf Books, Ltd., 1987); S. Kammerman and A. Kahn, *Privatization and the Welfare State* (Princeton, N.J.: Princeton University Press, 1989).

4. See S. Hatch and J. Mocroft, *Components of Welfare* (London: Bedford Square Press, 1983); N. Johnson, *The Welfare State in Transition: The Theory and Practice of Welfare Pluralism* (Amherst: University of Massachusetts Press, 1987); Gilbert and Gilbert, op. cit.

5. A. Walker, *Community Care in Western Europe and the New Challenges* (Hong Kong: Department of Social Work and Social Administration, University of Hong Kong, 1992), p. 2.

6. N. Glazer, "Welfare and Welfare in America", in *The Welfare State East and West*, edited by R. Rose and R. Shiratori (New York: Oxford University Press, 1986), p. 51.

7. R. Pinker, "On Rediscovering the Middle Way to Social Welfare", in *The State and Social Welfare, The Objective of Policy*, edited by T. Wilson and D. Wilson (London: Longman, 1991), pp. 280–300.

8. N. F. Cui, *Explorations in the Work of Civil Affairs* (Beijing: People's Press, 1988), pp. 162–63.

9. SSB, *China Statistical Yearbook* (Beijing: China Statistical Publishers, 1993), p. 127.

10. N. Glazer, op. cit., pp. 48–80.

11. J. Dixon and D. Macarov, *Social Welfare in Socialist Countries* (London: Routledge, 1992), pp. 1–8.

12. World Bank, "China: The Economic System", in *The Chinese: Adapting the Past, Building the Future*, edited by R. Dernberger, K. De Woskin, S. Goldstein, R. Murphey, and M. Whyte (Ann Arbor, Michigan: Center for Chinese Studies, The University of Michigan, 1986), pp. 485–97.

13. R. Mishra, *Society and Social Policy* (London: Macmillan, 1977), p. 124.

14. J. Adam (ed.), *Economic Reforms and Welfare Systems in the USSR, Poland and Hungary, Social Contract in Transformation* (London: Macmillan, 1991), p. xi.

15. Z. Ferge, *A Society in the Making: Hungarian Social and Societal Policy 1945–75* (Harmondsworth: Penguin, 1979), p. 55.

16. Ferge, op. cit.; J. R. Townsend, *Politics in China* (Boston: Little, Brown, 1980); V. George and N. Manning, *Socialism, Social Welfare and Soviet Union* (London: Routledge, Kegan and Paul, 1980); B. Page, *Who Gets What From Government* (Berkeley: University of California Press, 1983); C. Taylor and D. Jodice, *World Handbook of Political and Social Indicators* (New Haven, CT: Yale University Press, 1983); R. Morris, *Rethinking Social Welfare: Why Care for the Strangers* (New York: Longman, 1986).

17. I. Szelenyi, *Urban Inequalities under State Socialism* (Oxford: Oxford University Press, 1983); T. Cliff, *State Capitalism in Russia* (London: Pluto, 1974); B. Deacon, *Social Policy and Socialism: The Struggle for Socialist Relations of Welfare* (London: Pluto Press, 1983).

18. B. Deacon and J. Szalai (eds.), *Social Policy in the New Eastern Europe* (Aldershot: Avebury, 1990), p. 92.

19. G. Esping-Andersen, *The Three Worlds of Welfare Capitalism* (Cambridge: Polity, 1990).
20. Q. Y. Zhu, *Social Security System in the Soviet Union and East European Countries* (Beijing: Huaxia Publishers, 1991); Deacon and Szalai, op. cit.
21. P. Rosenstein-Roden, "Problems of Industrialization in Southern and Eastern Europe", *Economic Journal*, LIll (1943), pp. 205–11; W. Rostow, *The Stages of Economic Growth: A Non-communist Manifesto* (Cambridge: Cambridge University Press, 1960).
22. G. V. Rimlinger, *Welfare Policy and Industrialization in Europe, America and Russia* (New York: Wiley, 1971); C. Kerr, J. Dunlop, F. Harbison, and C. A. Myers, *Industrialism and Industrial Man* (Cambridge, Mass.: Harvard University Press, 1960); H. Wilensky, *The Welfare State and Equality: Structural and Ideological Roots of Public Expenditure* (Berkeley, Cal.: University of California Press, 1975); R. Mishra, op. cit., pp. 33–42; A. Kahn and A. Kammerman, *Social Services in International Perspective* (Washington: US Department of Health, Education and Welfare, 1976).
23. Wilensky, op. cit., p. xiii.
24. D. Bell, *The End of Ideology* (Glencoe, Ill.: Free Press, 1964); J. Galbraith, *The New Industrial State* (Harmondsworth: Penguin Books, 1967); *The Affluent Society* (London: Hamish Hamilton, 1969); Kerr et al., op. cit.; S. Lipset, *Political Man* (London: Heinemann, 1960).
25. Esping-Andersen, op. cit.
26. G. W. Wang, *The Chineseness of China* (Hong Kong: Oxford University Press, 1991).
27. J. Spence, *To Change China* (Boston: Little, Brown and Co., 1969), p. xiii.
28. S. Ogden, *China's Unresolved Issues: Politics, Development, and Culture* (Englewood, Cliffs, N.J.: Prentice Hall, 1989), p. 7. The attachment to this identity is not only intensive but it is also pervasive. Lucian Pye has noted:

    > The Chinese see such an absolute difference between themselves and others that even when living in lonely isolation in distant countries they unconsciously find it natural and appropriate to refer to those in whose homeland they are living as "foreigners".

    L. Pye, *The Spirit of Chinese Politics* (Cambridge, Mass.: The MIT Press, 1992), p. 56.
29. R. Murphy, "History and Geography, Introduction", in Dernberger et al., op. cit., pp. 5–36.

Abbreviations

Currency

The official currency in the PRC is yuan. In November 1994, the official exchange rate was: US$ 1 = 8.05 yuan.

Abbreviations

BR	*Beijing Review*
CCA	*China Civil Affairs*
CCP	Chinese Communist Party
COE	Collectively-owned Enterprises
CS	*China Society*
CYL	Communist Youth League
MP	*Ming Pao*
MCA	Ministry of Civil Affairs
NEZ	New Economic Zones
NPC	National People's Congress
OW	*Outlook Weekly*
PD	*People's Daily*
POE	Privately-owned Enterprises
PRC	People's Republic of China
SOE	State-owned Enterprises
SCMP	*South China Morning Post*
SEZ	Special Economic Zones
SSB	State Statistical Bureau
WF	Women's Federation

Acknowledgements

We wish to express our thanks to the Marden Foundation of Hong Kong for a generous grant which enabled Professor Nann to return to Hong Kong to work on this book. We also wish to acknowledge the assistance provided by the Department of Social Work and Social Administration at The University of Hong Kong.

Two persons who provided invaluable help with electronic data processing were Floyd Bolitho and Sander Nann. We are indebted to both.

Last but not least, we wish to thank our many friends in the People's Republic of China whose work in education and training and in social welfare administration comprise an important part of the story presented in the following pages.

J. C. B. Leung and R. C. Nann

Historical and Cultural Legacies

The various streams and strands of thought that have contributed to a Chinese view of the world are, in the mind of the historian, W. T. Chan, like parts of "an intellectual symphony in three movements":

> The first movement, from the sixth to the second century B.C., was essentially a period of development of the three major themes of Confucianism, Taoism, and Moism, and the four minor ones of Logicians, Neo-Moism, the Legalists, and Yin-Yang Interactionism, all with their contrasts and harmonies, to the accompaniment of the others of the "Hundred Schools". The second movement was characterized by the intermingling of the different motives which resolved into the dominant chord of medieval Chinese philosophy, while the note of Buddhism was introduced from India, giving it the effect of counterpoint. In the third movement, the longest of all, from the eleventh century to the present day, the characteristic notes of Chinese philosophy have been synthesized to transform the persistent chord of Confucianism into the long and unique melody which is Neo-Confucianism.[1]

It is not our intention to engage in a discourse on Chinese philosophy. However, as traditional concepts and ways of thought have an important influence in the social affairs of current-day China, we will in this opening chapter, look at those ideas and practices that have a significant bearing on contemporary social development and social welfare in the PRC.

Familism

Traditional Chinese society comprised a multitude of family groups which formed the basic unit of the social, economic, and political structure. Few secondary organisations existed outside the family to serve an individual's social needs. The Chinese family, and its extended set of blood-related kinships, operated as a self-sufficient, self-regulating and self-governing "little society" upon which one had to depend for job, education, support, and assistance in times of difficulties.[2]

The dominant principle of filial piety (*xiao*) prescribed a moral obligation upon junior members of the family to respect and to take care of their elderly parents, as expressed by a cherished saying — *lao you suo yang* (the elderly are cared for).[3] On their part, family elders were obliged to look after the welfare of other members, which included the settling of domestic disputes, disciplining non-conformists, arranging marriages and careers, assigning social and economic responsibilities, distributing income to family members, and allocating relief to those in need. The elders held what could be called an omnipotent authority. In return, junior members enjoyed complete protection and security. The continuation of this family tradition required the care of children by parents and later, the elderly parents by their grown-up children — a "feedback model" of family care, in the words of one Chinese sociologist, as contrasted with a "relay model in the West."[4]

The family in China served as the prototype of all social organisations including that of government. This stemmed from Confucian principles[5] which prescribed an hierarchical order of status and roles, and a clearly defined system of vertical relationships within society.[6] The five specific sets of relationship included: King-minister; father-son; husband-wife; older brother-younger brother (or sister); and friend-friend. Of these relationships, three are specifically family-based and blood-related, but even the other two are modelled after the family because the nation was regarded as an extension of the family order: the emperor as *tianzi* (son of Heaven); benevolent officials as *fumu guan* (parental officials who love their subjects as children); and friends as "brothers". The nation was regarded as a big family, and the family as a small nation. In fact, the

Figure 1.1. The Family-centred Network of Relationship

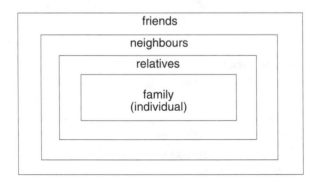

Chinese term for the state *guojia* literally means "state-family".

Traditionally, as shown in Figure 1.1, the family was put at the centre, and according to an hierarchy of relationships, one learned to relate differentially to others, depending upon their distance from the family centre. Family relationship ranked above relationship with relatives, relatives over friends, and so on:

> There are different lines in the treatment of other people. The most basic is for family members, between parents and children and among brothers, where the morality requires piety towards parents and respect for older siblings as the hallmarks of humaneness. The next line is for friends, and there the moral element stresses loyalty and trust: "When working for some you must be loyal, with friends you must be trustworthy." The tenets of Chinese morality and law all change in accordance with the degree of intimacy of the personal relationship. Because of this, in this sort of society general models of behaviour have no utility. You first evaluate who it is you are dealing with, and then you can decide what standards to use.[7]

The boundary of a family in fact could be flexible; the relational network might include colleagues at work, mates, friends and neighbours. But once formed, the obligations to care and to provide assistance to those within the social network would apply. These obligations were based on the notion of *renqing* (human feelings or human obligation) which are considered to be above man-made rules or even laws. To give somebody a *renqing* means offering assistance; the person being assisted would owe the helper a *renqing*, and is obliged to return the favour in the future. This practice, then, is a form of social exchange.

However, one was not expected to give assistance to strangers, nor vice versa. Thus, a Chinese person can be compassionate and humanistic to people within their personal family network, and inconsiderate, inhuman, and even cruel-hearted to strangers. This paradox, or inconsistency in behaviour, seems to arise from the fact that Confucianism is very vague about relationships with strangers who fall outside the five basic sets of relationships. Consequently, a Chinese person often finds it difficult to know how to relate to strangers. Moral constraints and discipline would no longer apply in relating to persons lying outside a person's social network, or living outside the Chinese society. It is in this context that Chinese people have at times been described as selfish, individualistic, and lacking unity.[8]

In describing the lack of public virtues and public spirit outside the family network, a Chinese scholar, Lu Xun, gave as an example the common occurrence in China of pedestrians not giving assistance to people falling on the ground because of illness or injury in accidents. He described it as the "spectator phenomenon" (*kanke*).[9] In all probability, this also explains the absence (until very recently) of community-wide charity drives, or general public appeals, to support health, education and welfare services in China. The people would feel no compunction to contribute to programmes that serve "strangers". The family-centred culture was reinforced by a self-sufficient agricultural economy in which one had limited mobility.[10] Inhabited usually by people with the same surname and the same clan, a natural village was governed by elected elders. Control over the village economy strengthened the authority of the elders over other members of the clan but the unity of the land-based agricultural economy required the mutual help and cooperation of every person. Thus, the collective economy held the family together as a production unit and reinforced the ideology of familism and self-reliance. This basic ideology would be echoed in the 1950s when, under Communist rule, mass collectivisation of the Chinese countryside into rural communes could only be accomplished with the ready compliance of the peasant population.

The Individual and the Collective

The family orientation of the Chinese culture has led some to the conclude that the individual is insignificant in such a system.[11] We believe this judgment is incorrect, and would concur with Mei, Fairbank and King that it comes from an inappropriate application of Western concepts of individualism.[12] Traditional Chinese society is neither individual-based nor society-based; rather, it is relation-based.[13] An individual achieves humanism through interaction with other people, especially family members.[14]

To be sure, under the collective family and clanship system, the Western idea of individualism is conspicuously absent. An individual, with his/her identity rooted in the relations, is not perceived as an independent and isolated entity but as a social being in the context of relationship with other people. Accordingly, no human could exist away from people. All moral virtues had to be practised and developed in relating with others.

Although socialisation practices stressed the cultivation of harmony and cohesiveness of the group, this did not mean there was no room for individual and private interests. Individuals were encouraged to strive for self-cultivation but this would be achieved through self-discipline and self-control, rather than self-autonomy and self-direction.[15] However, one had to realise that one's fate was intimately tied to the development of the collectives, and individual value could only materialise through collective life. Such a belief system of course could colour the meaning of such concepts as individual and civil rights, subjects that we will look at in later chapters.

Authoritarian but Minimal State

Inspired by Confucian ideals, government in traditional China operated through a centralised imperial bureaucracy administered by an officialdom of scholars (with the emperor at the top of the hierarchy). As the supreme ruler, the emperor derived his governing mandate and legitimacy to rule from "Heaven".[16] The emperor or the state in fact had virtually complete control over the population, the armies, the economy, as well as over religious communities and worship. However, the power of the Chinese emperors was limited by a vast jurisprudence made up of rites, customs, and rules of which the body of civil servants, or "mandarinate", functioned as the defender and interpreter.[17]

The concept of a professional civil service, based on competitive entrance examinations, regularised evaluations, and systematic promotions began as early as the Han dynasty (206 B.C.–A.D. 221). Opportunity for upward mobility, and recruiting and assigning people to responsible positions according to merit, rather than birth, had features of a modern civil service.

The size of the traditional civil service was small, and the government administration only reached "down" to the county level. The state, despite having absolute power over the people, usually avoided direct interference in family and local community affairs. Most affairs at the local level which concerned the day-to-day lives of the masses were left to the village elders to handle. But often, the family heads and village elders would be held responsible for the misdemeanours committed by their dependents. With limited governmental penetration into everyday society, a remote relationship existed between the state and the family. In China, the rules of conduct in the daily lives of the people were based on customs and mores rather than on state legislation.

When domestic conflicts arose, the government would support the authority of family elders over their kin.[18] In turn, leaders of local organisations would not challenge policy decisions of government. For the ordinary person, a direct contact with government officials usually occurred only when there was a problem. Thus, one avoided interaction with the state as much as possible. A colloquial Chinese saying equated going to a government office with "visiting hell".

In theory if not in practice, the role of the state on the one hand was to provide a favourable social environment for people to cultivate their morality, and on the other, to be the guardian of the moral order. The state that internalised the Confucian ethic and abided the code of proper behaviour would be a just and benevolent government. If the state failed to keep the society in a good moral order, a "crisis of faith" would ensue undermining the foundation of state power. At such times, people would have the right to rebel.

The emperor and his officials were expected to act as models of virtue for the people. Since the Han dynasty, emperors had emphasised the work of *jiaohua* (moral socialisation), and local officials had been recruited to specialise in the work of promoting cultural norms, customs and morality.[19] The Chinese did not develop impersonal standards of justice based on a system of laws. Society is governed by man and not by laws. The latter were seen as punitive instruments or as something that invites people to be tricky, and therefore are to be distrusted. Moreover, a good leader should govern by setting a good example, not by relying on laws. Indeed, a government that must rely on the application of law is not only neglecting its duty to teach and to nurture but is also admitting to moral deficiency.

Spiritualism, Secularism and Pragmatism

Not unlike people in other ancient civilisations, the Chinese also showed an interest and fascination with the spiritual and the metaphysical. Religion in China has so interwoven with the broad fabric of family and social life that there was not even a special word for it until modern times. In spite of, or perhaps because of, the unyielding secularism and social ethics of Confucianism, Taoism and Buddhism became very popular among the Chinese:

> For nearly a millennium, roughly speaking from the time of Christ, Confucianism was overshadowed by Taoism and, more fundamentally, by Buddhism. The teachings of Buddhism brought from India proved to be refreshingly interesting to the Chinese mind. It is no exaggeration to say that for the greater part of the millennium the best thinkers in China were all Buddhist thinkers.[20]

Buddhist temples and monasteries are found everywhere in China as Buddhism came to touch every aspect of Chinese society. Of the various schools, the *Chan* (or Zen in Japanese) became the most popular. For some

Chinese, the family-based practice came to be moderated by the philosophy of Buddhism which encouraged every person to show mercy to people suffering from contingencies, such as poverty or old age. It was common for monks and nuns in monasteries to provide a variety of welfare services for the destitute. According to the Buddhist principle, helping others could build up or accumulate one's fortune or virtue. By being more charitable, one could expect a better life in the future, in one's next life, and with members of the family.[21]

However, like other ideas brought to China from the outside, Buddhism eventually came to be changed and absorbed into a Chinese form:

> Buddhist philosophy created a sense of awe among the literati, but it met resistance on two levels: it threatened the idea of the family and had to be countered; it threatened the literati monopoly of power and had to be integrated some way into the bureaucratic system. We might add that Buddhism appealed to the universalist side of Confucianism and enhanced the idealism in Chinese thought. But because it also challenged the particularist core of Chinese state and society and questioned its supremacy under Heaven, it had to be either ejected or domesticated and absorbed. That China succeeded in the latter by the Tang dynasty (A.D. 618–906) underlines the inclusiveness that was a key part of Chineseness for the first thousand years of imperial history.[22]

Not all Chinese have subscribed to the ideals of familism. Indeed, the Taoist influence went in the opposite direction, and would seem to uphold notions of an individualism that would appeal to many Westerners. W. T. Chan describes the Taoist as "the most rugged individualist among the Chinese":

> He would have as little government as possible. He would not be swayed by fear of other people's opinions. He meditates on nature, not to overcome himself by it but to enjoy himself therein. Under Taoist influence nature does seem to dominate in Chinese landscape painting where the human figure is dwarfed in the shadow of majestic mountains and rivers.[23]

The sinologist, Frederick Mote identifies the key difference between Confucianism and Taoism as follows:

> To identify the issue on which the two philosophies split most clearly, Confucianism believes that a person should live in harmony with nature and other people, but that a person is a measure of Confucian values. Hence, we call it a humanism — as unequivocal as the world has known. In contrast Taoism sees a person as ideally living in harmony with nature and if necessary isolated from other people. Nature, not people, is the touchstone of Taoist values. Hence, we would call it naturalism — and certainly an extreme one.[24]

The basic philosophy of Taoism is for each person to find his or her own way to live in harmony with nature. Confucianists considered Taoism (and Buddhism) as impractical, selfish and self-serving. Taoists in turn saw Confucianists as busy-bodies, meticulously observing and preaching rituals and forms that were considered by the former as nothing more than artificial devices.

Confucianism however remained the dominant and the mainstream philosophy in China. Often called the "civil religion",[25] it is a philosophy of the "here and now", stressing ethics aimed at solving immediate problems. It is practical rather than theoretical or metaphysical because it is concerned with practical matters. To Confucians, a virtue lacks meaning unless it is practised. Wisdom or intelligence, for example, is not merely the possession of knowledge but the ability to translate understanding into action. There is little speculation about the unreal or the impractical, and little interest in things that are too far removed from everyday practical life.

The foundations of Confucianism are secular; moral principles derive no authority from some supernature power but are self-justifying and self-obvious, or capable of being discovered by a wise person. Virtue is its own reward. People are not to be ethical for the sake of going to Heaven or to save their souls. Rather, people were ethical because it was their nature to be so. Persons who are ethical for the sake of some reward are considered as selfish.[26]

As family and religion were inseparable, the practice of ancestor worship made religion in China more a family matter than an individual choice. Ancestor worship was practised in most villages, and the ceremonies and rituals reinforced individual loyalty to the lineage and kinship group.

Education and Social Status

Language and education are intrinsic parts of any civilisation. Perhaps the one indicator that best reflects the richness of the Chinese civilisation is its written language which, according to available artifacts, goes back at least to about 1500 B.C. as a starting point.

Although ancient civilisations located in the Eastern Mediterranean regions apparently developed a written language before the Chinese, none left a body of literary materials as broad in content and as rich in quantity as did the Chinese. It is this written language and the careful attention given to written records that provided an important instrument for the continuity of Chinese culture over the millennia.[27]

A reverence for education is deeply rooted in the Chinese culture, as well as the notion that learning has a social purpose in promoting the public good. At the base is probably the Confucian tenet that man is perfectible, and that learning and knowledge is the route to self-realisation.

Confucius is credited with three innovations which did much to shape the characteristics of Chinese education and civilisation:

(a) The creation of the role of a professional teacher;

(b) The establishment of a foundation for learning that we would today call a broad liberal arts education that would prepare officials to deal with a wide range of issues and problems; and

(c) The acceptance of students from all social backgrounds, from aristocracy to common and humble backgrounds. (Hence, his famous words: "In education there should be no class distinctions.")

Up to Song dynasty (A.D. 960–1279), Chinese education was very much a private matter, depending almost entirely on the individual's family background and personal opportunities. After the founding of the Song, as a strategy to contain the influence of regional military governors, the state enhanced the prestige and power of civil officials by establishing publicly-supported schools as a training ground for examination candidates.

Block printing appeared in the first half of the 8th century, chiefly in Buddhist monasteries but the technique of printing books for popular use did not become significant until Song times. Large-scale printing of books occurred in the Ming dynasty (A.D. 1368–1644). By late Ming times, not only were basic texts and references readily available to the nation but repeated reproductions of early rare and often voluminous works became available to scholars.

Under the Ming dynasty, social mobility (based on education and the civil service examination) reached a level unparalleled in Chinese history. A quota system was established in A.D. 1441 to ensure students from various provinces. The examination and academic degree system became more elaborate, and the school system truly nationwide.[28]

The Confucian state was also acknowledged to be a "physiological" state in the sense that peasants were recognised to be primary producers of wealth on whose labour the governing class depended for sustenance. Hence, peasants were entitled to take civil service examinations. Artisans and merchants, on the other hand, were regarded by the traditional Chinese state as secondary producers of wealth and as middle-men. As such they were subjected to sumptuary and discriminatory laws among which the most serious was the denial of their right of entry into the official governing class. Up to the end of the Song period, the law forbade artisans and merchants and their families to take government examinations. The common impression that Chinese society traditionally looked down upon and discriminated against artisans and merchants has persisted to modern times.

Exposure to Western schooling practices began through missionary schools founded in the third quarter of the 19th century, and about this same time, students were allowed to seek education abroad. Around the turn of the present century, a dualistic system began to emerge — modern state-controlled schools in the cities, and in the rural areas schools that more or less remained loyal to the traditional texts and methods of learning.

Health and Health Care

It is generally acknowledged that one of the most notable accomplishments of the PRC is in field of health. By emphasising preventive health care and by encouraging both traditional and modern medicine, the PRC was able to quickly turn around communicable diseases, and to increase life expectancy to a level equal to, or better than, countries with much higher per capita incomes.

Traditional medicine is still widely practised and receives strong government support. Ancient Chinese writings indicate that the development of traditional healing arts can in part be traced to a search for immortality, a concept that appears in prehistoric Chinese legends. Later, emperors became fascinated with finding an elixir which would bring "ever-lasting life in this world". The attempt to transmute base metals into gold also became part of this enterprise as it was believed that gold-making was the first step towards the attainment of immortality.[29]

Maintaining the "vital powers" of one's body is a central concept to Taoism as a way to everlasting life. Needham lists six categories of techniques employed by Taoists: respiratory, heliotherapeutic, gymnastic, sexual, alchemical or pharmaceutical, and dietary.[30] And, because of the Taoists concern with nature and the metaphysical, magic and fortune-telling became very popular.

In the history of Chinese healing arts, physicians and magicians were both respected alike — when a rational explanation for healing was found, it was called medicine; otherwise it was called magic. Modern writers date the first practice of alchemy to the 4th century B.C. The earliest book written on alchemical theory appeared during the Han dynasty in the year A.D. 142. A "Golden Age of Chinese Alchemy" followed (from approximately A.D.

400 to 700). It was during this period, if we may digress briefly, that an alchemist, in attempting to make the elixir of immortality, hit upon the inflammable nature of proto-gunpowder.

The heritage of Chinese medical and pharmaceutical science can be found today in practices such as acupuncture, use of herbs, and in the area of food and nutrition. The belief persists that every food has a *yin* or *yang* quality, and that a balanced diet is required for good health.[31] Perkins and Yusuf identify several other "noteworthy health-related characteristics of traditional Chinese eating habits":

> Water is generally boiled before it is drunk.... This tradition is linked with tea-drinking.... A great emphasis on fresh vegetables and meat is another feature of Chinese eating habits, as is the aversion to raw foods. The reliance on stir frying with high heat preserves vitamins apart from conserving fuel and cooking oil. A peasant diet, which traditionally has contained a preponderance of grain, vegetables, and tubers and only small quantities of meat and fat, has minimized the intake of cholesterol and sugar, while providing large amounts of complex carbohydrates and roughage. Modern medicine has discovered that such a diet can offer useful protection against cardiovascular and metabolic diseases. Throughout the ages, Chinese peasants have consumed very limited quantities of dairy foods and have depended on grain, legumes, and soy beans for virtually all their protein, calcium and vitamins.[32]

Traditional Chinese Social Welfare

The traditional Chinese welfare system has been largely one of mutual help based on the family, the clan, and the local neighbourhood. Nevertheless, it did not mean that the role of the state was non-existent. There were situations like natural disasters for which need for assistance extended well beyond the capacity of families; and there were people who had no family or recourse to a family for support.

In case of famine or natural calamities, state assistance could take the form of providing food, clothing, loans, resettlement, reception centres, house repair, burial of the dead, work and tax exemption.[33] Apart from humanitarian reasons, government involvement was motivated by the threat of instability and unrest that could be brought on by natural calamities.[34] A new dynasty was often born when an emperor failed to provide workable remedies to natural disasters. In addition, the services were designed to demonstrate the paternalistic concern of the emperor towards his people.

It is recorded that long before Zhou dynasty (1100–770 B.C.), the government had recognised the responsibility for the care of the destitute. The scope of work included six aspects: child protection, care of the elderly, aid to the poor, social relief, medical health, and social security.[35] Since the Zhou dynasty, it is known that pensions for retired officials had been provided by some emperors.[36]

By the Han dynasty, the state began to provide care to the elderly who had no family support. In practice, the elderly were cared by the local clans and tribes which usually owned some common land and property to finance the welfare programme. During the Tang, Song, and Ming periods (A.D. 960–1644), residential homes for the single elderly people were built by local governments, and some form of tax exemptions were given to families who provided care to their elderly people.[37]

One of the prominent forms of state relief was the store house for grain (*changping cang*). In the Han dynasty, governments at the local county and city level set up store houses which purchased grain at times when prices were low, and resold them to the poor at a low price when the market price increased. The store houses were also used for relief in times of famine.

Another type of store house was called the *yi cang*, set up in towns and cities during the Sui dynasty (A.D. 581–618). The government collected taxes or donations in the form of grain from the rich, and re-distributed to the poor in times of emergency. Yet another version known as the *she cang* was organised mainly by the local people in villages which collected grain donations from all people for relief of the poor.

By the Qing dynasty (A.D. 1644–1911), another form of institution operated by the wealthy is the *shan tang* (benevolent society) which provided a variety of services such as operating schools, providing coffins and burial services, dispensing medical care, running shelters for the poor, the aged, the handicapped, the sick, abandoned babies, and victims of natural disasters. These services were often free of charge, but limited both in number and coverage.[38] Often the services were offered only to local residents or members of the community.

During the period of the Nationalist Government (1926–1949), relief and charity work came under the responsibility of the Department of Civil Affairs of the Ministry of Internal Affairs, set up in 1928. The Department issued regulations to encourage local governments to set up relief houses to provide care to the destitute. In 1933, there was a total of over 2,000 relief organisations, most of which were non-governmental organisations.[39]

The Traditional Ideals of *Da Tong* and *Xiao Kang*

Confucius, living in the times of political chaos, conceived of the world would progress through three stages of progress: The first stage is a world of disorder; the second is that of "minor peace" (*Xiao Kang*); and the third that of "Grand Unity" (*Da Tong*). Described in the *Book of Rites*,[40] the ideal of *Da Tong* represent Confucius' conception of the highest social order. It is a world characterised by the complete absence of self-interest and self-serving:

> When the Great Way was practised, the world was shared by all alike. The worthy and the able were promised to office and men practised good faith and lived in affection. Therefore they did not regard as parents only their own parents, or as sons only their own sons. The aged found a fitting close to their lives, the robust their proper employment; the young were provided with an upbringing and the widow and widower, the orphaned and the sick, with proper care. Men had their tasks and women their hearths. They hated to see goods lying about in waste, yet they did not hoard them for themselves; they used them not for private ends. Therefore all evil plotting was prevented and thieves and rebels did not arise, so that people could leave their outer gates unbolted. This was the age of Grand Unity.[41]

In perceiving the ideal of *Da Tong* as an utopia, Confucianists considered the *Xiao Kang* as a more moderate and practical goal.[42] Under the condition of *Xiao Kang*, self-interest and selfishness still prevailed. However, social order can be achieved by establishing a system of ethics to regulate the behaviour of institutions and individuals. The notion of *Xiao Kang* again reveals the realism and the pragmatism in Confucian thought. Indeed, the description of *Xiao Kang* is a summation of Confucius philosophy. Noteworthy is that the ideal of *Xiao Kang* is now being used by the PRC as the developmental target of China in the year 2000. (See Chapter 8)

Isolation and Remoteness from Foreign Influence

Before we conclude this quick tour of Chinese history, it is important to note, as have others, the effect of the remoteness if not the isolation, of China over the millennia. Nowadays, Europeans and North Americans might consider the Atlantic as "just another river to cross" but the Pacific Ocean has been, and remains, a vast expanse that provided an effective barrier on China's eastern coastal border. Great deserts served the same function in the northwest, as do lofty Himalayan mountains in the southwest.

Among the ancient civilisations, China undoubtedly was the most isolated from the others. Physical isolation coupled with the agrarian economy built up a culture of self-sufficiency. China, meaning the "middle kingdom", came to regard itself as the centre of the world, and foreigners as barbarians. This does not mean there was no contact, or China rejected influences from outside. Indeed, those who have investigated the substance of early Chinese science came to the conclusion that significant scientific interchange must have occurred between China and her neighbours, but not enough to erode the indigenous civilisation or threaten the political order. In his monumental work on Chinese science, Joseph Needham put it this way:

> It is probable that our final conclusion will be that there was far more intercourse between the Chinese and their western and southern neighbours than has often been supposed, but nevertheless, that the essential style of Chinese thought and culture patterns maintained a remarkable and perennial autonomy. This is the real meaning of the "isolation" of China; contacts there were, but never abundant enough to affect the characteristic style of the civilisation, and hence its science.[43]

The "other side" of isolation or remoteness is the development over several millennia of a great civilisation built on one's own resources. Given such a background, a policy of "self-reliance" and "self-sufficiency" as espoused by CCP leaders after coming to power is very consistent with traditional Chinese thinking and action, and thus cannot be taken simply as rhetoric. And, as we shall see later, the concept of self-reliance has significant implications for social development and social welfare in the PRC.

Notes

1. W. T. Chan, "The Story of Chinese Philosophy", in *The Chinese Mind*, edited by C. Moore (Honolulu: University of Hawaii Press, 1986), p. 31.

2. A. King and K. Bond, "The Confucian Paradigm of Man: A Sociological View", in *Chinese Culture and Mental Health*, edited by W. S. Tseng and D. Wu (London: Academic Press, 1985), pp. 29–45.

3. According to the *Scripture of Filiality* by Confucius, a son has to perform the following duties:

> In serving his parents the filial son is as reverent as possible to them while they are living. In taking care of them he does so with all possible joy; when they are sick he is extremely anxious about them; when he buries them he is stricken with grief; when he sacrifices to them he does so with the utmost solemnity. These five (duties) being discharged in full measure, then he has been able (truly) to serve his parents.

L. G. Thompson, *Chinese Religion: An Introduction* (Belmount, Cal.: Wadsworth Publishing Co., 1989), p. 42.

4. Fei identified two models of the parent-child relationship. For the "relay" type in the West, generation "A" takes care of generation "B" who in turn takes care of generation "C", and so forth. In the "feedback model" of China, generation "B" in addition to caring generation "C" must also support generation "A" when the latter gets old. The Chinese model forms the basis for providing support to the elderly. X. T. Fei, "Patterns and Issues of Elderly Support", in *Caring for the Elderly, Developing the Undertaking*, edited by the Policy Research Department, China National Committee on Ageing (Beijing: Science Press, 1988), pp. 112–16.

5. Confucianism is the philosophy of the school that acknowledged Confucius (551–479 B.C.) as its founder. Throughout most of Chinese history, Confucianism has been the dominant and what might be called the orthodox system of thought. Briefly stated, Confucianism has been characterised by its strong ethical sense, its emphasis on social responsibility, and its constructive, rational approach to immediate problems.

6. D. Munro, *The Concept of Man in Early China* (Stanford, Cal.: Stanford University Press, 1969), p. 23.

7. Y. F. Zheng, "Connections", in *The Chinese: Adapting the Past, Building the Future*, edited by R. Dernberger, K. De Woskin, S. Goldstein, R. Murphey, and M. Whyte (Michigan: Center for Chinese Studies, University of Michigan, 1986), p. 356.

8. A. King, "The Chinese Understanding of Privacy", *Ming Pao Monthly*, 2 (1994), pp. 56–62.

9. X. W. Zhai, "The Duality of Collective Orientation of the Chinese", *Jiang Hai Academic Journal*, 3 (1992), pp. 57–63.

10. The Confucius *Analects* prescribed that one should not travel afar when one's parents are still alive.

11. R. H. Solomon, *Mao's Revolution and the Chinese Political Culture* (Berkeley: University of California Press, 1971).

12. T. P. Mei, "The Status of the Individual in Chinese Social Thought and Practice", in *The Chinese Mind*, edited by C. Moore, op. cit., pp. 323–39; A. King, *Chinese Society and Culture* (Hong Kong: Oxford University Press, 1992); J. K. Fairbank, *China: A New History* (Cambridge, Mass.: Belknap Press of Harvard University Press, 1992).

13. S. M. Liang, *The Essence of Chinese Culture* (Taipei: Zheng Zhong Press, 1974), pp. 64–73.

14. W. T. Chan, "Chinese Theory and Practice, with Special Reference to Humanism", in *The Chinese Mind*, edited by C. Moore, op. cit., p. 319.

15. L. G. Thompson, op. cit., p. 15.

16. The Confucian concept of Heaven (*tian*) is not based on a religious notion of

some sort of paradise headed by a super-ordinate authority. Rather, it refers to the ultimate source of all nature which in the Chinese mind is part of a secular cosmos. *Tian*, in the Chinese understanding can have five different meanings: a physical *tian* (sky); a ruling *tian* (emperor); a fatalistic *tian* (fate); a naturalistic *tian* (nature); and a ethical *tian* (morality).

17. J. Gernet, "Introduction", in *Foundations and Limits of State Power in China*, edited by S. Schram (Hong Kong: The Chinese University Press, 1987), pp. xv–xxvii.

18. E. Croll, *The Politics of Marriages in Contemporary China* (London: Cambridge University Press, 1981), pp. 232–33.

19. Q. P. Yue, *The Structure of the State and the Chinese* (Hong Kong: Chung Hwa Book Co. Ltd., 1989), p. 150.

20. Y. P. Mei, "The Basis of Social, Ethical, and Spiritual Values in Chinese Philosophy", in *The Chinese Mind*, edited by C. Moore, op. cit., p. 161.

21. S. Zhang and Z. Gu, *History of Chinese Civil Affairs* (Harbin: Heilongjiang Educational Publishers, 1992), pp. 70–71.

22. G. W. Wang, *The Chineseness of China* (Hong Kong: Oxford University Press, 1991), p. 4.

23. W. T. Chan, op. cit. (1986), p. 25.

24. F. Mote, *Intellectual Foundations of China* (New York: McGraw Hill, 1989), p. 62. Mote explains that the terms are somewhat confused for us by the fact that in the West humanism promoted a romantic and idealistic view of nature, and in that pattern associated the two; in China, on the contrary, humanism and naturalism (in that special sense of idealising nature) mark the poles of philosophy.

25. Starr explains:

> Civil religion is seen as a set of beliefs, symbols, and ritual experiences that members of a society share and participate in that help to establish their identity as a group. Whereas these beliefs, symbols, and rituals may in some instances have a theological connotation, they are conceived of their adherents as distinct from beliefs, symbols, and rituals of a specific church. The collectivity united by the civil religion is broader than that of any single group of religious adherents. Just as individuals require ritual to satisfy certain psychological needs, so, similarly, a society can be said to require ritual as a binding force that brings together its members.

> J. Starr, *Ideology and Culture: An Introduction to the Dialectic of Contemporary Chinese Politics* (New York: Harper and Row, 1973), p. 33.

26. Mote attributes these attitudes to the absence of a creation myth in Chinese thought:

> ... the Chinese, among all people ancient and recent, primitive and modern are apparently unique in having no creation myth, that is, they have regarded the

world and humans as uncreated, as constituting the central features of a spontaneously self-generating cosmos having no creator, god, ultimate cause, or will external to itself.

Mote, op. cit., p. 13.

Mote goes on to note that an important consequence is that no institutionalised religion developed, people's religion remained a matter of private family practice, or any organised religion occured at the level of local organisation.

27. In an analysis of the intellectual foundations of China, Mote observed:

Mao Zedong and Jiang Jie-shi both acquired their basic literacy through the study of texts written well over two thousand years ago. The leaders of no other nation in our century have so directly inherited the mantle — or is it the pall? — of so ancient a cultural past, whether as proponents of its values or as rebels against them, or as both.

F. Mote, op. cit., pp. v–vi.

28. P. T. Ho, *The Ladder of Success in Imperial China* (New York: Columbia University Press, 1962), p. 17.

29. P. Y. Ho, *Li, Qi, and Shu: An Introduction to Science and Civilization in China* (Hong Kong: Hong Kong University Press, 1985), p. 184.

30. J. Needham, *Science and Civilisation in China* (Cambridge: Cambridge University Press, 1954).

31. T. Kaptchuk, *Chinese Medicine* (London: Rider, 1991); A. Kleinman, P. Kunstadter, R. Alexander, and J. Gale (eds.), *Medicine in Chinese Culture* (Washington: Department of Health, Culture, and Welfare, 1975).

32. D. Perkins and S. Yusuf, *Rural Development in China* (Baltimore: John Hopkins University Press, 1984), p. 150.

33. Z. H. Meng and M. H. Wang, *History of Chinese Civil Affairs* (Harbin: Heilongjiang Publishers, 1986), pp. 188–99; Y. T. Deng, *History of Disaster Relief in China* (Beijing: Shangwu Publishers, 1993), sections two and three.

34. W. H. Li and Y. Zhou, *Disasters and Famines* (Beijing: Higher Educational Publishers, 1991), p. 29.

35. S. Q. Jin, *China Civil Affairs History* (Changsha: Hunan University Publishers, 1989), pp. 51–60.

36. X. Y. Tian, *China Elderly Population and Society* (Beijing: China Economic Publishers, 1991), pp. 335–36.

37. Ibid., p. 336.

38. R. K. Feng and J. H. Chang, *Social Life in Qing Society* (Tianjin: People's Publishers, 1990), pp. 372–87.

39. S. Q. Jin, op. cit., p. 659.

40. The *Book of Rites*, *Li* is a collection of essays compiled during the Han dynasty from earlier writings. Some people suggested that the ideal was influenced by the Taoist conception of Grand Harmony. The book consisted of rituals that

governed the moral, social and religious activities of the entire aristocratic world.

41. C. Chai and M. Chai (eds.), *The Sacred Book of Confucius, and Other Confucius Classics* (New York: University Books, 1965), p. 338.

42. The *Xiao Kang* has been described as follows:

> Now the Great *Dao* (The Great Way) has fallen into obscurity, and the world is in the possession of families. Each regards as parents only his own parents and treats as sons only as his own sons; wealth and labour are employed for selfish purpose. The sovereigns take it as the proper *li* (rites) that their states should be hereditary; they endeavour to make their cities and suburbs strong, their ditches and moats secure. *Li* and *yi* are used as the norms to regulate the relationship between ruler and subject, to set up institutions, organize farms and hamlets, honour the brave and the wise, and bring merit to the individual. Hence schemes and plotting come about, and men take up arms. It was in this way that emperor Yu, Kings, Tang, Wen, Wu, and Cheng, and the Duke of Chou achieved eminence: all these six noble men paid attention to *Li*, and made manifest their *yi* and acted in good faith. They exposed their errors, made *jen* their law, and prudence their practice, thus showing the people wherein they should constantly abide. If there were any who did not follow these principles, he would lose power and position and be regarded by the multitude as dangerous. This is called *Hsiao-k'ang* .

Chai and Chai, op. cit., p. 338.

43. J. Needham, op. cit., p. 157.

Chinese Socialism: From Mao to Deng

The editors of *The Cambridge History of China* introduced the volume covering the post-Second World War period with the following statement:

> In 1949 a new stage was reached in the endeavours of successive Chinese elites to meet domestic problems inherited from the Late Imperial era and to respond to the century-old challenge posed by the industrialised West. A central government had now gained full control of the Chinese mainland, thus achieving the national unity so long desired. Moreover, it was committed for the first time to the overall modernisation of the nation's polity, economy, and society. The history of the succeeding decades is of the most massive experiment in social engineering the world has ever witnessed.[1]

In this chapter, we will look at the socialist transformation of the Chinese society in the context of its social policies and social welfare. In our subsequent references to the policies of Mao Zedong and Deng Xiaoping, we do not mean to imply that the policy-making process in the PRC is in the hands of a single individual. There are members of different factions within the leadership of the CCP who influence policy decisions, and the implementation of policies are in the hands of bureaucrats who are known to protect their own interests in translating policies made at the centre to action at lower echelons.[2] Nevertheless, from 1949 until his death in 1976, Mao and his supporters dominated the policy-making process; and since the late 1970s, the dominant force has come from Deng Xiaoping and his supporters.

Social Policy under Mao

On coming to power on 1 October 1949, the Communist leadership undertook the immediate need to rebuild a nation still reeling from the aftermath of World War II and the civil war. The CCP faced the formidable tasks of consolidating political and government structures, revitalising the economy, and maintaining law and order. The country had suffered a tremendous loss of both human and physical capital, leaving an economy near collapse. Heavy industrial production had fallen to only 30 per cent of pre-war levels, and output of agricultural consumer goods had fallen to about 70 per cent.[3] The number of unemployed people had reached almost five million, or 24 per cent of the employee population.[4] As an American-led blockade denied aid from the developed countries, the CCP relied heavily upon help from the Soviet Union in the form of trained technicians and limited capital loans.[5] The Soviet model of socialism also provided direction for state organisation and a strategy of industrial development. The adoption of the Soviet model seemed the only logical choice after the failure of earlier attempts by the Nationalist Government to modern-ise China along Western lines, and with the isolation of China following the Korean War.

The use of draconian measures brought about a remarkable reconstruc-tion within a few short years of Communist rule. Rates of savings and investment increased, as did life expectancy following the establishment of public health programmes and campaigns that effectively curbed infectious diseases and improved hygienic conditions. Social problems such as crime, unemployment, begging, prostitution, and drug addiction were removed through programmes of job placement and close supervision supplemented by heavy political education. Assistance to the unemployed included tem-porary assignments to public works, formation of small-scale enterprises, provision of assistance in returning to one's native village, and, if all else failed, pure relief.[6]

A strong centralised state emerged, and the nation's social system transformed according to Marxist precepts. Land reform in the countryside eliminated former rich landowners and landlords, redistributing plots to the poorer peasants. By 1952, over 113 million acres of land — plus draft animals and farm implements — were distributed to over 300 million landless peasants.[7] Industrialisation in the cities also proceeded based on a Stalinist model that placed emphasis on heavy industry funded by capital accumulated from the agricultural sector.[8] During this period, over 50 per cent of the state budget investment went to heavy industry, and only 6.2 per cent to agriculture.[9]

Chinese Communist leaders could proudly proclaim the economic success of their First Five-Year Plan (1953–1957). Indeed, the first decade under the CCP could, understandably, be claimed a creative period of reconstruction, growth, and innovation — a period of "the socialist high tide". Even the costly involvement of Chinese troops in the Korean war helped to consolidate Communist leadership at home, and established the PRC as a formidable military power abroad.

One important factor contributing to this early success was the presence of strong leaders, with skills forged by war and revolution over the preceding decades, combined with experience gained from the administration of regional bases under the control of the Communist before they achieved central power. Another asset came from the roots which the CCP had developed in rural communities during its formative years when operating guerrilla bases in the countryside.[10]

Gradual collectivisation of agriculture in the rural areas and nationalisation of enterprises in urban areas produced by 1958 the commune system in the countryside and a predominately state-owned industrial sector in the cities. Under the socialist command economy, processes of production, distribution, exchange, and consumption all came under the control of the state.

Along with this transformation of the Chinese political economy, social programmes were also put into place which would take differing approaches in the cities and countryside to provide social protection, social provision, and social welfare services. Although disparate, these social programmes, taken together, provided a safety net in welfare for the Chinese people.

Social policies had started to be formulated even before the CCP had come to power. Following the formation of the CCP in 1921, its prime concern focused on the recruitment of members, publicising the work of the party, and building up its military strength to combat Chinese Nationalist Government forces and the Japanese. Social reforms were pursued in areas controlled by the CCP to improve the conditions of working people. In championing the cause of the poor and the illiterate, Mao Zedong pronounced socialism and the new society as forces that would overthrow the traditional oppression of the "three big mountains" — imperialism, feudalism, and bureaucrat-capitalism. Bourgeois (that is, Western) social science teachings were withdrawn from the university curriculum, and welfare services provided by foreign missionaries and local charity organisations were nationalised or closed down.

One of the first social legislations took the form of a *Marriage Law*, promulgated in 1950, to break the traditional system of marriage arranged by parents and replace it with one in which young people would be free to choose their own partners. This law also promoted equality between the rights of men and women in choice of a marital partner.

The *Labour Insurance Law* (1951) provided unprecedented protection and benefits to workers in the urban areas. With nationalisation, most urban labour came to be employed in SOE, where wages were standardised and centrally controlled by the government. (See Chapter 4) In addition to life-long employment guarantee, urban residents also enjoyed the benefits of state subsidies in a number of essential commodities and public services.

In denouncing the theory of Malthus, Mao believed that a socialist revolution and increased production would solve the problem of feeding and employing a population that numbered 590 million people at the time of the first PRC census taken in 1953. However, at the end of the First Five-Year Plan, it became clear that the combined need to accumulate capital for industrial investment and to improve the living standards of the citizenry could not be so easily maintained. For example, consumer goods remained extremely scarce in the cities and rural income, which had started to improve, had become stagnant.

Not content with the pace of change, and recognising that the Soviet model emphasising heavy industry at the expense of agriculture did not suit a predominantly agricultural China, Mao envisioned "a great leap forward" based on a massive mobilisation of rural labour power that could make over the countryside and increase agricultural production. This in turn would implement a strategy that could simultaneously develop agriculture and industry. (In Mao's words, "Walking on two legs".) In the urban areas, Mao repeatedly called for the abolition of the wage system, and the re-introduction of the free supply system implemented during the war years in Yanan. He believed that the wage system was "a concession to the bourgeoisie", and its result had been "the development of individualism."[11]

There came a subsequent outpouring of work around the clock in irrigation and flood-control, land reclamation, and expansion of small-scale local industry to produce goods and equipment for agriculture.[12] The most publicised activity was the campaign begun in the summer of 1958 to produce steel from small backyard iron smelters. By autumn, 100 million people were involved. Unfortunately, the products turned out to be mostly unusable or uneconomic. But even worse, peasant farmers were diverted from doing their main task, that of growing grain.

A combination of factors led to catastrophe in 1959–1960 when millions of peasants were left hungry and dying of starvation. The massive engagement of corvée labour in public works had resulted in the neglect of harvesting a good 1958 crop; and bad weather the following year brought a poor crop. Unfortunately, this occurred just as authorities decided to increase state requisitions and collections of grain, influenced in part by exaggerated reports of abundant harvests (which lower echelon cadres were apt to make in order to ingratiate themselves with higher-ups). The peasants in some areas retained only half, or even less, of their usual subsistence grain supply. Before the central authorities could get a grasp of the real situation in the countryside, it is estimated that over 20 million people died of starvation, or of ills brought on by hunger and malnutrition.[13] For the first time, China recorded a negative population growth.

With the rise of pragmatists and moderates in the CCP leadership after 1961, some liberalisation of the economy occurred. The farming of private plots in rural areas, earlier prohibited, were restored so farmers could supplement their basic incomes. In industry, piece-rated labour and bonus systems were also restored. Just as the country was recovering from the Great Leap Forward (1958–1960), it was plunged into chaos by the Great Proletarian Cultural Revolution (1966–1975). With conflicts appearing among CCP leadership, and the growing power of a new bureaucracy, Mao launched an attack on the very establishment that he had earlier helped set in place. During the subsequent power struggle, Mao Zedong mobilised millions of youth, so-called Red Guards, to attack party structure, government departments and courts. Revolutionary committees were established to take charge of all units. The ideology of "politics in command" endorsed the principle of "red over expert", and political enthusiasm and correctness were pushed as more important than professional knowledge and formal education in guiding policy decisions. Intellectual and academic pursuits were now distrusted.

In education, the number of years in schools were cut short, medical training shortened, and admission to university education based on recommendations from work unit production leaders. In addition, an estimated 17 million unemployed urban youths were sent to seek jobs in the countryside. In brief, material incentives were de-emphasised, and self-reliance glorified. Under an egalitarian social policy, rationing became the major means of distributing scarce resources and regulating consumption.

The Cultural Revolution brought about more social disorder than perhaps even Mao himself had anticipated. Chaos followed in government departments, schools, factories, and welfare organisations. Little wonder that the populace, which had earlier imbued the Communist leadership with super-like powers, became disillusioned:

Belief in Mao had provided a secular form of faith that had given hope to many, and their disillusionment extended beyond individual leaders to the system they represented, including the Communist Party and the socialist system. Some Party leaders escaped the full brunt of public anger, for they too had been victims. But because Communist cadres had been in charge and had led China through the disastrous Great Leap Forward to the Cultural Revolution, at the very least the Party had lost the aura it had once enjoyed. Even the excitement of economic progress could not fully restore the faith or fill the spiritual void.[14]

Nominally, the period of the Cultural Revolution lasted from 1966 to 1969 when order was re-established by the People's Liberation Army, and millions of Red Guards were swept from the cities and "sent down to the countryside." However, some of the activities triggered by the Cultural Revolution continued for a whole decade until Mao's death in September, 1976. Before we take leave of the "Mao era", let us take a closer at his social values as these provide clues to his social welfare philosophy.

Mao's Social Values

A number of writers have identified Mao's social values to include self-reliance, hard work, diligence, self-sacrifice, mass line, and serving the people.[15] According to Mao, the building of a socialist man with self-discipline was considered as paramount. In learning about Communist ideals, every Chinese should be able to adopt an attitude of selflessness, to love hard work, to live a plain, frugal and austere life style, to love the party and the country, and to serve the people.

With limited contact with the outside world, China had assumed an independent policy of development both politically and economically. The policy line could be summarised as, "independence and self-direction; self-reliance and self-salvation." Each geographical location (from provinces to cities, from towns to villages), and each work unit (from urban factories to rural communes) would be self-sufficient, relying on one's own effort and resources.[16] Hard work rather than dependence on the state or collective for assistance would give a person dignity. The story of "the foolish old man removing the mountains" illustrated how will power, hard work and determination could remove obstacles to obtain a final victory.[17] Mao had two slogans for the communes: "The scale of the commune should be big, everything should be publicly-owned"; and, "Egalitarianism and voluntarism should be emphasised."

A typical example of self-reliance occurred after a devastating earthquake in Tangshan city in 1976 in which 242,000 people were reported to have perished, and 164,000 people seriously injured. In declining offers of humanitarian aid from the United Nations and other foreign relief organisations, China proudly proclaimed the rebuilding of a whole city through its own efforts.[18]

Mao was committed to the gradual elimination of the "three great differences" — income gaps between rural and urban areas, between manual and mental labour, and between industrial and agricultural sectors. This was through the establishment of public or socialist ownership of production means, and reduction of wage differences between occupations, ranks and types of work.

In agriculture, collectivisation had eliminated private plots, and income differences between villagers reduced. Although China had eliminated the very rich and limited the share of the rich, the Gini coefficient, as a measurement of personal income distribution was estimated to be 0.33 in 1979 which was not markedly more equal than those of some other low-income countries.[19] But if the availability of free or subsidised social services and basic necessities was included, the World Bank praised that "the poorest people in China are far better off than their counterparts in most other developing countries."[20]

According to Mao, egalitarianism would serve to provide work incentives than to make people lazy. Alternatively, he believed that differential financial rewards would give rise to economic inequalities and exploitation and would therefore, inhibit long-term economic growth. People who worked hard should be remunerated not by material rewards but by political rewards, such as recognition by their work units, by promotion, or by selection as role models.

In denouncing the importance of material incentives, Mao saw in the very poverty of his people a foundation for the transformation of society. Mao claimed that poverty and illiteracy were the "wealth" of China, and he saw in that very backwardness a reservoir of youthful energy and revolutionary creativity. He spoke of the outstanding features of the masses in China as being "poor and blank":

> Apart from their other characteristics, China's 600 million people have two remarkable peculiarities; they are, first of all, poor, and secondly, blank. That may seem like a bad thing, but it is really a good thing. People want change, want to do things, want revolution. A clean sheet of paper has no blotches, and so the newest and most beautiful pictures can be painted on it.[21]

Mao Zedong also emphasised volunteerism, the infinite capacity of the people to change the world by an act of will. Campaigns were popular means to mobilise the enthusiasm of the people in public works such as road construction, house building, and irrigation improvement. The idea of "serving the people" again promoted psychological and spiritual rewards while de-emphasising material incentives. Mao promoted as a "learning model" the person of Lei Feng, described as "a rust-free screw" who reportedly used most his hard-earned income to help others.[22] Another selfless hero put forward by Mao on serving the people was a Canadian doctor, Norman Bethune.[23]

In particular, Mao felt that cadres, operating under the principle of the mass line, should put the interests of the people before individual private interests. The government should follow the goal of the "public good", which is achieved through the mass line. Mass line is regarded as the style of work of the Communist Party — all work of the party/government should involve the people. The experience, ideas, feelings and views of the people should be respected and mobilised by the cadres in the process of carrying out government policies. The principle of "from the mass to the mass" involved a cycle of collecting opinion from the people, analysing the opinion by the cadres, and then returning it to the mass through action.[24]

During the period of Mao's failing health and subsequent death in 1976, a power struggle ensued for leadership. Any ambitions on the part of Mao's wife, Jiang Qing, and her cohorts (known as the Gang of Four) to continue the "Mao's line" were thwarted, and a relatively unknown Hua Guofeng took over, apparently as the personal choice of Mao. But Hua was unable to consolidate his leadership, and in the continuing manoeuvring for power a rehabilitated Deng Xiaoping (purged earlier in the Cultural Revolution) re-emerged in late 1978 to take over as the "paramount leader".

Economic Reform under Deng Xiaoping

Since 1978, under the tutelage of Deng Xiaoping and his supporters, China has been undergoing rapid change in its societal structure, in social norms and beliefs, and in life styles. This "Second Revolution" might be called an attempt to re-transform society after the Marx-Lenin-Mao approach had failed to bring about an egalitarian society with the promised economic achievements. Whereas Mao had previously emphasised political development and class struggle, Deng placed priority on economic and industrial development, with ideology downplayed. Consequently, Mao's old slogans, "politics in command" and "red over expert", gave way to

Deng's pragmatic "seek truth from facts" and "the colour of the cat is not important as long as it catches mice." With its priority on economic growth, Deng's policy might well be termed "economics in command".

Deng's concern about the state of the Chinese economy after taking over in the late 1970s was not without reason. The problems he encountered included high urban unemployment, deteriorating urban housing conditions, falling real wages, and sluggish economic growth. The economic condition of the countryside had become critical, and economic disparities between urban dwellers and rural peasants had further widened after decades under the "scissors pricing" policy.[25] Agricultural production was falling and peasant morale ebbing. The attempt to rejuvenate the countryside by organising farms and farmers into collectives had proven useful in some areas but had by and large failed due to poor incentives, ineffective leadership at lower levels, and resistance by many peasants to relinquish their individual household independence. Furthermore, there are apparently few, if any, economies of scale in wet rice agriculture where labour depends mainly on "hands and feet", and the most efficient production unit is the individual household.[26]

The turning point came in the Third plenum of the Central Committee of the 11th Party Congress in 1978 when Deng Xiaoping regained power, advocating the need to modernise agriculture, industry, defense, and technology. These would be accomplished by "one centre and two emphases" — under the central direction of economic reforms, the "two emphases" would be the adoption of an open-door policy to promote communication with the West, and the guidance in all reforms by "four cardinal principles" (which are the socialist road, Communist Party leadership, Marxism/ Leninism/Mao Zedong Thought, and democratic people's dictatorship). The cliche of "reform" came to replace the call for "revolution". In advocating the primacy of economic construction, Deng stated in 1978:

> From now on, economic work is the major politics. Leaving away from this main content, politics becomes empty-headed, and detached from the greatest interest of the party and the people.[27]

Emphasising a new regard for knowledge and expertise, Deng derided the idea of "red over expert". In order to win support for their programme of economic construction, Deng and his supporters formulated a new theory of national development. In the Sixth plenum of the Central Committee of the 11th Party Congress in 1981, the party acknowledged a basic contradiction between the underdeveloped productivity and the ever-rising cultural and material needs of the people.[28] This could be explained, according to the party line, by the uniqueness of China, and the need to find its own path of development. The notions of a "Primary Stage of Socialism", and "socialism with Chinese characteristics", were adopted at the 13th Party Congress in 1987 as benchmarks for the developmental direction of the nation.

According to this theory, China has evolved from a semi-feudalistic and semi-colonial society without a genuine proletariat revolution.[29] China, before 1949, was basically an agrarian society with a limited working class and an under-developed economy. The society, therefore, was not dominated by the contradictions between the proletariat and the bourgeoisie as envisaged by Marx, but by the discontent of the people towards a corrupt Nationalist Government. As a result, the revolution was not a genuine working-class revolution. Without attaining the level of advanced capitalism with high economic productivity and industrialisation, the basic conditions for a socialist revolution were not there.[30]

That is why, according to the new doctrine, neither orthodox Marxist theories nor experiences in other socialist countries can be directly and dogmatically applied to the Chinese situation. The previous attempts at radical reform during the Great Leap Forward and the Cultural Revolution were based on a dogmatic application of Marxist theory with little consideration to a Chinese situation which had not yet reached a mature stage of socialism. Thus, according to this theory, Mao made a mistake by declaring the attainment of communism during these periods.

Now, a "socialism with Chinese characteristics" will follow a flexible and pragmatic road of development, incorporating both the Marxist theory and the Chinese reality. Significantly, a certain degree of capitalism will be allowed to exist in order to facilitate economic development. The view is known as a "tolerance of capitalism".[31] In promoting economic reconstruction, work incentives are required. Deng rationalised his new approach in 1978 but was careful to placate Mao's supporters who were still around:

> We must have rewards and penalties, and the criteria must be perfectly clear. Those whose work is evaluated as good should be paid at a different rate from those who have done poorly. Our general policy is to place moral encouragement first, material incentives second. The awarding of medals and certificates of merit constitutes moral encouragement and represents a political honour. This is essential. However, material incentives cannot be dispensed with either. All related measures which have proved effective in the past should be restored. The bonus system should be reinstated. Money awards should be given to those who have made special contribution, including inventors and innovators.[32]

Deng's Social Policy

There are three major principles underlying Deng's drive to improve material incentives. First, a pluralistic economy with forms of economic enterprises (private and foreign ownership) other than public ownership are to be encouraged. Secondly, differences in pay should be widened, to allow some people to become wealthy so as to encourage individual enthusiasm and speed up the development of production. Thirdly, in denouncing the egalitarian principle of "everyone eating from the same pot", the principle of distribution is "to each according to his labour". Accordingly, reward should be linked to performance and effort.[33] In the Chinese saying: "More labour more benefit, less labour less benefit, and no labour no benefits."

Major social and economic reforms started in the rural areas. With experiments on the Household Responsibility System, communes were disbanded in 1983. Thereafter, the individual household again became the basic economic and social unit in rural areas. The reason why Deng started off his reforms in the rural areas is apparently because of his belief that this would maintain stability in the rural areas.[34]

Meanwhile, a responsibility system was also introduced in urban enterprises. Under a profit-retention system, enterprises would have the discretion to allocate their after-tax profit for re-investment, collective welfare, and payment of bonus.[35] A taxation system would radically changed the revenue sources and structure of the government which previously depended largely on direct profits from enterprises. Above all, a series of sweeping labour regulations were introduced in 1986 on dismissal, contract workers, bankruptcy, and unemployment insurance.[36] In addition, the *Enterprise Law* in 1988 prescribed the separation of public ownership from the operation. However, because the urban political situation is more complicated than that in the rural areas, urban reforms have tended to be incremental and cautious.

In the 14th Party Congress in 1992, ideological debate on capitalism and socialism was put aside, and the uniqueness of the Chinese background was emphasised. The development of the free-market was further endorsed under the concept of a "socialist market economy". Under this doctrine, welfare is considered a commodity. Thus, housing, education, medical care, and pensions are no longer treated simply as social services, but as personal consumption and commodities with marketable and monetary values. Privatisation and fee-charging are some of the emerging trends. Public housing are for sales. In medical care, there are 100,000 privately run hospitals and more than 300,000 doctors in private practice.[37] In education, private kindergartens, schools and colleges are a booming profit-making business.[38] Even in state-run universities, students can be admitted as private students (usually with lower admission standards, but have to pay higher fees).[39]

Currently, the government policy is committed to the restructuring of socialist welfare institutions, and to transfer some of the existing state and enterprise responsibilities in welfare to private and collective sectors. The traditional function of the family as a source of social protection is again emphasised. Pragmatically, the government is encouraging a more pluralistic approach to welfare, with responsibilities spread among economic enterprises, local neighbourhood communities, families and individuals, as well as the state. (See Chapters 5 and 6) Finally, some of the international relief organisations such as Oxfam and World Vision are allowed to operate relief projects in poverty-stricken areas. These projects include irrigation improvement, agricultural training and educational scholarship for orphans.[40]

As a consequence of economic reforms, state subsidies, rationing and price controls have inevitably given way to market forces. In relaxing price control of goods, the state has to increase allowances and wages to compensate for the rise in prices. This has accounted for the appearance of the item "price subsidies" in state government budgets after 1986. In drafting state budgets for 1994, over 38.3 billion yuan, or 6.3 per cent of the total budgeted expenditures have been allocated for subsidies to compensate for price rises.[41]

Under present circumstances, the traditional slogan of "only socialism can save China" has seemed to give way to the implicit acceptance that "only capitalism can save China". The vagueness of the concept of "socialism with Chinese characteristics" would allow an avowedly "socialist label" on the top, and a pragmatic and non-ideological operation in practice. To outsiders, China seems to be turning capitalist but to the Chinese leaders, there remains a steadfast commitment to socialism.

Both Mao Zedong and Deng Xiaoping have introduced new ideas and structures to social welfare in China. Despite attempts to break with the "feudalistic past", there are features which are very consistent with traditional social welfare practices.

Guanxi: Extension of a Family-based Relationship Network

Traditionally, Chinese people depended on a network of private relationships and connections to manage their lives and to get things done. This orientation is still strong. A discernable visitor to China would come to notice the operation of *guanxi*, which is described as follows by a Western reporter:

> We (Westerners) tend to see people as individuals; we make some distinctions, of course, between those we know and those we don't. But basically we have one code of manners for all. Chinese, on the other hand, instinctively divide people into those with whom they already have a fixed relationship, a connection, what the Chinese call guanxi, and those they don't. These connections operate like a series of invisible threads, tying Chinese to each other with far greater tensile strength than mere friendship in the West would do. Guanxi have created a social magnetic field in which all Chinese move, keenly aware of those people with whom they have connections and those they don't.... In a broader sense, guanxi also help explain how a nation of one billion people coheres.[42]

According to Butterfield, *guanxi* provides the lubricant for Chinese to get through life, particularly to get things done. To survive the rigid bureaucracy and the socialist system of having shortages in many essential commodities, people have to rely on their informal network which is also known as *zou houmen* (taking the back door) to realise one's private interests and personal gains. People see developing, cultivating, and "pulling" one's *guanxi* as a form of social investment or resource. In getting a job, admission to a school, obtaining a nursery place, or going overseas, one often has to rely on one's *guanxi*. Therefore, the *guanxi* network provides people with a feeling of security. Often, the network is maintained through the sending of gifts and invitation to feasts.

Guanxi network specifically refers to the expectations and obligations of mutual support and care between people who are relatives, or who come from the same localities. Perhaps they were classmates, or served in the same military unit. Similar to a family relationship, a *guanxi* relationship prescribes a moral obligation to those in the personal network to provide help when people find themselves in difficulties. The relationship is bounded by a connection of human emotions (*renqing* or *ganqing*). *Guanxi* is expected to operate even among people who have not known each other and have no warm personal feelings.[43] Furthermore, the giver of a service is not to expect an immediate favour in return from the receiver, but he may expect assistance from other people within the network. On the other hand, a receiver of favour is expected to remember it, and has an obligation to do something specifically in return, perhaps in favour of another person in the network.

With the coming of socialism in China, people were expected to treat one another equally and universally as comrades. Despite efforts in Mao's time to change traditional clanship relationships, the social phenomenon of *guanxi* still dominates in Communist China. One provincial official observed:

> No unit or individual lets you have something strictly according to regulations. Rather, you must have guanxi or you come up with nothing. This is true everywhere but especially in the South. The guanxi does not refer to old schools ties and so on. Rather, the guanxi is based on interest — strictly a you scratch my back and I scratch yours situation. The exchange of goods and favours seals the deal. This situation is pervasive because that is the way things are done at higher levels, and until they do things differently, nobody else will change.[44]

The impact of *guanxi* means that the notion of giving help to strangers is still unusual. The general response of the Chinese people in assisting flood victims in 1992 was largely apathetic.[45] People tended to see it as the responsibility of the government rather than a duty for all. Using another example of blood donation, the source of blood in China is still largely dependent on the private market. Voluntary blood and organ donation is rare. (The voluntary blood donation rate is only two per 1,000 people, whereas the international norm is five.) Over 77 per cent of available blood are by purchase.[46]

To the average Chinese person, *guanxi* is still a major important source of assistance, rather than formal government channels. Building up a reliable friendship network within one's work place, or neighbourhood, or village is of vital importance in protecting one's personal and family interests.

Welfare As a Gift from the State Rather Than a Citizen Right

Traditional China did not develop the notion of laws embodying impersonal standards of justice as did the ancient Greeks, or as a system of rights and obligations having its own moral force. Thus, there has not been a tradition of individual rights nor entitlements based on legal grounds.[47] The Chinese considered that the individual's status as a citizen derived from the state and therefore, the concept of individual considerations delimiting the power of the state is very alien.

The *Constitution of the PRC* (1982) mentions a number of social and political rights which include the right to work, to vote, to stand for election, to enjoy the freedom of speech, religion, association, demonstration, and privacy, and to social security benefits.[48] However, socialist human rights are viewed as rights of the majority, and are largely determined and limited by the economic conditions and system of the society.[49]

In the PRC, rights of the citizens are mixed with obligations, and individual rights are subsumed under the interests of the state and country. In other words, they are encouraged as long as they are consistent with state policies. They cannot infringe upon the interests of the state, of society and of the collective. Needless to say, China is against the notion of conceiving human rights as universal, natural, and given by God. An individual's status and rights are defined according to one's contribution towards the collectivity. Thus, welfare rights are seen as programmatic goals rather than as immediate claims on government.[50]

For example, the obligation to take care of the elderly, or the practice of the Single-child Policy represent more the concern of the state than the protection of individual rights. Rather than seeing welfare rights as natural and as entitlements founded in the human condition, they are treated as grants given by the state to enable the citizens to contribute energies to the needs of the nation.

Accordingly, welfare is a gift provided by the paternalistic and benevolent government or the CCP. People in need are not expected to demand services from the government, and it is up to the government to decide who deserves care according to the criteria of merit and contribution. Entitlements to services are to be earned, and not provided automatically. So it is the state that ought to be praised for its benevolence.

In responding to the international pressure to improve its human rights conditions, the State Council published a document to explain the human rights situation in China in 1991. China claimed that human rights were denied in traditional and feudalistic China, and only with the coming of the PRC that the Chinese enjoyed remarkable improvements in personal, political and economic rights (of which the right to subsistence is regarded as the foremost human right). The development of human rights must take into considerations the different stages of development and the different economic, political, and cultural conditions of the developing countries.[51]

Work Ethic

Traditional Chinese values emphasised hard working. The Communist morality requires a person to love labouring, especially manual labour. In addition to hard work, Mao also cherished the value of work-and-study programmes which required intellectuals, professionals, and government officials to involve in manual labour. The Chinese Communist ideology also put primacy to the meaning of work.[52]

For example, the strong work ethic implies that one must earn his social status through work. Work rather than dependence on the state for assistance would give a person dignity. In providing services for people in welfare need such as the poor or the disabled, job placement is perceived as the most important task. The setting of welfare factories for the physically handicapped and the therapy stations for the mentally ill and the mentally handicapped are popular forms of welfare services in China. (See Chapter 7) Work is perceived to have not only economic value but also a therapeutic and educational function.

Pragmatism

Pragmatism, or "seek truth from facts" was originally a basic principle cherished by Mao Zedong himself. But his idealism and passions often led him to embark on radical reforms along uncompromising ideological lines. Mao himself was not an orthodox Marxist, and often emphasised the importance of Chinese conditions and cultural predispositions to avoid a dogmatic application of universal Marxism. Various writers have pointed out the influence of traditional Chinese culture upon Mao's philosophy.[53] Being realists, Chinese are found to be highly adaptable to changing circumstances.

The pragmatism of Deng Xiaoping is marked by his "cat theory". In setting aside the debate over what is capitalist and what is socialist, Deng put forward three criteria for judging right and wrong, or gain and loss for all work. Does it facilitate: The development of the socialist productive forces? The overall national strength? The improvement of people's living standards?[54] In emphasising the pragmatic orientation of "making practice the sole criterion of truth", he advocated the further liberalisation of the Chinese mind from doctrinal politics.

According to Lucian Pye, a distinctive feature of Chinese pragmatism is the ability to tolerate and accept inconsistent and even irreconcilable beliefs:

> Chinese are relatively unperturbed at having to uphold logically inconsistent positions, and there may not be greater inner tensions when belief and fact do not readily coincide. Chinese pragmatism is almost by definition syncretic, based on a readiness to tolerate and accept what others might feel to be irreconcilable doctrines or beliefs.[55]

By stressing pragmatism in policy-making, the CCP today is cautious in introducing reforms, encouraging piecemeal innovations and experiments before making a commitment to major change. For example, economic reform after 1978 has not been based on a clear blueprint. The only "unifying" theme of the reform was to move away from a Stalinist economy.

Notes

1. J. Fairbank and R. MacFarquhar (eds.), *The Cambridge History of China*, Vol. 4 (Cambridge: Cambridge University Press, 1987), p. viii.
2. K. Lieberthal and M. Oksenberg, *Policy Making in China: Leaders, Structures and Processes* (Princeton, N.J.: Princeton University Press, 1989), pp. 16– 18.
3. M. Selden and V. Lippit (eds.), *The Transition to Socialism in China* (Armonk, N.Y.: M. E. Sharpe, Inc., 1982), p. 4.
4. *BR*, 4–10 November 1991, p. 8.
5. The Soviet Union made considerable contributions in the form of technical assistance, construction, and equipment for 154 modern industrial plants which were paid for by the Chinese, and the training of Chinese technicians. J. Wang, *Contemporary Chinese Politics: An Introduction* (Englewood Cliffs, N.J.: Prentice Hall, 1989), p. 10.
6. C. Riskin, *Chinese Political Economy* (Oxford: Oxford University Press, 1987), p. 61.
7. J. Wang, op. cit., p. 13.
8. Spence defined this urban-biased policy as "primitive accumulation" which forced the peasantry to sell more than a quarter of their total grain production to the state at extremely low prices. This policy left the peasants at subsistence level while it enabled the government to guarantee food supplies in the cities and keep wages down. J. Spence, *The Search for Modern China* (New York: W. W. Norton and Company, 1990), p. 544.
9. J. Gray, "The State and the Rural Economy in the PRC", in *Developmental States in East Asia*, edited by G. White (London: Macmillan Press, 1988), p. 199.
10. V. Nee, "Peasant Household Individualism", in *China Rural Development: The Great Transformation*, edited by W. Parish (Armonk, N.Y.: M. E. Sharpe, 1985), pp. 164–90.
11. S. Schram, *The Thought of Mao Tse-tung* (Cambridge: Cambridge University Press, 1989), p. 129.
12. Fairbank, op. cit., p. 371.
13. D. Goodman and G. Segal, *China at Forty: Mid-Life Crisis* (Oxford: Clarendon Press, 1989), p. 2.

14. E. Vogel, *One Step Ahead in China* (Cambridge: Harvard University Press, 1989), pp. 39–40.
15. B. H. Mok, "In the Service of Socialism: Social Welfare in China", *Social Work* (July/August 1983), pp. 269–72; J. Dixon, *The Chinese Welfare System 1949–1979* (New York: Praeger Publishers, 1981), chapter one.
16. Dixon, op. cit., p. 15.
17. The story was about an old man who determined to remove the mountains so that people could travel more conveniently. He claimed that while the mountains could not grow any higher, endless generations after him would one day achieve the goal.
18. J. K. Fairbank, *China: A New History* (Cambridge, Mass.: Belknap Press of Harvard University Press, 1992), pp. 404–405.
19. C. Riskin, op. cit., p. 250.
20. World Bank, *China : Socialist Economic Development*, Vol. 1 (Washington, DC: World Bank, 1983), pp. 94–95.
21. S. Schram, *The Political Thought of Mao Zedong* (New York: Praeger Publishers, 1966), p. 253.
22. Lei Feng (1940–1962) was made into a hero after his death in an accident. In insisting on learning from Mao Zedong's Thought, he claimed: "Life is short, but the cause of serving others is infinitely good. I have resolved to devote my limited life to serving the people."
23. Dr Bethune (1890–1939) was a member of the Communist Party of Canada, and he was sent to China to help the CCP in the war against Japan. The spirit of a foreigner selflessly adopting the cause of the Chinese revolution was praised by Mao.
24. S. Schram, op. cit. (1989), pp. 316–67.
25. As explained earlier, accumulation of capital occurred through an imbalance of trade between agriculture and industry. Peasants paid high prices for what they had to buy (such as fertilizer and farming implements) but received low prices for what they sold. This has been termed a policy of "scissors pricing". Over thirty years, under this artificial price mechanism, more than 600 billion yuan were transferred out of agriculture. This is a substantial portion of the total investment funds available during this period for capital construction in all sectors of the national economy. R. Kojima, "Accumulation, Technology, and China Economic Development", in *The Transition to Socialism in China*, edited by M. Selden and V. Lippit (Armonk, N.Y.: M. E. Sharpe, 1982), pp. 238–65.
26. V. Nee, op. cit.
27. X. P. Deng, *Deng Xiaoping, Speeches and Writings* (Oxford: Pergamon Press, 1984), p. 140.
28. P. Liu, Q. H. Li and A. P. Xia, *The Economic Thought of Deng Xiaoping* (Beijing: CCP Central Party College Publishers, 1992), pp. 86–93.

29. CCP leadership often regards that the pre-liberation China was a "semi-feudalistic" society. But traditional China in fact was not exactly under feudalistic rule.

30. Z. Y. Ding, X. F. Wang and X. C. Shang, *Introduction to Socialism with Chinese Characteristics* (Nanning: Guangxi Education Publishers, 1988), p. 18.

31. *BR*, 18–24 May 1992, p. 15.

32. X. P. Deng, op. cit., p. 118.

33. *BR*, 15–21 April 1991, p. v.

34. Deng said in 1987:

> From the point of view of the Chinese realities, 80 per cent of the population live in villages. The stability of China depends first of all on the stability of this population. Even the cities are becoming more beautiful, the foundation of stability cannot be possible without the village.

Liu and Li, op. cit., p. 254.

35. A system of taxation policy has been implemented with joint venture enterprises (1980), foreign-owned enterprises (1981), SOE (1984) and COE (1985).

36. These *Regulations* promulgated in 1986 concerned the following subjects: *Regulations on Bankruptcy of SOE, Regulations on the Dismissal of SOE Employees Violating Labour Discipline, Regulations on the Unemployment Insurance Scheme for SOE Employees, Regulations on the Implementation of Contract Worker System in SOE, and Regulations on the Recruitment of Workers in SOE.*

37. *SCMP*, 28 March 1994, p. 10.

38. It is estimated that there are over 1,200 private primary and secondary schools in China. Over 85 per cent of students are in private kindergartens and nurseries. In a private school in Guangzhou, each enroled student has to deposit 150,000 yuan as debenture, and annual fee is about 18,000 yuan. *CCA*, 3 (1994), pp. 36–37.

39. *MP*, 1 October 1993, p. 6.

40. *SCMP*, 20 May 1994, p. 8.

41. *Far Eastern Economic Review*, 24 March 1994, p. 48.

42. F. Butterfield, *China: Alive in the Bitter Sea* (New York: Times Books, 1982), p. 44.

43. L. Pye, "On Chinese Pragmatism", *The China Quarterly*, 106 (June 1986), pp. 206–34.

44. J. Spence, op. cit., p. 694.

45. *SCMP*, 17 July 1991, p. 8.

46. Recently, Beijing city followed the examples of Liaoning province and Shanghai city to make blood donation compulsory for residents. It was because

Beijing was only able to supply 51.5 per cent of its own blood need in 1990, and had to import blood from other areas. Under the new regulations, residents who donate blood would get a nutrition allowance and a day-off from work. Family members of donors would get priority in medical emergencies requiring blood transfusion. *MP*, 3 June 1991, p. 10; *SCMP*, 17 February 1992, p. 8.

47. A. Chen, "Human Rights in China: A Brief Historical Review", in *Human Rights in Hong Kong*, edited by R. Wacks (Hong Kong: Oxford University Press, 1992), pp. 176–201.

48. The Chinese *Constitution* does not have binding force in practice, and lacks concrete enforcement measures through legislative specifications. Often, constitutional articles represent only the intention and hope of the government.

49. *BR*, 10–16 January 1994, pp. 6–7.

50. R. Edwards, L. Henkin and A. Nathan, *Human Rights in Contemporary China* (New York: Columbia University Press, 1986), p. 125.

51. *SCMP*, 21 May 1994, p. 1.

52. The Chinese *Constitution* (1982), Article of 42 stipulates:

> Citizens of the People's Republic of China have the right as well as the duty to work.
>
> Using various channels, the state creates conditions for employment, strengthens labour protection, improves working conditions and, on the basis of expanded production, increases remuneration for work and social benefits.
>
> Work is the glorious duty of every able-bodied citizen. All working people in state enterprises and in urban and rural economic collectives should perform their tasks with an attitude consonant with their status as masters of the country. The state promotes socialist labour emulation, and commends and rewards model and advanced workers. The state encourages citizens to take part in voluntary labour.

53. J. Starr, *Ideology and Culture: An Introduction to the Dialectic of Contemporary Chinese Politics* (New York: Harper and Row, 1973); S. Schram, op. cit. (1989); G. W. Wang, *The Chineseness of China* (Hong Kong: Oxford University Press, 1991).

54. *BR*, 4–10 January 1993, p. 16.

55. L. Pye, op. cit., p. 217.

Modernisation: Soft Economy, Tough Government

We had indicated at the outset of this book that economics, politics, and social welfare in the PRC are so intertwined that it is not possible to discuss any one of these sectors without some appreciation of what is happening in the others. In this chapter, the major focus will be on economic developments in the PRC since 1978. However, we will also look briefly at subsequent pressures for political reform. These changes, in turn, provide a necessary backdrop for the following chapters which look specifically at the various social policies and social service programmes that make up China's current social welfare system.

Socialist Market Economy

Major economic reforms in the PRC, as noted in the previous chapter, began in 1978 with the Third plenum of the 11th Party Congress endorsing the principles of efficiency and profitability in economic development. At the following 12th Party Congress in 1982, the party put forward the principle, "the primacy of economic planning, supplemented by market adjustment." The 13th Party Congress in 1987 spoke of a "planned commodity economy", which was finally replaced by the concept of the "socialist market economy" at the 14th, and most recent, Party Congress in 1992. The importance attached to this development is reflected by its formal incorporation into the Chinese *Constitution* in the 9th National People's Congress (NPC).[1]

Since 1978, the CCP has repeatedly emphasised economic production as the top priority of the country. Under the concept of "market socialism", the role of the state is to strengthen the formulation of economic laws, to improve macro adjustments and control, and to forbid any units or individuals from interfering with the social economic order.[2] Under this policy, peasants in rural areas have a greater choice of crops to grow, and greater leeway to sell them at the highest prices; and industrial enterprises have more autonomy in decisions about production quota, allocation of funds, and recruitment of staff.

Turning to foreign sources for capital and technical aid represents, perhaps, the most significant shift in policy, for which Deng gave the following rationale:

> Backwardness must be recognised before it can be changed. One must learn from those who are more advanced before he can catch up with and surpass them. Of course, in order to raise China's scientific and technical level we must rely on our own efforts, develop our own creativity and persist in the policy of independence and self-reliance. But independence does not mean shutting the door on the world, nor does self-reliance mean blind opposition to everything foreign. Science and technology are part of the wealth created in common by all mankind. Every people or country should learn from the advanced science and technology of others.[3]

Under Deng Xiaoping's direction, China's economic policy has manifested three patterns of development:[4]

The first is found in urban areas and districts located along the eastern coastal province, characterised by rapid growth of both state-owned and collective industrial enterprises. Although only one-quarter of the country's population lives here, this coastal region contains over half of the state-owned industries and collective industries.

A second pattern of development is found in urban areas and districts located in the interior provinces. These regions hold another one-quarter of the nation's people, but there is less industry than in the coastal region, and the ratio of state to collectively-owned enterprises is higher than on the coast.

A third pattern of development has occurred in rural districts in both the interior and coastal regions, covering a vast expanse of the countryside where the remaining one-half of the population resides. The industrial development in these parts is not large, and unlike many enterprises found in the first two patterns, the relatively small industries are not subsidiaries or sub-contractors for larger urban enterprises.

Ezra Vogel has visited China on many occasions, and saw little change in the country up to 1980. However, he is struck not only by the transformations over the past decade but also by the rapid pace of change in the southern province of Guangdong:

> In annual visits to Guangdong since 1980, however, I have seen striking changes each time. By 1987 in Guangzhou, bicycles pulling carts had virtually disappeared and diesel tractors had been banned. Buses were more widespread, and almost no

one travelled standing in a truck bed. The streets were jammed with taxis, vans, cars, and motorbikes, in addition to bicycles. Stores, filled with goods and cus- tomers, lined the streets. Open food markets were large and noisy, with a far greater variety of goods for sale than before. New buildings and construction sites could be found in all parts of the city, and dozens of factories had modern production equipment .... More roads in the countryside were paved .... Trucks and vans had largely replaced the diesel tractors on rural highways.[5]

In other words, China is becoming modernised. Economically, China has recorded an average of 9 per cent in annual growth in GNP in the 1980s, and 12.8 per cent in 1992.[6] However, while elements of the Mao Zedong system are rapidly eroding, the new system espoused by Deng Xiaoping is not as yet institutionalised. Nevertheless, distinctive changes are discernable even while social, political, and economic contradictions abound.

The Opening of China

The opening of China to foreign investment and foreign products is a major turn-around from Maoist policies stressing a centrally controlled economy and self-reliance. For outsiders and the Chinese people alike, the opening of China after decades of isolation has consequences that are still unclear. An immediate impact is a dramatic increase in international trade. In the 1950s, the value of China's trade with other nations was small, limited mainly to the Soviet Union and Eastern European socialist allies. (Exports at the time equalled US$ 550 million, and imports US$ 580 million.) On a world-wide scale, China's international trade at the time ranked only 32nd amongst all nations.[7] By contrast, in 1993, the total value of import-exports had climbed to US$ 196 billion (US$ 92 billion in export value and US$ 104 billion in import value), ranking 11th in the world.[8] It is further estimated that by the year 1994, the annual total import and export volume is likely to hit US$ 200 billion.[9]

Being highly successful in attracting overseas investment, total foreign capital flow into China in 1993 reached US$ 27 billion, making the country the largest recipient of external finance in the world.[10] These statistics mainly reflect the establishment of special new economic zones (NEZ) to attract foreign investments. Five NEZ were created in the 1980s located in the southeastern sea coast of China (in Shenzhen, Zhuhai, Shantou in the province of Guangdong; Xiamen in the province of Fujian; and a fifth NEZ on the island province of Hainan). Subsequently, another NEZ has been established in the Pudong area of Shanghai. As well, some 300 cities, mainly along the eastern coastline and bordering rivers, have been designated as areas for foreign investments.

China's Ministry of Foreign Trade and Economic Cooperation shows that China currently has 4,497 enterprises operating in 120 countries and territories. Worldwide "official" direct investment added up to US$ 5.16 billion.[11] However, the Chinese Government has increasingly relied on borrowing both locally and overseas to finance projects. In 1993, the government issued 30 billion yuan of treasury bonds and foreign loans reached US$ 70 billion.[12]

The policy to open up China has manifested two other significant developments. Since 1978, over 190,000 students in various fields have been sent by the Chinese Government or as self-financed students to such countries as the United States, Canada, Australia, Japan, Russia, and western Europe. Admittedly, this programme has not worked out as well as expected as it is well-known that a significant number of these students have decided not to return to China.[13]

China's improved international relations are also reflected in a fast growing tourism industry. In 1978, less than 2 million travellers visited China. In 1992, this total had swelled to 38 million visitors, and it was estimated that foreign exchange income from tourism amounted to US$ 4 billion.[14]

The Household Responsibility System

One of Deng's first policies was to replace the rural communes with a system that gives individual peasant households the responsibility for its production. (See Chapter 6) This change affects both political and economic structures. It reinstates township governments, and strips the collective of all political, administrative, and non-economic powers and functions. Many households shifted from planting basic grain (still price-controlled) to planting cash crops that could be sold under free market prices. Furthermore, the change to individual household farming no longer required every rural household member to remain in the fields. Many took on work in nearby towns and cities while continuing to live in village home ("to leave the land but not leave the countryside"). Some energetic peasants worked on farms during the day or harvest seasons, and took casual jobs in nearby towns and cities during the night or non-harvesting period. Other peasants simply abandoned unprofitable farming for higher paying jobs in the new rural towns and cities. With the gradual mechanisation in agriculture, it is estimated that by the year 2000, approximately 200 million surplus labour will be released from agricultural work in rural areas.[15]

These changes in the rural areas of China have at least two major implications for its social welfare policies and programmes. First, the social safety net (however modest or generous) provided by the former rural commune system no longer exists; anyone needing help must now look to his or her household unit. Secondly, although large numbers of persons released from agricultural work have been absorbed into new rural enterprises as noted below, many others have become members of an unemployed and dislocated population. (See Chapter 9)

Urbanisation and Industrialisation of Rural Areas

In the PRC, the definition of an urban place has some peculiar characteristics. (See Chapter 5) The official definition of urban population refers to those people living in administrative districts of cities and towns. In recent years, the government has encouraged the development of rural townships. In the process of creating new areas of industrial growth, new rural towns serve to absorb surplus peasant labour which otherwise might stream *en masse* to the large built up urban areas.

Another feature of urbanisation is a significant growth in secondary and tertiary industries. Table 3.1 and Table 3.2 show that primary industry (farming and agriculture) is on the decline both in terms of employment and production values, whereas tertiary industries (commerce, tourism, entertainment, and services) are now emerging from their past neglect. Ironically, primary industry only constitutes 27 per cent of the gross national output, but it has employed almost 60 per cent of the labour work force.

Table 3.1: Gross National Product of Different Types of Industry in 1978 and 1992 (in billion yuan)

	1978		1992	
Primary industry	101.84	(28.4%)	574.4	(23.9%)
Secondary industry	174.52	(48.6%)	1,157.5	(48.2%)
Tertiary industry	82.45	(23.0%)	670.1	(27.9%)
Total	358.81	(100%)	2,402.0	(100%)

Source: SSB, *China Statistical Yearbook* (Beijing: China Statistical Publishers, 1993), pp. 31–32.

Table 3.2: Social Labour Force by Type of Industry in 1952, 1978,
and 1992 (in million yuan)

	1952		1978		1992	
Primary industry	173.2	(83.5%)	283.1	(70.5%)	347.7	(58.8%)
Secondary industry	15.3	(7.4%)	69.7	(17.4%)	129.2	(21.7%)
Tertiary industry	18.9	(9.1%)	48.7	(12.1%)	117.4	(19.8%)
Total	207.4	(100%)	401.5	(100%)	594.3	(100%)

Source: Ibid, p. 101.

In terms of output value, China can be recognised as an industrialised country, but China is basically an agricultural economy in terms of employment structure and degree of urbanisation.

A Multi-ownership Economy

Another area of significant change has been the transformation from a unitary structure of public ownership to a pluralistic and multi-ownership economy. Prior to 1978, public ownership monopolised the economic structure. Deng has since relaxed this policy to allow the development of other forms of ownership. In the early 1980s, he defended a policy of private ownership with important restrictions:

> ... private ownership of some means of production, such as farm cattle and small farm implements, is now permissable. There is nothing wrong with it. But private ownership is impermissable with regard to the land, water, conservancy facilities, important means of production, industrial enterprises and other large-scale sideline occupation run by the commune, production, brigade or team.[16]

In 1992, the *People's Daily* announced a new classification of enterprise: SOE (state-owned enterprises of the central and local governments); COE (collectively-owned enterprises in which the means of production are owned by a collective); Private Enterprises (where the means of production are owned by individual private citizens); Individual Entrepreneurs (where the individual's labour is the basis of production and the number of employees cannot exceed eight persons); Federative Enterprises (joint corporations of different types of enterprises); Foreign Investment; Hong Kong and Macau Investment; Ownership in shares; as

Table 3.3: Distribution of Labour Force in 1952, 1978, and 1992
(in percentage)

| | Percentage | | | |
	1952	1978	1992	Number (1992)
SOE	7.6	18.6	18.3	108,890,000
COE	0.1	5.1	6.2	36,210,000
Others	—	—	0.4	2,820,000
Individual labours				
Urban	4.3	—	1.3	8,380,000
Rural	88.0	76.3	73.8	438,020,000
	100.0	100.0	100.0	594,320,000

Source: Ibid, p. 97.

well as a category of "Others", which presumably is to take care of any new type of activity.[17]

Recent reforms giving more autonomy to enterprises include the separation of ownership (which may remain with the state) from management (which may be a collective or a private individual). Coupled with the selling of some money losing SOE to private investors, the issuing of shares in selected SOE reflect the trend towards greater privatisation. It is estimated that by the year 2000, the number of private enterprises would reach 300,000 (as compared to 130,000 in 1992), employing 50 million people and constituting 20 per cent of GDP.[18] Public ownership will remain the dominant form of ownership, but COE and private enterprises are growing. The magnitude of the changes brought about by Deng's reforms are reflected by shifts in the labour force and by production values among various types of enterprises. These are shown in Table 3.3 and Table 3.4.

The data in Table 3.3 show changes in the labour force which carries major implications for social welfare. In the year 1978, which denotes the end of the Maoist period, the majority of working persons (76.3 per cent) were engaged in rural agricultural labour where social needs were provided by rural communes. Another 19 per cent of the country's labour force, living mainly in urban areas, were engaged in SOE, which provide for its members a comprehensive cradle-to-grave social welfare coverage. (See Chapter 4) Only 5.1 per cent of the total working population were engaged in enterprises which did not have the equivalent kinds of welfare coverage.

Table 3.4: Distribution of Industrial Output Values by Ownership
(excluding farm output)

	1952	1978	1992	1992 Gross output value in billion yuan
SOE	41.5	77.6	48.1	1,782.4
COE	3.3	22.4	38.0	1,410.1
Individual business	20.6	—	6.8	250.7
Others	34.6	—	7.1	263.4
Total	100.0	100.0	100.0	3,706.6

Source: Ibid., p. 409.

By 1992, the proportion of workers still involved in SOE has remained approximately the same but the proportion of COE workers with little on-the-job welfare coverage had increased to 6.2 per cent. The large majority of workers remain in rural areas, but they no longer have the welfare umbrella provided previously by a rural commune.

The other noteworthy piece of information contained in Table 3.3 is that the 1978 figures show no one officially engaged in business as an individual. By 1992, however, 1.3 per cent of the total working population is listed in this category. Although this percentage is low, the raw numbers are significant given the enormous size of the working population.

Law Reforms

Historically, formal laws in China were employed mainly for punishment rather than for protection of individual rights. And, as we had noted in Chapter 1, traditional Chinese society was generally governed not by laws but by informal societal norms and procedures.

Following the Soviet legal system, the CCP's earlier policy put politics and party rule above the law which meant that the party, rather than an independent judiciary, determined what is right and what is wrong.[19] Most civil disputes were handled through mediation and administrative intervention by the state. Before 1978, all private practice of law was banned; the Ministry of Justice abolished in 1959, and law schools closed. The system was often marked by cruelty and abuses, especially during the Cultural Revolution. Only after 1979 were law schools reopened, a system of defense lawyer restored, the Ministry of Justice re-established, and the relationship between the party and the judiciary redefined.[20]

Along with the previously noted economic reforms has come a host of new laws. From 1978 to 1990, the NPC promulgated over 70 pieces of legislation; the State Council had issued over 700 regulations, and local People's Congress over 1,000 local laws.[21] Welfare laws include *Marriage, Law* (1980), *Protection of Women's Rights* (1991), *Protection of Juvenile* (1991), *Protection of the Rights of the Disabled* (1990), and *Trade Union Law* (1992). In 1989, the *Administrative Procedure Law* was promulgated which provided channels for ordinary citizens to take their disputes with the government to court. From 1990 to 1993, more than 70,000 law suits had been brought against the government. Of which 37 per cent were decided in favour of ordinary citizens.[22] Such basic law reforms, however, present Chinese leaders with a dilemma. On the one hand, there is acknowledgement that formal laws are essential for a stable modern economy, and for a favourable environment to attract foreign investments. On the other hand, law reform threatens to diminish the powers of the government and the party.

Maintaining a Tough Government

Economic reforms in the PRC have inevitably raised the issue of political reform and the role of the CCP. The issue centres generally on the connection between politics and economics, and particularly on the role of centralised power in the process of modernisation. Prior to the Tiananmen crackdown in June, 1989, the notion of neo-authoritarianism surfaced as a major topic among Chinese intellectuals and government officials.[23]

The experiences of other Asian countries became an important point of reference. Of special interest were the "Four Little Dragons", so-called because they were viewed as Chinese societies (Taiwan and Hong Kong) or, as societies heavily influenced by Confucian values (Singapore and South Korea). These states were prosperous, with governments perceived as highly authoritarian. A general perception of neo-authoritarianism by its proponents in the PRC is described in an excellent paper by Sautman:

> Chen Yizi, director of the State Council's Institute for Restructuring the Economic System, and two vice-directors, Wang Xiaoqiang and Li Jun, argued that there are four models of political economy in the world: tough governments and tough economies (the Stalinist model); soft governments and tough economies (e.g., India); tough governments and soft economies (the Four Small Dragons, Brazil, Turkey); and soft governments and soft economies (many contemporary western systems). Chen and his associates argued that the third system — tough

governments and soft economies had produced more successes than the first and second, while no developing country had succeeded with the fourth since the end of the Second World War. Their obvious implication was that China needed an authoritarian political regime that was capable of creating an expanding free market economy.[24]

Another proponent, Wu Jiaxiang, an economist at Beijing University, further argued that social development must pass through three stages: the first is a traditional autocratic authority in which a product economy prevailed; the second is an enlightened autocracy which creates a semi-market to replace the natural economy; and the third is a full market economy integrated with liberal democracy. According to Wu, no society has leaped directly from stage one to stage three. In other words, individual freedom cannot be developed in a society where the market economy is underdeveloped, and the development of the market economy requires the support of a strong authority.[25]

The doctrine of neo-authoritarianism contains a number of assumptions. One is a duality between economic freedom and centralised authority. A second assumption is that developing nations largely lack the conditions for promoting democracy, while neo-authoritarianism could create these through centralised power. A third is that democracy cannot be established immediately from imperial, colonial, or other "old" authoritarians regimes; a transitional period is required as the premature establishment of democracy would only impede economic development due to the disturbances and crises that would arise. During the discussions and debates among intellectuals prior to June 1989, many dissenting arguments were raised against the idea of neo-authoritarianism.[26] The essence of the opposing view is that rights and freedom (i.e., democracy) is never bestowed from above, they must be won by the people through political and economic struggle, as witnessed in examples taken from experiences in Western societies. A free market economy can only come with political freedom.

However, given the fact that no nation has entered the ranks of newly industrialising countries in the post-Second World War era through a soft government and soft economy, the proponents saw only two choices for developing countries. One is to have a weak leadership that will allow strong interest groups to carve up the market; the other is to have a hard-line leadership that can control forces for the effective introduction of a market system. (A Marxist-Leninist type of system evidently was no longer considered a relevant option.)

In recognising the danger that an authoritarian regime could simply shackle freedom, the proponents saw the need for certain conditions.[27]

    (a) The neo-authoritarian must promote legal commercial relations by contract that does not discriminate against non-governmental entities;

    (b) It permits an independent judiciary at least regarding economic mattters; and

    (c) It defines the legalities of relations between the central and local governments, between governments and enterprises, and between families and enterprises.

Whether or not the proponents were simply indulging in wishful thinking, the doctrine of neo-authoritarianism has an obvious appeal to the CCP leadership. It appears to be in tune with a strategy of "top-down" reforms. Moreover, it justifies a strong autocratic government for here is a theory that portrays a successful economic market system as compatible with an authoritarian political order.[28] The doctrine also appeals to the Chinese mind because it is consistent with some basic Confucian values.

Traditional Authoritarianism

In traditional society, people and their families could enjoy a relative autonomy in activities such as farming, trade, education, commerce, and religion. These however, depended on a harmonious and orderly environment that only a strong government could provide. In turn, respect for, and submissiveness to, authority became a distinctive feature of the Chinese civilisation:

> Officials were supposed to be sympathetic and understanding of the travails of individuals. A form of paternalism was the highest ideal of government, and everything was done to envelop transactions between government and the public in layers of diffuse human emotion. Citizens never demanded their rights; they sought instead the sympathy, and indeed the pity, of those more powerful than themselves. Officials, in turn, avoided as much as possible the confining discipline of any absolute and impersonal standards of treatment and demonstrated instead their capacity for human sentiment by giving free rein to discrimination in their treatment of each particular case. Above all citizens were taught that they should never be aggressive or demanding in their relations with public authorities; and officials were expected to be considerate and understanding of those who were docile and properly dependent.[29]

Influential Western social scientists such as Weber and Wright had posited the view that traditional Chinese culture blocked the emergence of capitalism and modernisation.[30] Later, Mao Zedong also denounced traditional Chinese culture as feudalistic. An anti-Confucianist theme permeated the Cultural Revolution (which implies that traditions were still strong among the populace in the late 1960s and early 1970s). Ironically, the chaos and tragedies created by the Cultural Revolution served to reinforce in the minds of people the great need for order and stability. In reinterpreting socialist ideology, Deng and his supporters have resurrected traditional values ("socialism with Chinese characteristics") as a base for introducing modernisation.

The Economics of Neo-Confucianism

With the break-up of socialist regimes in the former Soviet Union and Eastern European block, together with the economic success of Japan and the "Four Little Dragons", there has come a re-examination of the thesis that traditional Chinese culture is a block to modernisation. A number of writers now see certain aspects of Confucianism as not only amicable to the acceptance of Western knowledge but also instrumental in the development of an entrepreneurial spirit that has led to the economic prosperity of the Chinese in South East Asia.[31]

There is the further suggestion that "Post-Confucianism" is to the East what the Protestant ethic is to the West in promoting industrialisation and modernisation.[32] Kahn attributes four specific contributions of Confucian ethics to the economic success of East Asian nations:[33]

(a) The emphasis of the socialisation process of the family on self-control, education, skill learning, and attitudes towards work, family and obligations;
(b) Individual identification with the collectivity;
(c) Emphasis and acceptance of hierarchical structure;
(d) Emphasis on interdependence of human relations.

Other Neo-Confucian values that could promote industrialisation include the meritocratic selection of bureaucratic leaders; and the attachment of loyalty to groups such as family and local community, and workplace. The emphasis is on a group loyalty that puts the need of the group over individual interests. Under such a group orientation, people are more willing to limit their personal consumptions in order to save and to invest in the future of their family or firm.[34]

There is the interesting notion that it is the "political aspects", rather than the "economic aspects", of Confucianism which is the impedient to modernisation changes. If the government can provide a stable and secure environment which emphasises law and order, free trade, and efficient administration, successful economic performance can flourish.[35]

Contemporary Authoritarianism

Deng Xiaoping, learning from the lessons of Eastern Europe and the disorder caused by Mao's the Cultural Revolution, constantly reiterates the point that the single most critical variable affecting the viability of the new economic policies is a stable and unified political situation. Without this, he warned, economic development could not proceed. After the Tiananmen crackdown, he said in the *People's Daily*:[36]

> Before and above everything else, China needs stability. Without a stable environment, all other efforts will be in vain, and we will lose the gains we have already made. We need reforms, but we need stability before we can mount reforms. We will not be able to accomplish anything if we deviate from this point.

The developmental experiences of the Four Little Dragons have also had a profound effect on the Chinese leadership. Here is an Asian model to replace the Western model for a developing country. "To build a number of Hong Kongs on the Mainland," and "Turning Shenzhen (NEZ) into a 'socialist Hong Kong'", are some of the remarks now coming from the Chinese leadership.[37] Likewise, Chinese Government officials and Deng Xiaoping himself have suggested that China should learn from Singapore, a model of social order and discipline in the midst of economic modernisation.[38]

It is perfectly clear that Deng and his supporters see a tough government in control of the PRC, with efforts continuing to move in the direction of a soft economy. These would be the parameters within which modernisation of China would proceed. And the same macro conditions would be upheld in any reforms in the social welfare field.

Notes

1. This is a significant change from the *1982 Constitution* which proclaims that the state practices a planned economy on the basis of socialist public ownership, and ensures the growth of the national economy through overall economic planning with a supplementary role for market regulation. The amended constitution in 1993 states that China practises a socialist market economy. The state will strengthen economic legislation and perfect macroregulation and controls. *BR*, 26 April–2 May 1993, p. 1.

2. *BR*, 1–7 March 1993, p. 3.
3. X. P. Deng, *Deng Xiaoping, Speeches and Writings* (Oxford: Pergamon Press, 1984), p. 45.
4. D. Perkins,"The Influence of Economic Reforms on China's Urbanization", in *Chinese Urban Reform*, edited by Y. W. Kwok, W. Parish and A. Yeh (Armonk, N.Y.: M. E. Sharpe, 1990), pp. 78–106.
5. E. Vogel, *One Step Ahead in China* (Cambridge: Harvard University Press, 1989), p. 2.
6. *OW*, 28 June 1993, p. 3.
7. *MP*, 15 February 1992, p. 8.
8. *BR*, 11–16 April 1994, p. 22.
9. *BR*, 24–30 January 1994, p. 13.
10. *Hong Kong Economic Journal*, 17 December 1993, p. 9.
11. *BR*, 21–27 March 1994, p. 18.
12. *SCMP*, 8 July 1994, p. 9.
13. Only 60,000 of them had returned. *SCMP*, 19 January 1993, p. 9.
14. Of this figure, 90 per cent are tourists from Hong Kong, Macau and Taiwan. SSB, *China Statistical Yearbook* (Beijing: China Statistical Publishers, 1993), p. 654.
15. *OW*, 10 May 1993, p. 16.
16. X. P. Deng, op. cit., p. 95.
17. *PD*, 20 December 1992, p. 1.
18. *Hong Kong Economic Journal*, 29 January 1993, p. 10.
19. S. Odgen, *China's Unresolved Issues: Politics, Development, and Culture* (Englewood, Cliffs, N.J.: Prentice Hall, 1989), chapter six.
20. H. D. Chiu, "Chinese Law and Justice: Trends Over Three Decades", in *Power and Policy in the PRC*, edited by Y. M. Shaw (Boulder, Col.: Westview Press, 1985), pp. 203–28.
21. The Synthetical Study of Social Development Project Group, "A Synthetical Analysis of China's Social Development in the Structural Transition Period", *Sociological Studies*, 4 (20 July 1991), pp. 74–93.
22. *SCMP*, 13 July 1994, p. 10.
23. B. Sautman, "Sirens of the Strongman: Neo-Authoritarianism in Recent Chinese Political Theory", *The China Quarterly*, 129 (March 1992), pp. 72–102.
24. Ibid.
25. M. Ji, *Neo-Authoritarianism* (Taipei: Tangshan Publishers, 1991).
26. Opponents of neo-authoritarianism concentrated on seven counterpoints: the three-stage pattern of old authority, neo-authoritarianism and democracy is ahistorical; democracy can develop alongside a commodity economy; democracy should not be associated with anarchic social disturbances; the economic take-off of the Four Small Dragons resulted from *laissez-faire* and not from

government intervention; only democracy can abate official corruption, while authoritarianism cannot pave the way to democracy; neo-authoritarians confuse policy-making and policy implementation — the enforcement of policy is a matter of administrative responsibility, while the making of it should not be reduced to the world of the "chief"; and neo-authoritarians neglect the reform of the system and concentrate exclusively on the role of individuals. Sautman, op. cit., p. 83.

27. Ibid., p. 93.

28. C. A. Johnson, "Political Institutions and Economic Performance", in *Asian Economic Development — Present and Future*, edited by R. A. Scalapino, S. Sato and J. Wanandi (Berkeley, Institute of East Asian Studies, University of California, 1985), pp. 63–89; S. Huntington, *Political Order in Changing Societies* (London: Yale University Press).

29. L. Pye, *The Spirit of Chinese Politics* (Cambridge, Mass.: The MIT Press, 1968), p. 19.

30. M. Weber, *The Religion of China: Confucianism and Taoism* (New York: The Free Press, 1968); M. C. Wright, *The Last Stand of Chinese Conservatism: The T'ung-chih Restoration, 1862–1874* (Stanford: Stanford University Press, 1957).

31. D. Morawetz, *Twenty Years of Economic Development: 1950 to 1975* (New York: World Bank, 1977); E. Chen, *Hyper-growth in Asian Economics: A Comparative Study of Hong Kong, Japan, Korea, Singapore and Taiwan* (London: Macmillan, 1979); L. P. Jones and I. Sakong, *Government, Business and Entrepreneurship in Economic Development: The Korean Case* (Cambridge, Mass.: Harvard University Press, 1980); R. Hofheinz and K. Calder, *The Eastasian Edge* (New York: Basic Books, 1982); G. H. Huang, *Confucianism and East-Asian Modernization* (Taipei: Great Current Publishers, 1988); G. Redding, *The Spirit of Chinese Capitalism* (New York: De Gruyter, 1990); R. Appelbaum and J. Henderson (eds.), *States and Development in the Asian Pacific Rim* (London: Sage Publications, 1992). This is not to suggest that Confucianism is the only factor contributing to the modernisation of these nations. Under certain conditions, Confucian traditions supported by a modern form of political system could make modernisation possible. Some of the conditions include:

(a) Decentralised state administration: To minimise state intervention, a more decentralised administrative structure with delegated autonomy to make specific decisions concerning local problems;

(b) Authoritarian state: Authority is centralised in an hierarchy which can maintain stability and order, and efficient and clean government;

(c) Investment in human capital: The state has to ensure the abundant supply of human resources and educated manpower, and the maintenance of low unemployment.

32. R. MacFarquhar, "The Post-Confucian Challenge", *The Economist*, 9 February 1980, pp. 67–72.
33. H. Kahn, *World Economic Development: 1979 and Beyond* (London: Croom Helm, 1979), pp. 121–23.
34. G. Lodge and E. Vogel (eds.), *Ideology and National Competitiveness* (Boston, Mass.: Harvard Business School Press, 1987), pp. 14–23; E. Vogel, *The Four Little Dragons: The Spread of Industrialization in East Asia* (Cambridge, Mass.: Harvard University Press, 1991), pp. 92–103.
35. S. H. Alatas, "Religion and Modernization in Southeast Asia", in *Modernization in Southeast Asia*, edited by Hans-Dieter Evers (London: Oxford University Press, 1973), pp. 153–69; S. Goldstein (ed.), *Minidragons* (Boulder: Westview Press, 1991), p. 6.
36. *PD*, 10 October 1989, p. 1.
37. *SCMP*, 8 May 1992, p. 10.
38. *SCMP*, 20 July 1992, p. 9.

Employment-based Welfare —
The "Iron Rice Bowl"

According to Marxist-Leninist ideology, the working class or the proletariat is accorded a special or privileged position in a socialist society. With the means of production coming under public ownership, and the exploitation of workers removed, labour is no longer a commodity, and the relationship between management and labour would be harmonious as their interests are identical. The workers, now masters of the nation, would be motivated to be more productive. Labour welfare and protection would, therefore, facilitate economic growth.

These are the precepts upon which the CCP created an occupational welfare system that represented an unprecedented level of intervention by a Chinese government into the lives of its people, and brought into being a welfare institution previously unknown in traditional China. This development also served the new government's need to secure the support of urban employees for a Communist regime and its nationalisation programme during a period of economic recovery and nation building.

Even before coming to power in 1949, the CCP had targeted social security protection for workers as a major priority. For example, the party adopted the policy of an eight-hour workday in 1922; and in labour regulations promulgated in 1931, the Chinese Soviet introduced material and medical assistance to the sick, disabled, and elderly employees in the Communist revolutionary bases. In 1948, provisional regulations were enacted in the liberated areas of north-eastern China (Manchurian provinces) covering such matters as labour relations, labour insurance, the wage system, industrial safety, rights of women and children, and relief for the unemployed.[1]

Labour and Employment Policy under Mao

The CCP did not have to start their economic industrialisation from scratch.

They took over from the previous regime a significant amount of industrial capacity, skilled industrial labour, and entrepreneurial talent.[2] However, in 1949, as an aftermath of a world war and then civil war, industrial production had fallen to only 17 per cent of the GDP.[3] Nearly five million unemployed people, or 24 per cent of the non-agricultural workforce, presented the most urgent social and economic problem.[4] Lacking the resources to provide relief to the unemployed, the CCP pushed instead a policy of job creation through the development of heavy industry and the use of administrative procedures. All production and consumption came under the control of the central government, coordinated through a variety of plans prepared by different central planning commissions, and implemented by their counterpart units at the provincial and county levels. Not surprisingly, over one-half of the government ministries at this time were involved in economic functions.[5]

Regulations were also enacted to centralise control over the recruitment and allocation of employees. Subsequently, work units themselves were prevented from recruiting or dismissing workers, and graduates from schools and colleges did not have the freedom to choose their own jobs. Work assignment came under the Labour and Personnel Departments of local governments, which allocated workers to jobs on a permanent and life-long basis. Since enterprises were not responsible for their profit and losses, they showed little resistance to the government policy of assigning to them those "unnecessary employees".[6] During subsequent periods of high urban unemployment, young people would be assigned to seek work in the rural areas.[7]

Under the Chinese command economy, economic enterprises took the form of work units (*danwei*). The *danwei* became the pivotal mediating institution between the state and the individual, serving as a mechanism for the implementation of state policies and for the construction of a socialist society. Given the key role of government rather than the market in regulating economic processes, enterprises depended on the state for the supply of raw materials, the allocation of the work force, the sale and distribution of products, and for subsidies in times of deficits. The labour and employment policy of the CCP led to a rapid increase in the non-agricultural employee population, which swelled from 16 million in 1952 to 31 million in 1957, and to nearly 60 million in 1960.[8] Meanwhile, the unemployment rate dropped from 13.2 per cent in 1952 to 5.9 per cent in 1957.[9]

Not only were SOE workers guaranteed life-long employment, they also enjoyed generous welfare benefits and services. Functioning as a "small society" (*xiao shehui*) or "mini-welfare state", the *danwei* exhibited some basic characteristics of the traditional pattern of an extended family or clan bearing the total responsibility of taking care of all of the social and economic needs of their members.[10] The crucial difference is that the party leader now replaced the chief of the clan as the authoritarian, paternal and benevolent head.[11]

As we will later describe, a central part of the employment-based welfare programme is a social insurance scheme established in 1951 under the *Labour Insurance Law* (*Regulations regarding Labour Insurance in the PRC*). With a national development strategy patterned after the Soviet Union, the *Labour Insurance Law* was comprehensive in coverage, generous in the level of benefits, and non-contributory in its financing (did not require direct contributions from the workers). The unemployed, and the employees of the non-SOE, however were not included in the scheme. Perhaps the CCP regarded the existence of these two groups as transitory, diminishing as the socialist economy became fully developed. In fact, when the *Labour Insurance Law* was promulgated in 1951, nearly 98.6 per cent of the employed population worked in SOE.[12]

Various writers have emphasised the importance of the work unit in the PRC as not simply a place where one works.[13] Besides combining social, political and economic life, it is also a place where one acquires various forms of welfare services such as housing, medical care, education and social security. In addition to this basic protection, SOE workers came to enjoy a host of benefits, subsidies, and personal services. Taken together, these benefits and services formed a comprehensive system of "from-cradle-to-grave" protection and security. The work units had a pervasive and overwhelming influence on every aspect of an employee's life. At the same time, this dependency subjected the worker to the control of the state authority.

The Structure of Employment-based Welfare

The large majority of all organised social services in the PRC is found in enterprises or work units. For example, nationally, some 225,000 hospitals and three million primary schools are operated by SOE with only 60,000 hospitals and 830,000 primary schools by local governments.[14] In 1992, the total welfare expenditure in enterprises amounted to 131 billion yuan, representing almost one-third of the total nation's wage bill.[15] Typical welfare services within an SOE can be divided into four major areas:

(a) Labour insurance: This scheme provides benefits to cover retirement, sickness, injury (work related and non-work related), medical care, invalidity and death, funeral expenses, survivorship, maternity and sick leave.

(b) Allowances: China does not separate the difference between fringe benefits and welfare. Various benefits in cash include subsidies on food, meals, housing, bathing, haircuts, and transportation (and later), single-child families.

(c) Collective welfare: Most enterprises operate a number of service units which include clinics, primary schools, day care centres, nurseries, bathhouses, kindergartens, sports facilities, barber shops, canteens, club houses, recreational centres, libraries, theatres, and reading rooms.

(d) Individual welfare: The enterprises have the responsibility to take care of staff who have personal and family difficulties. These personal services, provided mainly by union cadres at the cell group level, include job placement for the physically disabled, mediation of family, individual and industrial disputes, promotion of family planning and family education, assistance to poverty-stricken households, care for the retired elderly, and the counselling of delinquent youth.

In order to understand the operation of the work-based system and the extent to which it penetrates into the lives of the workers, it is necessary to

Figure 4.1: A Simplified Organisational Structure of an SOE

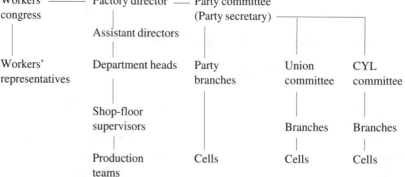

have a general picture of the structure of a typical SOE. This is shown in Figure 4.1.

Welfare Policy and Administration

The formulation and execution of welfare policy involves a complicated structure that interlocks an hierarchical network of committees and organisations. The integral parts of the SOE consist of the Communist Party representatives, the administration, the workers' congress and the union. Administratively, there is an assistant director who is responsible for the livelihood and welfare of the staff. In reality, the Communist Party committee, headed by a party secretary, is the most powerful decision-making body within the enterprise. There are parallel party committees side-by-side with the administrative structure at each level. These committees include departments concerned with the work of organisation, propaganda, military service, discipline, the Communist Youth League (CYL) and the union.[16] Generally speaking, the party controls all decisions regarding production, personnel (appointments, promotion, and transfer), finance, and welfare. And, the party committee is usually the final arbiter in making "correct" interpretations of government policies and directives in cases when disputes arise. The workers' congress is promoted as an important institution of democratic management in which industrial workers can participate in the management and decision-making of the enterprise. Comprised of elected workers' representatives, the functions of the congress include the responsibility to discuss, examine, and initiate proposals on enterprise management relating particularly to the enterprise's annual production targets and plans for the year. The congress is also involved in the formulation and administration of policies on labour protection and welfare, distribution of profits, and the rules governing the provision and allocation of housing, medical benefits, injury indemnity and retirement pensions.[17]

The Union and the Communist Youth League

Under the leadership of the party committee, there are two types of mass organisations, namely the union and the CYL. These organisations are viewed by the CCP as important bridges to facilitate communication between the party and the masses. The role of a "transmission belt" for party decisions is emphasised. Furthermore, the organisations are considered as "schools" for their constituencies to learn socialism, communism and Marxism.

Trade unions are found in major industries and at different geographical levels (province, city, county, and district). Their espoused task is to work for the rights and interests of workers and staff so they can play their part as a principal force in the building of a socialist material and spiritual civilisation.[18] Trade unions are supposed to be the key official channel where suggestions to the party on recruitment, wages, subsidies, welfare, industrial safety, and women's rights are made.

According to the official view, the fundamental interests of trade unions and the government are identical. Therefore, trade unions should safeguard government authority, which in return should respect and protect trade unions' legal rights and interests.[19] In contrast with the West, independent unions are suppressed, and the party-sponsored unions are not supposed to use industrial action. (In fact, the right to strike was deleted from the Chinese *Constitution* in 1982.) In 1992, there was a total of 617,000 grassroots unions with a membership of 103 million representing 92 per cent of the working population in enterprises with unions.[20] If the total employee population (148 million) is included, the rate of unionisation is 70 per cent. The percentage is further lowered to 17 per cent if the total working population including rural peasants (594 million) is used as the base. A national survey carried out by the All-China Federation of Trade Unions in 1986 showed that almost 60 per cent of the workers were not satisfied with the work of the unions, which were perceived to be preoccupied with recreational and cultural activities.[21]

The CYL accepts members aged between 14 to 28. It is also an hierarchically organised institution found in a variety of settings (schools, enterprises, army, neighbourhoods and government offices). In the past, CYL was an important organisation of political socialisation and party membership recruitment. In recent years, it has become less concerned with ideological and moral issues, and more involved in promoting members' personal interests, and solving practical problems. Recent activities, for example, focus on help in finding marriage partners, developing mutual interest groups, job training, sports and recreational activities, hot-line services for young people in trouble, and employment referrals.[22] By 1989, CYL membership had reached 56 million, which represented less than 20 per cent of the youth population.[23]

A number of functional committees operate at the level of the enterprise, the shopfloor, and the production team. The members of these committees include party secretaries, union secretaries/chairmen and CYL secretaries at the corresponding level. A typical SOE would have:

— A livelihood committee to look after the day-to-day living needs of employees and their families;

— A labour insurance committee to assist in the management of the labour insurance programme;

— A propaganda committee to organise cultural, educational, and recreational activities; and

— A women's committee to look after the special needs of women employees, many of whom are mothers of young children, including the establishment of nurseries, breast-feeding rooms and kindergartens.

To summarise, it can be seen that the welfare network provides a wide variety of benefits and services that integrates a mixture of political, welfare and economic functions. The work units are highly organised, and every person is protected and served, and also monitored, by a myriad of party-controlled networks. All the officials of the party, CYL and unions are state cadres, with wages and welfare paid fully by the enterprises.

Key Features of Employment-based Welfare

The work-based welfare system provides a level of coverage that would be considered comprehensive and generous in comparison with the most advanced welfare states in the West. Within the Chinese context, social security benefits are particularly generous given the generally low levels of income in the PRC. Depending on their former employment, a retiree usually can obtain 60 to 90 per cent of his or her standard wage. In addition to the monthly pension payment, a retiree and family retains other welfare benefits such as housing, medical care and other subsidies.[24]

Another important feature is the non-contributory system of insurance and benefits. Social security expenses are neither financed by taxation nor contributions from employees, but by the income of each individual enterprise. Welfare benefits are regarded as a social wage to compensate for low monetary wages. Thus, expenditures on housing have consistently accounted for less than one per cent of the monthly expenditure of a family.[25]

There are, however, internal discrepancies in welfare benefits as their levels are neither flat-rated nor based upon actual needs. Rather, they are usually calculated according to the rank and status of an employee.

Consequently, discrepancies can account for a substantial difference in living standards between the upper and lower ranks in the enterprises, and between enterprises with different financial situations.[26] For example, in recent years, the average annual social security expenditure per worker in the metropolitan centres of Beijing, Shanghai, and Tianjin was 600 to 700 yuan, whereas it was only 400 to 500 yuan in the poorer Gansu, Qinghai and Xinjiang provinces.[27]

Due to its manifold programme areas, twelve government ministries, commissions and organisations are involved in the administration and policy formulation of the occupational welfare system. They include the Ministries of Labour, Finance, Civil Affairs, Personnel, and Health, as well as the State Economic Organisation Reform Commission, State Planning Commission, Bank of China, and the All-China Federation of Trade Unions. This is a cumbersome feature of the welfare structure as the policy-making dynamics are complicated, and it is often difficult to establish an overall coherent policy when issues arise.

Perhaps the main limitation of the occupational welfare system as a social institution is its inaccessibility to the general population. The system serves the employees of the SOE and the various government departments. Together, they included almost all urban workers at the start of the programme in 1951, but by 1992, these workers accounted for 74 per cent of the employee population, and only 18 per cent of all economically active persons including rural peasants.[28] In brief, among the 567.4 million total working population in China, some 82 per cent are outside this social security and welfare network. The "divided" welfare system gives the SOE a privileged job status, and strongly favours urban residents.[29] With continuous diversification of the economy, the SOE employee population is expected to decrease even more.

The fact that an SOE, until recent reforms, was not responsible for profits or losses turned out to be another vulnerable feature. In cases where an enterprise lost money, it would fall upon state subsidies to indirectly pay for the services. Welfare benefits, as a result, were often distributed indiscriminately to employees as a means to supplement the policy of "high employment, high welfare, and low wages". On the other side of the ledger, enterprises were allowed to devote a proportion of their income to "unproductive investment", primarily housing for employees.[30] This often became a way for enterprise managers to "finesse" the system. As Walder points out:

> When faced with administrative controls on cash disbursements managers turned to distributions in kind through welfare funds, rapid construction of housing, and other strategies to distribute income to their workers.[31]

The significance of occupational welfare becomes apparent when considered in the context of the austere life endured by the large majority of the Chinese population. Similar to other socialist countries, the priority of the government during the Maoist era was on the development of heavy industries. Capital accumulation and investment absorbed most of the economic surplus rather than it being used for improving the living standards and consumption of the people.[32] The CCP slogan: "production first, livelihood second" indicated the policy priority of promoting economic productivity while suppressing consumption and rationing commodities.

The CCP policy on controlled low wages resulted in an average annual increase of only 0.37 per cent in wages between 1953 to 1978.[33] The centralised control of the wage system was intended to limit the difference in income between high and low ranking staff. Under the labour policy of "total government responsibility and centralised government assignment" (*tongbao tongpei*), the state shouldered the responsibility of providing comprehensive work-based welfare and guaranteeing jobs. Consequently, job mobility and dismissals, and to a certain extent, "unemployment" were more or less impossible in the Chinese context for several decades. In official terminology, there are only people "waiting for employment".

Cracks in the "Iron Rice Bowl"

For more than three decades after the establishment of the PRC, government commitment to occupational welfare was unanimously perceived as a superior feature of socialism, and was never challenged or even in doubt. Problems with the social security system began to be recognised by the government in the early 1980s. This was mainly due to a dramatic rise in welfare expenditures. The insurance and welfare fund soared from 7.81 billion yuan in 1978 (14 per cent of the total wage bill) to 131 billion yuan in 1992 (33 per cent of the total wage bill).[34] In fact, standard wage as a percentage of the total SOE employee monetary income dropped from 86 per cent in 1978 to only 54 per cent in 1992.[35]

The growth in welfare expenditure correlated with increasing numbers of people retiring from work. The number of retirees leaped prominently from 3 million in 1978 to over 26 million in 1992, and the ratio of employees to retirees decreased from 30:1 in 1978 to only 5.7:1 in 1992.[36]

This is an average figure; the ratio, in fact varies from 90:1 in some young enterprises to a mere 2:1 in some older enterprises.[37] Consequently, expenditure on retirees rose from 1.7 billion yuan in 1978 to 79.5 billion yuan in 1992.[38] Far worse, demographic projections put the number of retirees by the year 2000 at 40 million, representing 17 per cent of the employee population, with retirement expenditure expected to amount to 150 billion yuan.[39]

In addition to expenditure on pensions, enterprises also have to pay for other welfare expenses of the retirees such as housing and medical care. It is estimated that the pension itself accounts for only one-half of the total expenditure on retirees.[40]

Employment-based welfare represents a comprehensive form of social security for the urban working population, and is an integral part in the building of socialism in the PRC. By and large, it reflects the priority given to the ideology of egalitarianism. Yet the egalitarian employment and wage policy came to be viewed cynically by the Chinese as the major reason for creating the phenomenon of "the Three Irons and One Big". The "iron rice bowl" means that employment for workers is permanent and life-long; the "iron chair" means that the work position is permanent and workers have no worries about dismissals or demotions; and the "iron wage level" means the workers get paid whether or not they show up for work. The "big rice pot" refers to the egalitarian policy of rewarding every person equally without regard to their contribution and performance. The phenomenon is marked by restricted labour mobility or a stagnant work force, prevailing hidden unemployment, and low work incentives and productivity.[41] The Chinese sayings of "work for five persons, but livelihood for three" or "the rice for three persons is shared by five" summarise the inefficiency of the economic enterprises. In the words of an Hungarian economist, the phenomenon is described as "unemployment on the job."[42]

Economic and Labour Reforms Since 1978

As we have indicated, the Chinese Government, under the leadership of Premier Deng Xiaoping and his supporters, is attempting to move the centrally planned economy towards a market orientation. The new economic approach is: the state regulates the market and the market guides the enterprises. Instead of remitting all their profits to the state, or asking for subsidies from the state to cover deficits, economic enterprises, in theory at least, are now accountable for their own finances. With the coming of the profit-retention scheme and the taxation system in 1983, enterprises can retain their profits after paying all the required taxes. With the promulgation of the *Enterprise Law* in 1988 which prescribed the separation of ownership and management, enterprises are supposed to have more autonomy to decide on their policy on labour welfare (wages, bonuses, benefits), person-nel, production, marketing, and investment.[43] But along with greater autonomy, the enterprises now must also take up a larger share of the welfare responsibility. Thus, the issue of how welfare policy affects the efficiency and productivity of the enterprises becomes salient. Labour insurance expenses are still counted as operational expenses, and the after-tax profit would be divided according to the following ratio: 50 per cent for re-investment, 30 per cent for bonus, and 20 per cent for collective welfare.[44]

With the economic diversification in the 1980s, as many as nine categories of enterprises are now recognised, but they can be classified into four main types; namely the SOE, the COE, the Individually-owned (private enterprises), and others (such as joint ventures with foreign partners). The COE are economic enterprises organised by local neighbour-hood governments and organisations in both rural and urban areas, and (in contrast to the SOE) are not bound by the state to provide occupational welfare. Employees in COE not only receive fewer welfare benefits but, on average, also earn less than their counterparts in SOE.[45] And, in 1992, a COE retiree, on average, received only 66 per cent of the pension given to a counterpart in SOE.[46]

The size of the non-agricultural employee population reached nearly 148 million in 1992. The proportion of SOE employees decreased slightly from 78.4 per cent in 1978 to 73.6 per cent in 1992; whereas the COE increased from 21.6 per cent to 24.5 per cent over the same period. The significant change is found in the figures for private enterprises and joint ventures. Almost non-existent in 1978, their figures are still relatively small but they are looked upon as the growth areas in the coming years (Table 4.1).

Significant changes are revealed in the respective outputs of the various types of enterprises. SOE accounted for over three-quarters of the total industrial output in 1978. However, in 1992, its share had plummeted to only 48 per cent. (See Table 3.4 in Chapter 3). Despite massive credits and protection for the SOE, industrial growth in recent years has been fuelled largely by COE (mainly in rural industries), and especially by individual private enterprises and foreign joint ventures.[47] It is reported that at least

Table 4.1: Changes Since 1978 in Distribution of Employee Population in
Different Economic Sectors (in percentage)

	1978	1982	1989	1992
SOE	78.4	76.5	73.6	73.6
COE	21.6	23.5	25.5	24.5
Others	—	—	0.9	1.9
	100.0	100.0	100.0	100.0

Source: SSB, *China Statistical Yearbook* (Beijing: China statistical Publishers, 1993),
         p. 97.

one-third of the SOE were suffering losses in 1993, and in the beginning of
1994, the figure was increased to over 50 per cent. Output by SOE grew
only 2.2 per cent, compared with 32.1 per cent for the COE and 79.1 per
cent for other sectors. SOE losses amounted to 100 million yuan a day.[48]
Direct state subsidies for losses by these enterprises came to 20.5 billion
yuan which was about 5 per cent of the state revenues in 1993.[49]

In order to spread the financial burden of welfare costs, the government
has encouraged work units to participate in joint funding of the retirement
scheme (pension pools) in 1985.[50] (Actually, experiments on funding pools
have been carried out in several provinces since 1984.) The intent is for
young enterprises to share the welfare burden of the older enterprises. The
funds are managed by the insurance agencies of the local labour bureaux,
and they are usually deposited in banks and invested in government bonds.
Therefore, soaring inflation would lead to substantial losses of these funds.
At the end of 1992, about 58 per cent of the employee population were
included in the scheme, and 59 per cent of pension expenditures are paid
through these funding pools.[51] Participation in the funding pools is still
voluntary, reflecting the reluctance of the government to assume an overall
responsibility through legislation in the management of the fund. The
average contribution rate by enterprises to these funds is 19 per cent of the
total payroll, whereas expenditure on pensions is only 15 per cent.[52] Therefore, the funds, even though are operated on a "pay-as-you-go" principle,
they can usually pay for the pensions expenses, and there is currently a
small surplus.[53] In cases of deficits, the local government would intervene
to cover the losses. Furthermore, since most of these funds are organised
at the county and city level, there lacks a senior level authority to achieve
the purpose of pooling risks on a nation-wide, or even a provincial-wide

basis. Currently, several provinces including Guangdong, Beijing, Tianjin, Shanghai and Fujian are organised at the provincial level.

Other than pensions, medical care is the second largest item of expenditure in occupational welfare. One recent report noted that the state only provides 14 per cent of the total medical expenditure in hospitals, while the rest has to come from user fees.[54] Medical expenses for employees increased dramatically from 3.18 billion yuan in 1978 to 22 billion yuan in 1992, more than a seven-fold increase.[55] Increased expenditure is attributed to wastage, problems in management and the rising cost of medical care.[56] Not surprisingly, the system of free medical treatment for employees is under criticism. An official Chinese newspaper reported:

> Free medical treatment, a system started 39 years ago in China to serve government and enterprise employees, must undergo reform because it has reached an impasse. The situation now is such that many enterprises are virtually unable to reimburse all medical costs incurred by their employees and many non-business state institutions have run into debt.[57]

Recently, there have been experiments all over China to cut down soaring costs and alleged wastage in medical care. Although no standardised model has emerged, the consensus is that the system of free medical treatment must be abandoned, enterprise commitment in medical care be delimited, and individual employees should contribute partially to their medical bills.[58]

It is the desire by the CCP leadership to diminish the responsibility of the enterprises in providing collective welfare to their employees. Such a move may have been influenced by a report produced by consultants from the World Bank in 1985, indicating that the "continued heavy reliance on pensions paid directly by employers would be an obstacle to intensive growth."[59] The report recommended the separation of the enterprises' general finances from its pension fund, and noted that the ideal would be to turn the latter over to a state-run scheme financed by compulsory wage-related contributions from workers and their employers.

To facilitate economic reforms, the state promulgated regulations in 1986 on dismissal, recruitment, bankruptcy, and the introduction of a labour contract system. In effect, the government has endorsed the following as new operating principles: economic enterprises that are not profit-making should declare bankruptcy; employees with undesirable performance should be dismissed; and new recruits should be employed on contract rather than on a permanent basis.

The stated intent of the "labour contract system" is to facilitate labour mobility and work incentives. In contrast to permanent employees, contract employees and their employing work units are required to make monthly contributions to a trust fund. The individual worker contributes 3 per cent of his/her standard wage, while the work unit gives 15 per cent of the total payroll to the trust which would pay for pensions.[60] Understandably, the contract system has raised much anxiety among the working population. The system has therefore been implemented with great caution in selected provinces. There were only 6.2 million contract workers in 1986; but by 1992, the figure had increased to 25.4 million, representing 17.2 per cent of the employee population.[61] There are predictions that this figure will reach 50 per cent by the year 2000, and 95 per cent by 2010.[62] If this is to be the case, the Chinese Government will have to pursue a rapid universalisation of the contract system for all workers and cadres in the SOE. At the present time, the labour system tolerates the co-existence of several labour types, namely permanent employees, contract employees and temporary employees.

Layoffs due to redundancy, bankruptcy of the work units, or termination of contracts, are now possible in principle. However, since unemployment in socialist China entails immense political risks, a concomitant unemployment insurance scheme has been implemented to cushion the change. Based on an experiment in Shenyang city in 1985, unemployment insurance schemes are now organised by labour service companies at the level of the cities and towns. These schemes are financed by contributions (0.6 per cent of the total payroll) from the enterprises to a common trust fund.[63] The fund provides assistance to employees of the participating enterprises who become unemployed because of redundancy, dismissal or termination of contract.[64] In 1991, revenue amounted to 837 million yuan. Among the 250 million yuan in expenditure, only 9.6 per cent was allocated as direct cash relief to the unemployed, while 29 per cent was for management expenses. In 1992, a total of 71 million employees had participated in the scheme, and 420,000 people received relief assistance.[65]

The heavy reliance of employees on their work units for the satisfaction of economic and social needs means that bankruptcy and dismissal embodies high political risks and is, therefore, difficult to put into practice. Even though the number of enterprises losing money is only the rise, and the government is determined to support the practice of declaring bankruptcy, enterprises that declare bankruptcy are still unusual, left alone dismissal of employees.[66]

It is estimated that between 1991 and 2000, the annual number of new entrants into the labour market each year will reach 20 million, not to mention the existing surplus labour force of 200 million in the rural areas and 20 million in the SOE.[67] Before 1978, most of the new jobs created by the government were in SOE. Among the 7.4 million new jobs created by the government in 1992, less than half were in SOE.[68] To rationalise the employment structure, under-employed people are encouraged to make their own arrangements for jobs, extend their maternity leave and no-pay leave, go through re-training programmes, or take early retirement. In short, the Chinese Government has partially abandoned its commitment to full employment and the strategy of job creation through administrative procedures.

Future Welfare Reforms

The PRC's Seventh Five-Year National Plan for Economic and Social Development (1986–1990) had for the first time incorporated a chapter on social security. The plan explicitly acknowledged the necessity to reform the existing social security system, but gave no specific blueprint for this. Instead, it proposed:

> During the period of the Seventh Five Year Plan, we shall try to gradually put in place a socialist social security system with Chinese characteristics.
>
> We shall establish a social insurance system, promote social welfare under-takings, continue to give preferential treatment to families of servicemen and revolutionary martyrs and provide relief to the needy.
>
> Social security funds will be raised through various channels. We shall reform the social welfare management system by integrating socialised administration with work unit administration, but emphasising the former. We shall continue to foster the fine tradition of mutual assistance among relatives, friends and neighbours.[69]

World Bank consultants, invited back to China in 1989, submitted another report to the State Council.[70] As in its first report, there was again the opinion that the existing social security system in China is a major impediment to the effective operation of the SOE. Furthermore, the progress of economic reform had reached a stage where major changes in the social security system were considered pivotal to further the reforms in price, wage and mobility of labour force, and in turn, support the growth and development of the national economy. The World Bank made a list of recommendations on the social security reforms, including the following:

(a) In the short-term, permanent workers, similar to the contract workers should be required to participate in contributory retirement insurance schemes; the standard of the pensions has to be improved so that it corresponds to the actual monetary income of the workers (at least 40 to 60 per cent of the total income); insurance funds can be invested in government bonds; contract workers and permanent workers should share the same insurance fund; and central government should introduce insurance tax on wages and bonuses.

(b) In the long-term, pension schemes should extend to cover all sectors of employees and the current age of retirement should be extended.

However, the Chinese Government remains cautious and hesitant in implementing such changes. Its current Eighth Five-Year National Plan for Economic and Social Development (1991–1995), and a Ten-Year Development Programme (1991–2000) have vaguely stated:

> A social insurance system for the aged should be established for people of different occupations in cities and towns, with the state, collectives and individuals sharing the cost in a rational way. The scope of insurance for people waiting for jobs should be enlarged, and a multi-level social insurance programme be practised.[71]

In 1991, the State Council issued a number of "directives" on the reform of the pensions system. These "directives" are in fact guidelines rather than compulsory policy regulations with a schedule for implementation. They imply a decentralised, gradual, and pluralistic approach to reform. In general, the major issues on social security reforms include the following:

(a) To introduce an element of contribution from employees to social insurance schemes on retirement, medical care and work injury;

(b) To widen the existing occupational welfare to cover other economic sectors;

(c) To consolidate a national social assistance scheme for people whose income falls below the poverty line; and

(d) To replace hidden welfare subsidies to workers by increasing wages so as to encourage the workers to obtain services from the market. Raising rents, encouraging the workers to buy their own houses, and cutting food allowances are some examples.

In addition, the proposed pension plan can consist of three main types. First, basic pensions insurance regulated through state legislations can be found in all SOE. The benefit level is set at a minimum. The basic pension can be supplemented by a second type of pension, the enterprise pension which is largely financed by enterprise profits. The last type of pension is individual savings or private insurance which is voluntary.[72]

Despite pressure to reform occupational welfare, no comprehensive action plan has been introduced. Instead, piecemeal and tentative changes such as the contract labour scheme, the *Bankruptcy Law* and pension pools have been implemented at the discretion of enterprises and local governments. A number of experiments are being tried to lessen the financial pressure on the SOE. Some of the existing welfare facilities such as canteens, kindergartens, nurseries, hospitals, and bath houses have been opened to fee-paying non-employees.[73] To reform the policy on housing, enterprises are beginning to sell some of the housing quarters to their employees at a relatively low price. In this way, the welfare responsibility of the enterprises can be reduced, and in return, they can obtain additional income for welfare. (However, it seems that only the senior and well-off cadres can afford to buy these houses.)

In general, there is a definite move away from an individual-enterprise-centred welfare, based on a Leninist model of full state and employer responsibility. However, there is reluctance on the part of government, which is already plagued by continuous budget deficits, to assume a financial commitment to a more broad-gauged social security programme. In place of a universal model for the country, the present policy is to encourage local governments, especially those in the SEZ, such as Shenzhen, Zhuhai and Hainan to experiment with their own approaches through localised legislations and regulations.[74] These provinces and cities all promulgated their own laws on social security provisions, covering areas such as minimum wage, and social insurance in work injury, medical care, maternity leave, and unemployment.[75] By and large, the incremental and cautious policy reflects less a coherent ideological direction than the pragmatic need to cope with political implications and risks, and the realities of economic constraints and changing demographic pressure. It is reported that a leading group comprising of several related ministries has been preparing the "social insurance law" which tries to extend the practice of contributory social insurance to cover contingencies.[76]

Social Stability and Welfare Reforms

Since the establishment of a socialist regime in China, occupational welfare has been a vital mechanism for providing social stability. Moreover, the heavy reliance that employees have come to expect from their work units for the satisfaction of economic and social needs means that bankruptcy and dismissal embodies a high risk of creating social instability. A rising number of labour disputes has already been perceived as a threat to the maintenance of social order.[77] Most of the labour disputes occur in foreign-invested and private enterprises involving violation of labour contracts, wages, working time, working conditions and safety. Industrial relations are particularly poor in joint ventures.[78] Currently, there are 6 million Chinese workers being employed in 47,000 foreign-funded enterprises along China's booming eastern coast. Poor working conditions, callous factory management and inadequate supervision are to be blamed for a number of industrial accidents happened in the SEZs.[79] Furthermore, only 12 per cent of these enterprises have unions.[80]

Significantly, a party news organ has felt it necessary to reiterate the point that the maintenance and guarantee of social stability is paramount during the process of economic reforms.[81] The Chinese press in general has been active in reassuring the people that reform would ultimately benefit China's workers. For example, the *Economic Daily* reported:

> Many people now fear that smashing the three irons means shattering their rice bowl. This is incorrect. It is just the opposite. Those workers who truly love their enterprises and who think both about the good of the company and their own personal benefit will be able to win the rewards they deserve through "smashing the three irons".[82]

In contradiction to the pledge by the CCP to regard the working class as the masters of the enterprises, the findings of a survey in 1988 by the Chinese Academy of Social Sciences (in 21 cities covering 47 SOE and 15,472 workers) showed that only 24 per cent of the respondents believed in their superior status; and only 39 per cent in this group felt satisfied with their relationship with management.[83] With the introduction of enterprise and market reforms, labour is more an economic commodity in exchange for wages. The issue of deteriorating labour relations will undoubtedly be a thorny problem for the Chinese authorities.

Another problem facing attempts in welfare reform is the issue of state control and influence over employees. Traditionally, work units were assigned the important mission of providing ideological education and influencing the behaviour of the workers through administrative discipline. The primacy of economic growth and productivity in work units will erode and undermine the authority and credibility of the CCP. With the collapse of

Communist regimes in the former Soviet Union and the Eastern European countries, the CCP has recognised the difficulties in maintaining a national consensus and state legitimacy simply through political education and control. Rapid social changes and reforms have already induced rising expectations and unsettling tensions brought on by social inequalities. As a result, welfare issues have been uncharacteristically put on the political agenda for the mitigation of social conflicts and the maintenance of social stability. The role of the CCP as a paternal protector of the people's interest and welfare must be sustained at all costs.

Employment-based Welfare: Enlightened Social Policy or Scapegoat for the Failure of the SOE?

In the early decades of the PRC, occupational welfare was depicted as a social and political asset but today, it is held responsible for depressing economic growth. However, the financial difficulties of the SOE may be symptoms of a larger problem rooted in an ossified and monolithic state bureaucracy. Undeniably, welfare costs add to the burden of the SOE but not all SOE losses can be attributed to the welfare system. Various economists who have studied the Chinese command economy have identified such cost-related matters as bottle-necks and delays in supply of essential production materials, miss-matches between the materials required and available, a poorly-developed transportation infrastructure to move finished products to markets, the notorious lack of mechanisms for horizontal coordination required by modern industries, and so on. The assaults on occupational welfare in fact have not been fully supported with objective evidence. The crux of the problem lies in the future of the SOE. There are already suggestions to sell more SOE to collectives or foreign companies. But because of ideological reasons, resistance among CCP leadership to sales is still strong.[84]

Given the abiding importance of occupational welfare to the maintenance of political stability, it is likely that the iron rice bowls will remain largely intact but with changes, particularly in the financing of pensions, medical care, and housing.

In the debate over this issue, one argument put forth is that economic enterprises should put their emphasis on production improvement rather than in non-economic pursuits. A concomitant to this argument is that existing welfare functions should be, as far as possible, transferred to society, notably to local urban neighbourhoods and rural villages.

Notes

1. J. L. Gong, S. Wu, and Q. Li, *Textbook on Labour Laws* (Beijing: Beijing Institute of Economics Publishers, 1989), pp. 56–60.
2. World Bank, "China: The Economic System", in *The Chinese: Adapting the Past, Building the Future*, edited by R. Dernberger, K. De Woskin, S. Goldstein, R. Murphey, and M. Whyte (Ann Arbor, Michigan: Center for Chinese Studies, University of Michigan, 1986), pp. 485–97.
3. Contemporary China Workers' Wage, Welfare and Social Insurance Editorial Committee, *Contemporary China's Wage and Social Insurance* (Beijng: China Social Science Publishers, 1987), p. 3.
4. *BR*, 4–10 November 1991, p. 18.
5. For example, there were 81 ministries in the state council in 1956, and 50 of them were related to economic functions.
6. B. W. Yin, W. H. Xu, and H. C. Cao, *China Social Insurance System Reform* (Shanghai: Fudan University Publishers, 1992), p. 109.
7. Some 20 million redundant urban employees in the early 1960s and 17 million urban young people during the Cultural Revolution were sent to the rural areas for jobs. *PD*, 19 August 1992, p. 5.
8. SSB, *China Statistical Year Book 1992* (Beijing: China Statistical Publishers, 1992), p. 79.
9. Ibid., p. 100.
10. S. D. Yue, "The Reform of the Chinese Social Welfare System", *Management World*, 4 (1991), pp. 171–76.
11. Another aspect of the employment-based welfare system relating to family values was the practice of the *dingti* (replacement), that enabled the children of retirees to take up jobs of their parents in work units. This had been established with two intentions; to encourage early retirement so that more work places would be opened up for young workers; and to protect family values as the phenomenon of "employment of relatives" (*jinqin jiuye*) is common in China. This practice was abolished in 1986 as it came to be considered an impediment to the promotion of economic efficiency and rationality. C. D. Jian, "Attempt to Discuss the Causes, Problems, and Responses of Employment of Relatives", *Labour Economics and Personnel Management*, 7 (1991), pp. 38–40.
12. SSB, op. cit., p. 97.
13. F. Schurmann, *Ideology and Organization in Communist China* (Berkeley: University of California Press, 1971); T. Saich, "Workers in the Workers' State: Urban Workers in the PRC", in *Groups and Politics in the PRC*, edited by D. Goodman (Cardiff: University College of Cardiff Press, 1984), pp. 152–75; A. Walder, *Communist Neo-traditionalism: Work and Authority in Chinese Society* (Berkeley: University of California Press, 1986); "Factory

and Manager in an Era of Reform", *The China Quarterly*, 118 (June 1989), pp. 242–64; O. Laaksonen, *Management in China During and After Mao in Enterprises, Government and Party* (New York: Walter de Gruyter, 1988).

14. F. Yuan,"Contemporary Labour and Employment Problem", *Journal of Beijing University*, 4 (1990), pp. 6–13.

15. The welfare expenditures in SOE broke down as follows:

— pensions of retired workers	51.8%
— medical expenses of workers and their families	20.2%
— sanitation	6.6%
— collective welfare facilities	4.2%
— collective welfare subsidies	3.8%
— transportation	2.8%
— single-child allowance	1.3%
— cultural and sports activities	1.3%
— subsidies to poverty-stricken employees	0.9%
— relief and funeral expenses	0.8%
— others	6.2%

SSB, op. cit., pp. 815–16.

16. Despite recent reforms to separate the functions of the party and the administration, and to provide more autonomy to the enterprise director to manage the enterprise professionally, major decision-making power remains in the hands of the party structure and its secretaries at all levels.

17. H. Ma, *China's Economic Situation and Prospects* (Beijing: China Development Publishers, 1990), pp. 129–30. In 1991, there was a total of 373,000 workers' congresses, representing 118.8 million workers. Of a total of nearly three million proposals initiated by management, these workers' congresses endorsed 74 per cent. Over one-half of the endorsed proposals were related to the improvement of productivity. Experiments were carried out to give authority to the congresses to elect factory management, but this power was shortly withdrawn.

18. Foreign Languages Press, *Trade Unions in China* (Beijing: Foreign Languages Press, 1987), p. 6. For a brief history of trade unionism in China, see M. Warner, "Chinese Trade Unions, Structure and Function in a Decade of Economic Reforms," in *Organized Labor in the Asia Pacific Region*, edited by S. Frenkell (Ithaca: Connell University Press, 1993), pp. 59–81.

19. *BR*, 7–15 November 1988, p. 4.

20. SSB, op. cit., p. 806.

21. All-China Federation of Trade Unions, *The Survey on the Existing Conditions of Workers* (Beijing: Workers' Publishers, 1987).

22. Each Youth League branch at the shopfloor level has a number of departments including organisation (recruitment of new members and membership management), propaganda (learning of political theories and state policies),

culture and sports (organising cultural, recreational and sports activities), production (enhancing productivity and the learning of advanced technology by members).

23. SSB, *China Statistical Yearbook* (Beijing: China Statistical Publishers, 1990), p. 808.

24. X. W. Wei, "Social Security System in China", in *Status Quo, Challenge and Prospect: Collected Works of the Seminar of the Asian-Pacific Region Social Work Education*, edited by the Asian-Pacific Association of Social Work Education (Beijing: Beijing University Press, 1991), pp. 65–70.

25. China Statistical Information and Consultancy Service Centre, *China Report (1949–1989)* (Hong Kong: Influxfunds Co. Ltd. and Zie Yongder Co. Ltd., 1990), p. 458.

26. C. Chan, "Inequalities in the Provisions of Social and Occupational Welfare in Urban China", *Hong Kong Journal of Social Work*, XXIV (1990), pp. 1–10.

27. Q. F. Zhu, "The Relationship between Social Security Enterprise and Economic and Social Development", paper presented at the Conference on Social Welfare Development in China and Hong Kong, *Into the Nineties* (30 October–3 November 1990, Beijing).

28. SSB, *China Statistical Yearbook* (Beijing: State Statistical Publishers, 1993), p. 97.

29. In 1992, 84 per cent of the total welfare insurance expenditures of the whole country went to employees in SOE. SSB, op. cit., p. 815. A survey in 1989 in Beijing showed that only 8.8 per cent of the employees in privately-owned sectors provided employees with full payment of wages and medical care expenses, while 23.3 per cent had nothing provided. M. X. Han, *The Existing Conditions and Development of Contemporary Chinese Privately-owned Economy* (Beijing: Reform Publishers, 1992), pp. 278–82.

30. Yuan, op. cit., pp. 6–13.

31. Walder, op. cit., p. 243.

32. H. Davis and R. Scase, *Western Capitalism and State Socialism: An Introduction* (Oxford: Basil Blackwell, 1985), pp. 86, 152.

33. China Statistical Information and Consultancy Service Centre, op. cit., pp. 453.

34. SSB, (1993), op. cit., p. 815.

35. The distribution of the monetary income of the workers in SOE consists of: 54 per cent standard wage, 20 per cent bonuses and 24 per cent subsidies, and 2 per cent others. Ibid., p. 127.

36. Ibid., p. 817.

37. *BR*, 2–8 September 1994, p. 20.

38. SSB, (1993), op. cit., p. 817.

39. *OW*, 30 March 1992, p. 12.

40. SSB, (1993), op. cit., p. 815.

41. *BR*, 24–30 October 1988, p. 25; *OW*, 2 March 1992, p. 7.

42. J. Kornai, *Economics of Shortage* (Amsterdam: North-Holland, 1980), p. 254.

43. The *Enterprise Law* of 1988 defined the SOE as a socialist commodity production and accounting unit which operates independently, assumes sole responsibility for gains and losses, and conducts independent accounting according to the law. Property of SOE are owned by the people, but the state grants enterprises their management power in accordance with the principle of separating ownership from management. To further the implementation of the *Enterprise Law*, the State Council issued in 1991 the *Regulations concerning the Management Mechanism Transformation of SOE*. Accordingly, SOE are given more power to manage and plan production, set prices to their products and services, make investments, determine wage and bonus distribution, and control the hiring and firing of its work force. *BR*, 16–22 November 1992, p. 8.

44. P. Yun and W. H. Wang, *China Finance, Wage, Insurance and Welfare Encyclopedia* (Shenyang: Liaoning People's Publishers, 1991), p. 1033.

45. On average, a COE employee was 73 per cent in wages, 50 per cent in bonuses, 55 per cent in subsidies of a SOE employee in 1992. SSB, (1993), op. cit., p. 122.

46. Ibid., p. 817.

47. Despite massive credits for the state sector, industrial growth was fuelled largely by collectively-owned rural enterprises, which enjoyed 28.5 per cent year-on-year growth in output, and foreign joint ventures, which had 48.8 per cent growth in production. SOE had only a 14.4 per cent year-on-year increase in production in 1992. *SCMP*, 28 June 1993, p. 15.

48. *SCMP*, 18 March 1994, p. 18; 19 April 1994, p. 1; 20 May 1994, p. 9. Ailing industrial sectors include coal, metallurgy, electricity, petrochemical and lumbers.

49. It is the practice of the state budget to include subsidies to money-losing enterprises as revenues, rather than expenditures. *BR*, 11–17 April 1994, p. 30.

50. Before 1969, each enterprise had to reserve 3 per cent of the total payroll for the labour insurance fund. While 70 per cent of the fund was devoted to expenditure on labour insurance in each individual enterprise, the rest had to be submitted to the All-China Federation of Trade Unions which would then redistribute the fund to those enterprises unable to pay their expenses. In this way, there was an element of redistribution in social security expenses among the enterprises. The practice was however abolished after 1969, and welfare expenditure thereafter was included under the operational cost of each individual enterprise. In effect, occupational welfare became individual-enterprise-centred welfare.

51. *BR*, 8–14 March 1993, p. 40; M. K. Wang, *China's Social Security System Reform* (Beijing: Social Science Publishers, 1992), p. 35.

52. The contributory rate is considered as relatively high, particularly for those money-losing SOE. Wang, op. cit., p. 35.

53. *Reform Monthly*, 12 (1993), pp. 20–21.

54. *MP*, 22 January 1992, p. 8.

55. SSB, (1993), op. cit., p. 815.

56. H. Y. Zhang, "Several Basic Questions on Enterprise Medical Insurance Reforms", *Social Work Research*, 1 (1993), pp. 15–22.

57. Quoted from *SCMP*, 26 July 1991, p. 8.

58. N. Y. Zhang and Z. L. Shi, *Nanchang City, Labour, Wage and Social Insurance, Research on the Reform of These Three Systems* (Beijing: China Labour Publishers, 1991), p. 331.

59. World Bank, *China — Long Term Development Issues and Options* (Baltimore: The John Hopkins University Press, 1985), p. 141.

60. Ministry of Labour and Personnel, *Unemployment Insurance Manual* (Beijing: Labour and Personnel Publishers, 1988), pp. 107–11.

61. SSB, (1993), op. cit., p. 117.

62. Y. C. Dai and H. M. Li, "The Dual System of Labour Mobility and the Distribution of Wages", *China Social Science*, 5 (1991), pp. 93–108.

63. Contribution was one per cent before 1993.

64. According to the regulations, an unemployed person with more than five years of working experience can obtain 60 to 75 per cent of his/her salary for a year, and then, 50 per cent of the salary for another year. Those with less than five years of working experience can obtain only one year of assistance.

65. Wang, op. cit., p. 222.

66. *BR*, 17–23 August 1992, p. 9. From 1986 to 1994, more than 900 enterprises have declared themselves bankrupt, and within these enterprises, only 20 were SOE. *SCMP*, 1 July 1994, p. 3.

67. J. J. Shen and Y. Pan, "The Challenge and Response to the Problem of Unemployent in the 1990s", *Journal of China Labour Movement Institute*, 3 (1991), pp. 25–29.

68. SSB, (1993), op. cit., p. 119.

69. N. Chow, "Modernization and Social Security Reforms in China", *Asian Perspective*, 13.2 (Fall–Winter 1989), p. 60.

70. World Bank, Asian Division, *Social Security Reforms in Chinese Socialist Economy* (16 October 1989).

71. *BR*, 18 February–3 March 1991, p. 21.

72. China Labour Report Editorial Committee, *China Labour Report 1988–89* (Beijing: China Labour Publishers, 1991), p. 111.

73. Ibid., p. 118.

74. N. Chow, *Social Security Reform in China: An Attempt to Build Up a Socialist Social Security System with Chinese Characteristics*, Monograph Series No.

4 (Hong Kong: Department of Social Work and Social Administration, University of Hong Kong, 1994).

75. *SCMP*, 23 June 1994, p. 14.

76. *MP*, 27 June 1994, p. 10.

77. It was reported by the All-China Federation of Trade Unions that about 37,450 workers took part in 1,620 protest actions all over China in 1990. These actions included strikes, go-slows, rallies, petitioning local governments and sit-ins. *SCMP*, 30 August 1991, p. 10. Another compilation shows that there were 250,000 labour disputes between 1988 to 1993. *SCMP*, 2 March 1994, p. 1. In 1993, the Ministry of Labour recorded 12,358 labour disputes, up from 8,150 in 1992. *SCMP*, 16 July 1994, p. 3. These actions reflect the dissatisfaction of the workers over the socialist system's failure to meet their basic needs. Furthermore, official newspapers have been sensitive to the news about violence against enterprise managers and property committed by workers dismissed by the enterprises. Rising labour conflict seems inevitable with the increasing power of the individual enterprises to employ, dismiss, and discipline workers, as well as to allocate welfare benefits, bonus and wages.

78. Industrial disputes are common in joint ventures in which work disciplines are enforced, working conditions are reportedly poor, and dismissals are frequent. *Economic Daily*, 30 December 1993, p. 5.

79. *SCMP*, 8 June 1994, p. 8; 20 June 1994, p. 8.

80. *SCMP*, 29 June 1994, p. 4.

81. *PD*, 29 April 1992, p. 1.

82. Quoted from *SCMP*, 29 July 1992, p. 8.

83. P. S. Zhang, "Investigation and Analysis of the Employee Cohesiveness in Large and Middle SOE", *Sociological Studies*, 5 (20 September 1991), pp. 60–70.

84. *SCMP*, 11 June 1994, p. 7; 20 June 1994, p. 8.

Neighbourhood-based Welfare in the Urban Areas

Cities in China have a long history not only as places for economic and commercial enterprises but also as governmental and military centres. Their early development occurred along the two major rivers, the Yangtze River and the Yellow River, and the Grand Canal. Song dynasty (A.D. 1077) records show two cities (Kaifeng and Hangzhou) already with populations of over one million people.[1]

From the time of the Qin dynasty (221–206 B.C.), successive regimes in China have relied on a decentralised system of local organisations to help govern and control its people.[2] Rulers in the Song dynasty (A.D. 960–1278) introduced the *bao-jia* system (in which ten households formed a *jia*, and ten *jia* formed a *bao*). This system in essence institutionalised the practice of self-governing and self-managing units under informal local community leadership. Formal government departments penetrated only to the county or district levels whose officials served as supervising agents over the local *bao-jia*. As an extension of a centralised bureaucracy, this system served to assist the government in the administration of law and execution of policies. The *bao-jia* responsibilities included tax collection and military conscription, as well as regular reports to government officials on births, deaths, marriages, movements of people, and any unlawful activities.

The neighbourhood system in China has remained basically unchanged. Under the Nationalist Government, the neighbourhood system was used for four main functions: neighbourhood management, political education, taxation, and military defense.[3] In particular, the Nationalist Government issued an instruction in 1939 that local governments should recruit young and loyal party members as neighbourhood officials.[4]

Immediately after the establishment of the PRC in 1949, the People's Liberation Army and the People's Government set up neighbourhood governments organised under Street Offices and Residents' Committees. The primary functions of these grassroots units were political, serving to identify and locate counter-revolutionaries, run-away criminals and land-lords. In particular, they mobilised the people to support the political movements and educational campaigns in the early 1950s. Other tasks of these neighbourhood organisations included the improvement of sanitation and public security, and the provision of relief and mediation services.[5] It was also a mechanism to redistribute and control urban population, and to alleviate the social problems of unemployment, crime, beggars, poverty, drug addiction and prostitution. The *Regulations on the Organisation of the Street Office* and the *Regulations on the Organisation of the Residents' Committee* were both promulgated in 1954.

As we know, Mao launched communes in the countryside to develop self-sufficient agricultural enterprises. Likewise, he also attempted to de-velop urban communes into self-sufficient industrial complexes in 1958. However, unlike the rural collectives, the experiment on urban communes never really got off the ground.[6]

Definition of an "Urban Place"

Today, the definition of an "urban" place in China has some peculiar characteristics. The designation of a place as a town or city is open to political bargaining and manipulation.[7] There are three ways to interpret the degree of urbanisation in China.

First, urbanisation can be a measure of the proportion of non-agricul-tural population. The status of agricultural or non-agricultural residents is determined at birth according to household registration regulations.[8] Generally, agricultural and non-agricultural residents "live" in rural or urban areas respectively, but this distinction neither reflects the nature of an individual's actual residential location nor occupation. The status is largely related to access to state rations, jobs, and urban services (e.g. schooling for children). This privilege is retained even when a non-agricul-tural resident moves to a rural area. On the other hand, many agricultural residents may reside in a city but their status will remain "agricultural". In recent years, as cities have annexed an increasing number of rural counties, the percentage of agricultural residents in the urban population has also increased. In 1991, 19.5 per cent of the population was classified as non-agricultural.[9]

Another way to look at urbanisation is as a referent of the popula-tion living under the jurisdiction of a city administration. If the population of city-administered counties is included, 62.8 per cent of the national population are now living in cities. However, if counties are excluded, the percentage drops to 27.6 per cent.[10]

The third way is often used as the basis for an official definition of urban population. Under this definition, city people refers to the population living in the administrative districts of cities and towns.

Prior to 1978, China pursued three urban goals: to control the growth of cities; to restrict growth within smaller urban places; and to shift urban development from the eastern coast to the less developed interior regions.[11] By and large, the Household Registration System had been effective in controlling rural to urban migration. Because of the policy to limit city growth through the control of population movement, urbanisation was slow before 1978.[12]

But the picture has changed dramatically in the 1980s. The 1982 census showed a total of 236 cities and 2,664 towns; 38 cities contained populations of more than 1 million people; and the three centres (Shanghai, Beijing, and Tianjin) had populations over 5 million. Following the relaxed restrictions on developing new cities and towns, the number of cities had increased to a total of 458 in 1991; of which 95 had populations over 1 million; and the number of towns increased to a total of 11,882.[13]

Also with relaxation of residential mobility, more rural migrants are moving into cities for jobs and better life chances.[14] The major strategy to reduce population growth in cities is to develop towns and rural industries so as to absorb surplus labour and keep them from moving into cities.[15] Production values in cities constitutes 59 per cent of the national production value, and contributes 77.7 per cent of the government taxation revenue received.[16] In short, national development is highly city-centred.

Current Urban Structure

According to the Chinese *Constitution* (1982), the government administration is divided into four main levels:

Central (*zhongyang*)
|
Provinces (*sheng*)
|
Prefectures (*diqu*)
|
Counties (*xian*)

Developments in the 1980s have made the overall administrative structure much more complicated, as shown in Appendix 1 on the administrative divisions of the levels of government in 1992.

According to the administrative structure, cities are the main mid-level structure of the government. But there are cities at the level of the province (municipalities), prefecture, and county. Beijing, Shanghai, and Tianjin are the three municipalities at the provincial level, administered under the central government. There are 191 prefectural level cities reporting directly to the provinces. Finally, there are 323 county level cities which report to prefectures.[17] In the movement to promote city-centred administration, a rural county or town can be converted into a city status if the values of production and concentration of non-agricultural population reach the defined criteria. A typical city is divided into administrative districts. Under each administrative district, there are street offices and residents' committees.

The Work of the Street Offices

According to the *Regulations on the Organisation of the Street Office* (1954), Street Offices are mandatory in cities with population over 100,000 people, optional in cities with population between 50,000 to 100,000 and not required for cities with population less than 50,000 people. A Street Office is the agency of the district people's government, and government officials are assigned to their Street Office posts by the district people's government, which is the lowest official level of government. It is called the Street Office because local neighbourhoods are identified by the main thoroughfare running through the area. A street also implies a "grassroots" connotation.

Although not officially a part of the formal government bureaucracy, a Street Office in essence, serves as the lowest level of government in the PRC (called the grassroots political organ). Generally speaking, Street Offices and their various departments and working committees are responsible for a number of political, environmental, cultural, social, economic and welfare functions. A typical Street Office would govern a population of 50,000 to 100,000 neighbourhood residents. The work of a Street Office can be divided into 7 aspects:

(a) To manage and construct urban services, including public facilities, environment, sanitation, control of legal structures and buildings;

(b) To provide advice and guidance to Residents' Committees on the election of office-bearers, coordination of the work of the committees and assignment of duties;

(c) To execute and promote family planning policy and the implementation of the Single-child Policy;

(d) To work with other departments in the areas of market management, tree planting, cultural work, hygiene, public order and security, fire prevention and civil affairs;

(e) To manage and promote COE at the level of the Street Offices and Residents' Committees which provide the required financial resource to support social programmes;

(f) To register the unemployed youth, and assist them in finding new jobs;

(g) To organise civic and legal education programmes to publicise government policies, laws and communist ideologies.[18]

Thus, the Street Offices are the front-line organs to administer the official functions of urban service management, and to serve as a go-between for the central government and the residents. Official regulations do not prescribe any standardised organisational structure for all Street Offices, and their staffing arrangements can also vary in different cities. Under each Street Office, there are on average 10 to 20 departments and 30 to 100 staff, depending on the size of the city.[19]

The Work of the Residents' Committees

The organisation and establishment of the Residents' Committees is based on the *Regulations on the Organisation of the Residents' Committee*, implemented in 1954, and amended in 1989. As self-management, self-education and self-service mass organisations, their tasks include:

(a) To publicise the Chinese *Constitution*, laws, regulations, and state polices; to protect the legal rights and benefits of the residents; to educate the residents on the obligations of conformity to laws, protecting public property; and to promote a variety of activities on socialist spiritual civilisation;

(b) To manage the public affairs and welfare of the residents;

(c) To mediate civil disputes;

(d) To assist in the maintenance of law and order;

(e) To assist the people government in implementing the work of family planning, public sanitation, public relief, and educating the young people;

(f) To communicate the views of the residents to the people's government, and to make recommendations for improvements.[20]

A Residents' Committee may represent from 100 to 700 households. Their elected officers (chairman and vice-chairmen) are recognised as state cadres — paid staff who carry out most of the day-to-day work. Figure 5.1 shows the structure of a typical district organisation.

Welfare Provisions for City Residents

As mentioned in Chapter 4, urban residents enjoy the benefit of state subsidies which is part of the government's basic policy to keep the costs of essential goods and services at an affordable level to consumers. In the Chinese system, most subsidies are not "given out" as such. The central government "buys" essential goods and services and pays a certain amount to producers. It then "sells" them to consumers at a controlled price. Particularly in the case of agricultural products, cost of production is not a major factor in the determination of price. This is referred to as a "hidden subsidy". Some examples are:

Figure 5.1: The Organisation of the Neighbourhood-based
Service System

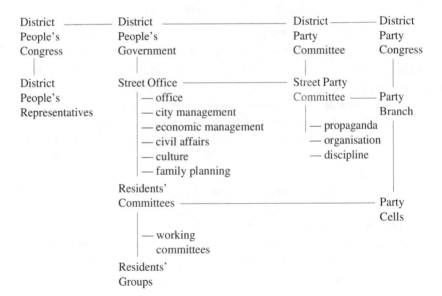

(a) Subsidies for agricultural products such as grains, edible oil, cotton, eggs, meat, and vegetables; and industrial products such as coal, soap, and detergent. It is estimated that there were over 120 commodities subsidised by the state. In 1994, such subsidies represented over 6.3 per cent of the total state budget (7.2 per cent in 1993).[21]

(b) Subsidies for public services by local governments, such as housing, transportation, and electricity, gas, social services and water supply.

(c) Indirect subsidies through SOE in free medical, educational services, and cultural services.

The controlled price system obviously affects the living standards of both the peasants who produce the basic food supply and the urban resident consumers. Apart from the "hidden" subsidies, there are "visible" subsidies in the form of direct income transfers which are given directly to workers employed in SOE, most of whom live within city jurisdictions. With the policy to relax government price control, the state has turned some of the hidden subsides into cash subsidies through the SOE to compensate for the price increase.

Street Office Welfare Services

The welfare services currently provided by urban Street Offices are generally rehabilitative and ameliorative. Apart from this generalisation, there is no standardised pattern so that differences in service context and service emphasis are invariably found between cities, and even between local units within a city. According to the Three-Year Plan launched in Beijing in 1988, basic welfare facilities of each Street Office should include the following services:

— an elderly home
— a welfare factory[22]
— a day care centre for the disabled children
— an elderly activity centre
— a daily life service station
— a work therapy workshop for mental patients[23]
— a service station for families of the martyrs

In 1988, of the 95 administrative streets in Beijing, some 76 had reached the proposed standard listed above.[24] In Shanghai, the standard for each administrative street is a welfare factory, an elderly home, caring groups for the elderly and mental patients, a service station for the childless elderly, a work therapy station for the mentally ill, and a day care centre for the physically handicapped children. By the end of 1992, about two-thirds of the Street Offices had developed community services, and there were altogether 112,171 neighbourhood-based welfare units. Of these, about 22 per cent were services for the elderly, 8 per cent for the disabled, and 15 per cent for the ex-servicemen.[25]

Perhaps the very absence of a standardised and bureaucratic approach is one of the unique strengths of the Street Office and welfare programmes. For one thing, this facilitates innovations and experimentation. These are manifold. One office, for example, makes much use of volunteers in assisting disabled persons with domestic tasks such as shopping, and house cleaning. Another puts emphasis on providing social and recreational activities. In Jin Hua Street, Guangzhou, a neighbourhood-based rehabilitation programme for the physically disabled was launched in cooperation with a teaching hospital. A large-scale family life education programme, including classes on child rearing, family relationship and marriage is delivered in another Street Office.

In addition to the supervision from the district government "on the top", the work of the Street Office, like any other government organisation, is also closely supervised horizontally by the corresponding party committee. The work of the party cells at the lower level includes the formation and management of party cells, election of party officials, political education to members as well as the masses, guidance to party cells, CYL, Women's Federations, and trade unions, and discipline of members. As in the case of all enterprises, the party secretaries of the Street Offices and Residents' Committees in reality have the real power in policy decisions.

In principle, Street Offices come under the district governments but in operation, they have to be responsive to over 40 government departments who have a direct or indirect interest. The Chinese use the vivid description of "a thousand threads on the top and a needle at the bottom" to describe the multiple accountability of Street Offices.

Personal Services Provided by the Residents' Committees

Each Residents' Committee has at least five working sub-committees. The latter are usually engaged in the following areas:

(a) Social welfare (civil affairs): This includes taking care of the elderly, job placement for the disabled, assistance for families or individuals in financial hardship, care of retired and demobilised servicemen, and help to families of the martyrs.[26]

(b) Public security: This includes prevention of fire, theft, gambling, prostitution and assaults; organisation of security patrol; working with delinquents. The work with delinquents at the grassroots level is called "education and assistance" which involves the setting up of a monitoring group for each individual delinquent and ex-criminal, or young people with identified undesirable behaviour. Under a contract for a specified period, the client would receive assistance in terms of job placement and counselling from the monitoring group members.[27]

(c) Culture and public health: Residents' Committees are authorised to establish public regulations governing the conditions of the area environment. For example, each household is responsible for improving sanitation, planting of trees and maintaining the public order in front of its own unit. Public regulations also control the rearing of poultry, dogs, cats and pigs. Violation of the regulations are subject to fines by the Residents' Committees. Furthermore, Residents' Committees can make efforts to beautify the neighbourhood through building of parks, rest-areas and playgrounds, and planting of trees. The provision of libraries, activity rooms and reading rooms is another area of function, together with the organisation of sport and recreational programmes.

(d) Mediation of local disputes: This includes any area of personal conflict such as marriage, family, housing, debts, fighting, property, land, love affairs, caring of the older parents, assault, personal problems of suicide, low work morale, and emotional problems.[28]

(e) Aid to women: One of the main tasks of this committee is the implementation of the "five good" family campaign. The aim is to promote model families by emphasising: love of country and respect for the law; productive work for workers or learning for students; respect the old and care of the young; good living arrangements; and good civilised family attitudes. The Residents' Committee is responsible for the running of the day care centres and kindergartens; and execution of family planning and population control policy.[29]

Financing Urban Neighbourhood Welfare

The major source of income for neighbourhood welfare is from the profits gained by commercial enterprises operated by the Street Offices. Thus, it is not surprising to find high priority placed on the development of profitable enterprises and businesses which hold the promise of a secure and stable income for services as well as for wages of cadres. In serving the residents, Street Offices and Residents' Committees also offer a wide range of practical services as a means of earning income. Such services are manifold, including simple repairs, collection of electricity and water bills, laundry, shops (selling cigarettes, daily necessities), bicycle stations, cookfood stalls, dress making, delivery of milk and coal, and household cleaning. Charges are also levied on residents for the planting of trees in the neighbourhood, collection of garbage, and organising security patrols.

Financial assistance from the higher government offices is both limited and unstable. Hence, the provision of welfare services in the neighbourhood system is, to a large extent, dependent on the ability of the neighbourhood itself to develop a profitable local economy.

Staffing Problems

Because of the low status and low salary of the work of the Street Office, it is very difficult to attract young staff with high educational qualifications. More often than not, jobs are taken by demobilised soldiers, redundant staff transferred from other enterprises and retired staff.[30] As the cadres of the Residents' Committees are elected among the residents, and wages are low, only those who are old, weak and poorly educated would be willing to take up the job. A survey in Shanghai showed that 63 per cent of the cadres in Residents' Committees were over 56 years old, and only 20 per cent of them had their education above the secondary school level.[31]

There are no cadres (paid staff) who perform solely welfare functions. They must carry a mixed load of responsibilities, and inherent in their various functions are role conflicts. For example, they must respond to the interests and needs of the residents and, in this regard, are expected to stimulate and mobilise self-help efforts towards neighbourhood improvement. At the same time, they represent the central government in implementing government policies which may be unpopular with the residents. Moreover, the cadres also have the role of providing political education as they are considered to be representatives of the party.

The official line is that no substantial conflicts exist between the interests of the party/government and the residents, so that any role confusion in community development is not a problem. (A local conflict would simply be a manifestation of a lack of communication, or the result of incorrect ideological attitudes of the residents.) In any case, the vitality of the local neighbourhood system is largely dependent on the initiatives and qualities of the cadres, and the ability of the units to develop profitable industries and businesses.

Up to now, the concept of a professional community worker is not recognised in China. Training in cadre colleges places high emphasis on ideological education with the assumption that enthusiasm and correct political thinking are more important than learning social science theory and problem-solving skills.

Democratic Centralism

In principle, the local units reflect a philosophy of the "mass line" which purportedly pays great attention to the needs and wishes of the mass. An ideology of "democratic centralism" expects the conformity and subordination of the minority to the majority, and also expects subordinates to give way to their superiors. Not surprisingly, such a system often turns out to be highly antithetical to the values of local initiative and self-direction. In operation, the neighbourhood structure does not encourage the articulation and representation of interests of the residents when these are considered to be in conflict with those of the official/party line. Thus, it is no surprise to find that the support of the residents for the neighbourhood system is not whole-heartedly positive.

The neighbourhood structure represents a grassroots political organ which forms the linkage between residents and government. This structure supposedly provides opportunities for residents to participate in the governing process, and to engage in self-help and mutual-aid efforts to improve neighbourhood conditions generally and to meet particular welfare needs. However, these functions are more often than not dominated by a priority given to exert political control on behalf of the government. The approach of "community development" in China is a "top-down" process which tries to obtain, with minimum deviations, grassroots support and acceptance of policy goals established by senior cadres and party officials. In current operation, the Street Offices and Residents' Committees are an "instrument of the state" to secure ideological consensus and unity.

There is no better example than actions taken in the aftermath of the student movement crisis in June 1989. Street Offices and Residents' Committees were immediately mobilised to support the government policy through organising political study groups, putting up supportive banners, and assisting the police in tracking down political dissidents.

A recent survey by a sociologist from Beijing University on the participatory culture of local neighbourhood residents found a low level of participatory orientation, and genuine resident participation is limited.[32] The findings are attributed to traditions of centralised government administration which assumed a "top-down" control over neighbourhood affairs, and the failure of the residents to communicate their needs to the upper levels.

Future Welfare Development

According to a survey in 1989, the municipalities of Beijing, Shanghai, Tianjin together with the city of Wuhan scored high on the indicators of community service provisions; whereas the cities of Guangzhou and Chengdu were low, and the NEZ of Shenzhen was a blank. The findings also indicated that the level of community service provision is not correlated with the level of economic affluence. Thus, there is the conclusion that the commitment of, and priority given by, the local city governments to community services are more important than general economic conditions in the development of community services.[33]

At the present time, the pattern of neighbourhood-based welfare in the urban areas is haphazard, and suffers from a lack of adequately trained staff. There is also a lack of authority to implement programmes. In operation, the system is overloaded with demands from higher government departments to implement "top-down" policies. However, there is evidence of deliberate efforts to improve the public image of the system as one that represents the interest of local residents and provides the necessary services to improve their quality of life.

As organs of self-management, self-education and self-service, Residents' Committees can be an important base for mobilising local resources to meet welfare needs. As we have already noted, economic reforms pushed by Deng Xiaoping have placed the future of occupational welfare under question. If the current system of the work unit as the main source of welfare for city dwellers is dismantled or diminished, it would undoubtedly lead to the transfer of some welfare responsibilities to the neighbourhoods, particularly in areas such as care for the elderly, the disabled, the unemployed, and youth at risk. Some of these welfare centres are beginning to be established at the district level, and in some Street Offices, volunteer groups are formed to assist the delivery of welfare services. But high residential and work mobility, rapid urban renewal and redevelopment, and privatised life style may impede the further development of this neighbourhood-based welfare system.

Significantly, a larger role for local neighbourhoods in the provision of welfare service has already been advocated by the Ministry of Civil Affairs (MCA) after a conference on community service in 1987. To consolidate the financial basis of the Street Offices and Residents' Committees, social and public services in the neighbourhood is recognised as "tertiary services", to be included under the overall city developmental plans.[34] In August 1993, 14 government ministries and commissions issued a joint policy paper on the future development of community services. The paper encouraged the establishment of companies in neighbourhoods to integrate together the development of profit-making community services and welfare services. Under the slogan of "to use service to support service", it is expected that profits generated from those fee-charging community services can subsidise the welfare services for people who cannot afford to pay.[35]

Notes

1. Z. L. Gu, *Chinese City and Town System: History, Situation, and Prospects* (Beijing: Commercial Publishers, 1992), p. 90.
2. For a detailed history of the transformation of the neighbourhood structure, see H. A. Zhang and Y. H. Bai, *The Evolution of the Chinese Village Grassroots Construction* (Chengdu: Sichuan Peoples' Publishers, 1992), pp. 1–84.
3. M. H. Lu, *Introduction to Civil Affairs* (Beijing: Civil Affairs Cadre Administration College, 1984), pp. 39–43.
4. A compilation by the government in 1942 showed that there were a total of 268,052 *bao*, 2,984,086 *jia*, and 39,991,132 households. On average, there were 13.4 households per *jia* and 11.1 *jia* per *bao*. Zhang and Bai, op. cit., p. 148.
5. M. Zi, *Regulations on the Organisation of the Residents' Committee in China* (Beijing: China Democratic Legal Publishers, 1990), chapter four.
6. Urban commune movement was initiated in 1958 in five major cities, with a Street Office as the basis for the organisation of a commune. In the process, Street Offices organised production cooperatives, canteens, nurseries, etc. J.

Q. Zhao and Y. Z. Cheng, "Exploration on the Establishment of Urban District and Street Organisations", in *Local Governmental Organisation Reform Research*, edited by Y. T. Su (Beijing: CCP Central Party College Publishers, 1992), p. 297; J. Starr, *Ideology and Culture: An Introduction to the Dialectic of Contemporary Chinese Politics* (New York: Harper and Row, 1973), p. 90.

7.   There is often tension between central and local governments over control of taxing authority and finances. When a place is certified as an urban centre, the local government gains control; when an urban centre is decertified, it loses control. R. Kwok et al. (eds.), *China Urban Reform* (Armonk, N.Y.: M. E. Sharpe, 1990), p. 8.

8.   The system of household registration was implemented in 1958, supplemented by a system of identity card in 1985. With each individual household as a unit, the registration records the name, sex, age, birth place, death and migration of the person. The system divides the people into two categories, namely the agricultural and non-agricultural population. Non-agricultural population is entitled to all kinds of subsidies on agricultural products from the state whereas the agricultural population has to sell their product to the state at a lower price. In employment, enterprises in the urban areas would discriminate against employing people from the rural areas. The system further restricts the mobility and migration of the rural population, and inter-marriages between rural and urban residents. Even marriages cannot change the household status. S. Goldstein and A. Goldstein, "Town and City: New Directions in Chinese Urbanisation", in Kwok et al., op. cit., pp. 19–44.

9.   SSB, *China Statistical Yearbook* (Beijing: China Statistical Publishers, 1992), p. 73.

10.   SSB, *China Statistical Yearbook* (Beijing: China Statistical Publishers, 1993), p. 81.

11.   A. Yeh, and X. G. Xu, "Changes in City Size and Regional Distribution", in Kwok et al., op. cit., pp. 45–61.

12.   P. Y. Gao, *A Comparative Study on Urbanisation between China and Foreign Countries* (Tianjin: Nankai University Press, 1992), pp. 87–91.

13.   SSB, (1993), op. cit., p. 72. Between 1984 to 1989, there were on average 29 new cities each year, and the number was increased to 45 in 1990 and 1991. *MP*, 15 June 1994, p. 10.

14.   Mobile population in cities is estimated to reach 60 million. Gao, op. cit., p. 134.

15.   Ibid., p. 238.

16.   Ibid.

17.   Ministry of Civil Affairs, *Simplified Administrative District Division* (Beijing: China Map Publishers, 1993), p. 1.

18.   Ministry of Civil Affairs, *To Improve the Work of the Residents' Committees in the New Era* (Beijing: Legal Publishers, 1987), p. 129.

19. Zhao and Cheng, op. cit., pp. 306–307.

20. The functions of the Residents' Committees are spelled out in the *Constitution of the PRC* (1982), Article 111. Included in their duties as "mass organisations" at the grassroots level, are:

> The residents' and villagers' committees establish committees for people's mediation, public security, public health and other matters in order to manage public affairs and social services in their areas, mediate civil disputes, help maintain public order and convey residents' opinions and demands and make suggestions to the people's government.

PD, 29 December 1989, p. 1.

21. *Far Eastern Economic Review*, 24 March 1994, p. 28.

22. Welfare factories (see Chapter 7) are production units which have over 35 per cent of their employees classified as disabled so that they can be eligible for tax exemptions.

23. Work therapy stations are places for patients to participate in social and production activities.

24. *Social Security Bulletin*, 22 March 1988, p. 4.

25. SSB, (1993), op. cit., p. 809. Another illustration is the city Guangzhou where there were 80 administrative streets and 1,329 residents committees. Altogether, they provided the following services:
    — 717 welfare factories (1,172 handicapped persons)
    — 45 elderly homes (236 old people)
    — 72 community centres
    — 71 work therapy stations (for mentally ill patients)
    — 1,153 care groups for the mentally ill
    — 1,394 elderly care groups
    C. H. Zhu, *Community Service in Urban China: A Case Study of a Street Office in Guangzhou* (M.Soc.Sc. dissertation, University of Hong Kong, 1993), p. 62

26. A common form of serving the need of the elderly and the mentally ill is the setting up of a caring groups for each eligible client. The caring groups are made up of local volunteers who would provide care to people in need. The services include delivery of food, home help, social support, and reminding patients to take medication.

27. J. Ma, *Introduction to the Work of Education and Assistance* (Tianjin: Mass Publishers, 1986).

28. Traditionally instead of taking their disputes to the government officials, Chinese preferred to invite people with authority in the neighbourhood and the clan to arbitrate their disputes. The Communist Government promulgated the *Regulations on the Organisation of Mediation Committee* in 1954 which was amended in 1990. According to the *Regulations*, mediation committee, staffed

by elected residents' representatives would be set up in each neighbourhood. In 1992, there were over one million mediation committees with 10 million mediators. Of the 6 million cases involved, family disputes (marriages, inheritance, care of the elderly) accounted for 40 per cent. The rest were mainly neighbourhood and business disputes. J. Leung, *Family Mediation with Chinese Characteristics: A Hybrid of Formal and Informal Service in China* (Department of Social Work and Social Administration, University of Hong Kong, 1991); SSB, op. cit., pp. 814, 816.

29. To implement the Single-child Policy, women cadres at the neighbourhood level pay door-to-door visits to spread the message of family planning and to investigate the situation in each household — whether women are using contraceptives, who is eligible to give birth and who has become pregnant. Information is collected, and estimation of birth rate and population increase would be submitted to the Family Planning Committee at the district and city level. According to the set quotas for the year, the neighbourhood family planning committees would decide which couples are eligible and authorised to have a child, and be provided with planned birth certificates. All unauthorised births are defined as unplanned, and the parents would be disciplined by a fine and the denial of medical care.

30. *Social Security Bulletin*, 11 September 1987, p. 4.

31. G. H. Ren, "The Method and Content of Training Frontline Elderly Social Workers", in *Conference on Social Work Education in Chinese Societies: Existing Patterns and Future Development*, edited by Asia and Pacific Association for Social Work Education (1994), p. 317.

32. X. B. Wang, "An Exploration on the Resident Awareness and Participation in China", *Social Work Research*, 2 (1991), pp. 30–36.

33. J. Tang and Y. Wang, "Concerning the Quantitative Study on the Existing Conditions of Urban Community Services", *Social Work Research*, 3 (1991), pp. 47–50.

34. *Sociological Studies*, 2 (1994), p. 122.

35. *CCA*, 12 (1993), pp. 28–29.

Locality-based Welfare in the Rural Areas

The organisation of rural areas in China can be traced back to the Shang dynasty (1766–1121 B.C.). Throughout the millennia, the lowest level of government had been the county. Beneath the county were villages, where residents more or less had to rely on self-established structures for the management of local affairs. Usually, villages contained people of the same clan where families lived in separate compounds but in close proximity. Prior to the Communist take-over, villages were governed by their rich elders and the scholar gentry, who undertook responsibility for official duties such as household registration and tax collection, and were also involved in the coordination of economic production, irrigation and public works. When necessary, the clan would also dispense welfare, and made loans to members who found themselves in financial difficulty. The practice of ancestor worship helped to hold villagers together, as did the performance of communal ceremonies and rites. The kinship system served to maintain social control, so that the loyalties of village members usually came to be attached to the kinship relationship rather than to remote national government.

Villages could have a population ranging from as few as 100 residents to several thousand people. Located nearby is usually a small market town where peasants could sell their surplus crops in exchange for specialised products. Villages were self-governing, self-contained and self-sufficient "little worlds" into which villagers were born, and where they then lived, and died. In fact, the homogenous and immobile nature of the community and the relatively simple and tradition-bound character of agrarian life rendered superfluous the existence of formalised laws and regulations, which in any case were uncomprehensible to the average peasant.

With the Communist takeover in 1949, county People's Governments were established to facilitate land reform and the development of collectives and cooperatives. In order to avoid the sorts of problems associated with runaway urbanisation that plague many developing countries, the

CCP, as noted in earlier chapters, controlled the growth of urban areas in China through a tightly-administered system of household registration which kept rural people from migrating to the cities.

Rural Areas Today

Just as urban places in China may be defined by different criteria, the same may be said of rural areas. Reference may be made to the latter as "non-city places", that is, territories lying outside the administrative boundaries of cities. Or, they can be defined according to population engaged in agricultural production. Yet again, rural population may refer to those living in counties (*xian*) which are made up of towns (*zhen*), and villages (*xiang*). The picture is complicated by the fact that many rural towns today are rapidly-growing centres taking on a distinctively urban character both physically (modern structures including sky-scrapers), and socially (modernised life styles). Further confusion arises from recent reforms that have placed some counties (i.e., their towns and villages) under the administration of a nearby city. The reforms have also allowed many rural residents to have non-agricultural jobs so that type of employment is not always a reliable base to distinguish between urban and rural people.

The 1990 census figures showed that 72.4 per cent of the national population lived in non-city places. Of the 438 million economically active persons living in the rural areas, 78 per cent of them were engaged in agricultural work.[1] Paradoxically, agriculture only constituted 24 per cent of the total value of production of the country in 1992.[2] As a proportion of the total output in rural areas, gross output value of agriculture decreased from 69 per cent in 1980 to 36 per cent in 1992.[3] Rapid development of towns was driven by thriving rural industries. By 1992, there was a total of 21 million rural enterprises, employing 106 million employees, with a production values reaching 1,797.5 billion yuan.[4] One of the major concerns today is the loss of cultivated areas due to industrialisation, afforestation and pasturing.[5]

During the early decades of the PRC, the Maoist policy of a rigid wage system had compressed income levels so that the discrepancy between the highest and lowest was not that large. One of the consequences of economic reform under Deng Xiaoping is a growing difference in rural incomes. This is shown in Table 6.1.

Another dimension shown by Table 6.1 is the extent of people living in poverty. Using the poverty line of 200 yuan, there are about 20 million

Table 6.1: Distribution of Annual per Capita Income of Counties in 1991

Annual per capita income	Number of Counties	Population	Percentage
Under 200 yuan	38	19,598,000	2.2
200–300 yuan	165	61,304,000	7.0
300–400 yuan	336	115,633,000	13.1
400–500 yuan	381	145,265,000	16.5
500–600 yuan	383	146,970,000	16.7
600–700 yuan	355	138,739,000	15.8
700–800 yuan	270	91,813,000	10.4
800–1,000 yuan	299	96,394,000	11.0
Over 1,000 yuan	275	64,879,000	7.4
	2,502	880,595,000	100.0

Source: Ministry of Agriculture, *China Agricultural Statistics Material* (Beijing: Agricultural Publishers, 1992), pp. 378–81.

people living in poverty. Most of these poor counties are located in the Western region. One report shows the average gap between the highest and lowest rural income increased from a ratio of 2.9 to 1 in 1978, to 4.8 to 1 in 1989. In the rural areas of Gansu province, for example, average annual income was only 490 yuan in 1992, whereas in the rural areas around the municipality of Shanghai, it was 2,226 yuan.[6]

Such figures show that economic development and modernisation is not evenly spread among the rural areas. Indeed, available data suggest that most development is taking place in only a few concentrated areas (in the NEZ, and along the eastern sea coast). Most rural regions of the country remain barely touched. Indeed, there are many parts of rural China that not only remain in utter poverty but also still lack even the most basic of public utilities. Such a picture is portrayed by Vogel of villagers in a mountainous part of Guangdong province:

In 1987 Dongshan had a population of 11,658 with an average per capita annual income of 118 yuan. People consumed an average of 104 kilograms of unhusked rice a year, about one-third of the province's average consumption. At best the villagers averaged one bowl of rice per day, with various kinds of mixed grains for their other food. Their overall intake was below normal daily requirements. Of the natural villages in Dongshan, about 60 per cent were connected by dirt road, the rest were not. About 20 per cent of the population had electricity. Dongshan had telephone service, but none of the smaller natural villages did. Water had to be carried to the village from some distance.[7]

Overall, about one-third of the rural villages in China do not have safe water supply; 56 per cent are not connected by telephone; 33 per cent had no post office (some cannot even be reached by mail); television is available to only 38 per cent; and over 90 per cent of all villagers have to rely on wood and grass as burning fuel.[8]

Rural Welfare Policy under Mao

When the Communist took over China in 1949, land reform and redistribution of small plots to poor peasants were followed immediately by the collectivisation of rural areas through the formation of mutual-aid teams, and later cooperatives. Meanwhile, the state also exerted control over the pricing and marketing of agricultural products in order to extract capital to implement the development of heavy industry.[9] As we have discussed earlier in this book, by 1953, a system of compulsory delivery of agricultural products at fixed prices was instituted. Despite the reliance of the CCP on the support of the rural peasant during the revolution, it put into place an urban-biased policy patterned on a Stalinist model. This policy was undoubtedly influenced also by the desire of the CCP leadership for rapid industrialisation.

However, the basic needs of the rural peasant were not overlooked. In addition to the land reforms, a rural welfare system came into being in 1956 under the government's *Model Regulations for an Advanced Agricultural Producers' Cooperative*:

> Rural cooperatives will provide care to those who do not have working ability or have lost their working ability, and those single elderly and handicapped people who do not have any source of dependency.[10]

The commune system became the vehicle to provide collective welfare which included facilities such as communal dining halls, nurseries and kindergartens, and specialised teams for sewing, shoemaking, laundering, and the such. These welfare services were free of charge. One of the espoused intentions of these collective programmes was to replace, or to reduce, the function of the traditional family as Mao desired to win over the loyalties of peasants to the state. In 1958, some 740,000 production cooperatives in rural areas were organised into 26,578 communes (120 million households). On average, there were 4,600 households in each commune.[11] The policy organised the rural population into a three-tier structure with communes at the top, then brigades, and finally, production teams.

A "five-guarantees" scheme was established to provide care for needy people, particularly elderly persons who had no source of help. In 1958, there were altogether 3.13 million households, or over 5 million people under this scheme which was intended to guarantee the provision of food, housing, clothing, medical care and burial expenses.[12] As the plan called for a portion of the income of a production team to be deducted as the means to finance the welfare scheme, the standard of provision varied a great deal among the communes, depending upon the financial situation of each unit.[13]

During the Cultural Revolution, a cooperative health insurance scheme was implemented with financial contribution from individual members as well as from the commune.[14] These contributions paid the salary of barefoot doctors, and financed the operation of local clinics.

Lacking the legislative authority underlying the occupational-based programme in urban areas, the health and welfare provisions of the rural collectives were difficult to institutionalise. Furthermore, the low operational level of the welfare schemes made the pooling of funds and risks among communes difficult. Often, programmes which were expected to operate for a year ran out of funds after only a few months.[15] Notwithstanding these anomalies, the PRC did nevertheless attain for its peasant population a higher level of social care than any country at a comparable level of economic development. Ahmad and Hussain summarised the operation of the commune system as follows:

> The commune system integrated political, economic and social functions into one. It was marked by the centralised allocation of labour and the collective disposal of income. Allocation of income in cash and kind was done according partly to need and partly to work. In this way, each rural household is provided with an "iron rice bowl" of secure livelihood.[16]

Rural Reform under Deng

Although collectivisation succeeded in removing social and economic inequalities within some communes, it had little impact on differences between regions.[17] As part of Deng's new directions for economic reform, the collective commune system was disbanded in 1983, to be replaced by the gradual commercialisation and privatisation of the rural economy.

By 1984, some 54,000 communes and 170,000 production brigades were decentralised into 767,395 villages and 3,136 ethnic villages. Under the new responsibility system, the use of the land (but not the ownership) was assigned to family households in proportion to their size. Peasants would pay various taxes and charges, and would be obliged to sell to the government a portion of their product.[18]

This decollectivisation turned the rural areas into market-oriented, outward-looking economies with a diversified mixture of grain and cash crop farming. Along with this change, peasants were encouraged to undertake sideline productions such as the rearing of pigs for the market-place, and to seek non-agricultural employment. As independent agricultural producers, the family or the household became the basic rural economic unit. Now, individual household has to be responsible for the procurement of raw material and production inputs, the transportation to market, storage, capital, loans, technical knowledge and information. The function of the family (which had been reduced by the collective commune system) becomes revitalised. With diminished administrative control from the central state and the traditional collectives, new forms of economic cooperatives in specialised farming (specialised households) and industries, organised along the family or clanship line begin to flourish.[19] There has also been a revitalisation of traditional beliefs and cultural practices such as *fengshui*, idol and ancestor worshipping, rebuilding the clan ancestral halls, widening the genealogical records, arranged marriages, and concubineship.[20] The economic reforms also dismantled the system of collective welfare provision in rural areas. There is now the particular problem of finding an alternative source of funds which the communes had previously provided for this welfare purpose.[21] As this problem has not been successfully resolved, rural social welfare has become a "vacuum territory". One writer summarised the situation as follows:

> For various reasons, the five guarantee or honour old age homes are at present still not well run. With the dividing of land, cooperative brigade medical clinics in many areas were discontinued, frequently being leased to paramedics who then charged fees for their use. The welfare fund, which supported the care of indigent elderly has in many areas remained in name only. The decline in collective support of social services implies that families have had to turn increasingly to their private incomes to finance education and health care.[22]

To be sure, the rapid development of rural industries and the establishment of towns have presented greater employment choices for the peasants, and increased income to many rural households. As the Household

Responsibility System no longer required every family member to farm, the policy of "leave the field but remain in the village" attempts to retain the surplus labour in rural areas to be absorbed by newly emerging rural industries. However, in contrast to SOE in urban areas, rural industries classified as COE are not obligated to provide welfare protection for employees. And a job with COE does not guarantee a life-long tenure.

A foreboding sign is evidence that growth in the rural economy has become stagnant. A modest rise in state purchase prices for agricultural products cannot compensate for the increasing costs of agricultural inputs such as fertilizers, pesticides, and farm machineries. Furthermore, rural areas have been plagued by the practice of local officials trying to squeeze funds from the peasants in the form of taxes, fines and contributions to public works. The situation is further aggravated by the situation that some local governments are unable to pay for the agricultural products in cash.[23] There are reports of increasing tensions and conflicts in the rural areas.[24] The minister responsible for agriculture summarised the current plight of the rural areas:

> The biggest problem in China's agriculture is how it has fallen behind industry. Purchase prices for farm goods are low, while farm inputs are more expensive. The profitability of farming is declining and farmers are losing their motivation. In the four decade since the Communist revolution, annual industrial growth had been as much as four times as fast as agricultural growth and the gap was growing. Since 1984, the cost of fertilizer, pesticide, fuel and plastic sheeting had risen 92 per cent but the prices of grain had increased only 59 per cent.[25]

Current Rural Administrative Structure

The re-organised rural administrative structure consists of county (*xian*) and township (*xiang/zhen*) people's governments. These are grassroots political organs appointed by the local people's congresses. Beneath them are village committees, self-governing mass organisations. In 1992, there were altogether 1,848 county governments, 34,115 *xiang* governments, 14,135 town governments, and 806,032 village committees.[26]

Overall responsibility for welfare policy in rural areas now rests in the hands of the Ministry of Civil Affairs (MCA) and its departments. (See Chapter 7) Operationally, welfare services in township are usually co-ordinated by a local committee on civil affairs and social security, with the cadre who is responsible for civil affairs coming under the direct super-vision of the township director.[27]

The village committees, as mass organisations based on mutual-help, comprise representatives elected directly by the residents.[28] Their overall responsibilities include economic production and management, maintenance of political order, and provision of social, cultural, educational and welfare services.[29] Under the former Maoist regime, local governing units and their staff of cadres wielded a great deal of power. However, Deng's decentralisation policy has made their roles less powerful, and less enviable as they have responsibility to implement such unpopular tasks as collecting fees for technical services, environmental hygiene, and water supply, as well as levying fines on families who violate public regulations such as bearing a third child.

Current Rural Welfare Services

Under Mao's regime, an egalitarian policy manifested a redistributive welfare approach using such instruments as the sharing of wages, income transfers, and provision of welfare by the collectives. Under Deng's new policies, the provision of welfare has mainly fallen back onto the individual family. Current welfare concerns in the rural areas focus on a number of areas:

Care of the Elderly

Caring for the elderly is an age-old tradition in China, and it remains an area of vital concern today. The Five Guarantees Scheme is supposed to provide financial support to elderly people who can no longer work, who have no income, and are without family support (i.e., the "three nos"). The Scheme also has the task of trying to help orphans, and the physically and mentally disabled. Some residential homes have been established at the township level for the homeless elderly. For those who prefer to live separately, "caring groups" (often referred to as the "scattered form of care"), are set up by local volunteers who regularly pay visits to older persons, delivering food and medicine, and helping with household chores.

In 1992, an estimated total of almost 2.3 million people were eligible for the Five Guarantees Scheme (3 million people in 1985), about 77 per cent of them were elderly people. However, only 82 per cent or so of the eligible persons actually received help, as also shown in Table 6.2.[30] The total number of elderly homes in rural areas increased moderately from 23,662 in 1985 (caring for 261,669 residents), to 26,472 in 1992 (caring for

Table 6.2: The Situation of the Five Guarantees Scheme in 1985,
1989 and 1992

	1985	1989	1992
Number of people in need	3,008,407	3,217,420	2,318,384
Elderly	2,501,073	2,553,328	1,782,865
Orphan	113,626	120,868	} 535,519
Disabled	393,708	543,224	
Supported by the local community	2,237,533	2,224,367	1,893,757
(Percentage of the total need)	(74.4%)	(69.1%)	(81.7%)
Residential care in %	11.7	15.5	18.5
Care in scattered form in %	88.3	84.5	81.5
Those without service in %	25.6	30.9	18.3
Expenditure in million yuan	528.54	749.22	755.58

Sources: SSB, *State Statistical Yearbook* (Beijing: China Statistical Publishers, 1993),
p. 808; SSB, *China Agricultural Annual Report* (Beijing: China Statistical
Publishers, 1993), p. 303.

350,570 residents).[31] Compared with the 70 million elderly people living in
the rural areas, the number of elderly people under formal care of any sort
is in fact minuscule. Furthermore, elderly homes can be found only in 57
per cent of the township areas.[32]

A very small proportion of the elderly, as we will discuss below, have
pensions, so that the majority of the rural elderly must rely on their own
savings and family support for livelihood. Unfortunately, the situation
is aggravated by the Single-child Policy. Although the effectiveness of
this policy in rural areas is still in doubt, it nevertheless carries the great
threat of "the 4-2-1"; that is, a married couple has to take care of four
elderly parents and one child. In short, there is the threat that even the
family as a welfare supportive system is becoming more fragile and unreliable. One of the reasons, among others, for strong resistance to family
planning in rural areas is because of the poorly developed social security
protection for old age. A family with more children means more old age
protection.

Retirement

The 1990 census showed a total 8.2 per cent of the rural population is of
retiring age or older. This population is expected to increase by 3 per cent

each year.[33] Peasants in rural areas do not enjoy a social security programme which includes the provision of pensions on retirement. As noted earlier, most of these elderly persons must continue working beyond the state's official age limit, or rely on their families for livelihood.[34] In actual fact, some 60 per cent of the rural elderly apparently continue to work while receiving some family help.[35]

Recent research findings confirm that informal care provided by the family is still the most important source of help in rural areas. A research officer in the Guangzhou Academy of Social Sciences summarises the three categories of elderly persons:

(a) Those with working ability continue to work for their income;
(b) Those without working ability must depend on their family members for their livelihood;
(c) Those without working ability or family members must depend on relatives and friends, and lastly, on the local governments (Five Guarantees Scheme) for livelihood.

Relief for the Poor

Relief work can consist of two aspects: assistance to poverty-stricken households, and assistance to victims of natural disasters. Much rural poverty is caused by natural circumstances, such as poor soil, inhospitable climate, and geographical isolation. Financial assistance includes direct payment or interest-free loans to poverty-stricken households and to ex-servicemen and dependents of martyrs. Or it can be in the form of reduction or remittance of taxes, priority in purchasing the products of those in living in poverty, supplying them with improved seeds and farm inputs, subsidies to buy such inputs, and the provision of technical education and advices. Relief assistance generally comes under the responsibility of the MCA, and will be discussed further in the next chapter.

The current government policy in disaster relief is to encourage people either to participate in disaster insurance schemes, or to contribute to a savings fund set up by Village Committees. The annual allocation by the central state government for disaster relief has remained at one billion yuan, which apparently can cover only one-third of total annual losses.[36]

Medical Care

On the eve of decollectivisation in 1979, it was estimated that 90 per cent of the rural population had some form of cooperative medical insurance

Table 6.3: Payment of Medical Fees (in percentage)

	National	City	Town	County
Self-paid	71.7	26.7	45.1	94.7
Half-paid	9.9	22.1	19.2	3.1
Free of charge	18.4	51.2	35.7	2.2
Total	100.0	100.0	100.0	100.0

Source: *BR*, 14–20 November, 1988, p. 8.

Table 6.4: Perceived Problems of Medical Care between City
and Village Residents (in percentage)

	No problem	Financial Problem	Hospital far away	Others	Total
City	68.47	14.27	4.08	13.18	100%
Village	5.27	61.88	17.47	15.38	100%

Source: X. Y. Tian, *China Elderly Population and Society* (Beijing: China Economic
Publishers, 1991), p. 290.

through the production brigades. By 1985, after the dismantling of the
communes, only 5 per cent of villages had retained the medical schemes.[37]
Henderson reported that the organisation of medical clinics in rural areas
has been diversified; about one-third of the facilities are still collectively
run as a COE at the township level, others are contracted out to local
doctors, and the remainder are now privately run.[38]

A national survey showed that 18 per cent of the rural population, due
to economic reasons, could not receive medical treatment, and 56 per cent
of those requiring hospitalisation could not afford it.[39] Table 6.3 shows the
sharp discrepancy between rural and urban areas in the payment of medical
expenses. In the case of urban employees, the work units would pay for
all the medical expenses of their employees and one-half of the expenses
of their family members. But in the rural areas, peasants are treated the
same as individual entrepreneurs, who must pay full medical expenses out
of their own pockets.

Financing Rural Welfare

Except in a few very underdeveloped areas, the central government does not give direct subsidies to rural welfare. At the present time, money to finance rural welfare programmes comes from a variety of other sources. They include:

(a) Income from profits of COE enterprises.

(b) Income from profits of welfare factories. (See Chapter 7)

(c) Subsidies from local government at the township level (funds allocated for civil affairs purposes).

(d) Funds from collective incomes of peasants reserved for welfare purposes.

(e) Private donations.

(f) Individual contribution.

Since there is little centralised or standardised control over the allocation of welfare funds, the amount of revenue that can be devoted to welfare purposes varies tremendously among different rural areas. For those which are economically better off, particularly with well-developed collective enterprises, substantial allowances can be given directly to welfare recipients.[40]

An evaluation study by the staff of the Sociology Department, Zhongshan University in the rural areas of Zhuhai (located in the Pearl River Delta in southern China) summarises three main difficulties to assist the poor. They are:

(a) Only a limited number of poverty-stricken households (12 per cent) were in fact given assistance;

(b) Funds available for relief were both insufficient and unreliable; and

(c) The assistance was often not effective, and "getting rid of poverty" might simply mean bare survival.

The MCA was given the mandate by the State Council in 1986 to experiment on the provisions of social security in rural areas. The MCA recommends three levels of approach to tackle the problem of social security in rural areas.[41]

(a) The "Assistance Approach": For poverty-stricken areas, the major focus would be on providing direct relief and technical assistance while emphasising mutual help.

(b) The "Welfare Approach": For areas with stable income, peasants are encouraged to organise themselves into some form of mutual-aid trust fund.[42] Welfare services include homes for the elderly, welfare factories for the disabled, centres for the ex-servicemen and their families, and associations for burial affairs.

(c) The "Insurance Approach": For the more affluent areas, the development of cooperative insurance schemes on medical care and retirement are encouraged.[43]

At the present time, the pluralistic policy of "letting a hundred flowers bloom" has generated a variety of welfare models, especially involving those well-off communities. A closer look at some of these experimental models points up some major differences and problems:[44]

(a) Coverage: Some proposals are single-item, e.g., pensions only. Others include coverage for medical, education, accident, and natural disasters.

(b) Source of funds: Some propose financing mainly by the local government through the collective rural industries. Others propose different degrees of shared responsibility by the individual and local community.

(c) Levels: The experimental programmes are mainly operated at level of the township and the village, which unfortunately is too low to be effective in risk-sharing.

In 1993, a total of 800 counties had some form of retirement insurance in which 45 million people participated.[45] This coverage is still small, when set against a total of 400 million rural workers. In general, young people are resisting to commit themselves to some long-term investment to protect their livelihood in old age.[46] And the tradition of relying on the grown up children to take care of the elderly is still strong. In welfare services, it is expected that all township would in the future can have an elderly home, a welfare factory, and a social security trust fund.[47] Similar to the situation in the urban areas, these programmes, without strong support from the government, are found to have problems in management and losses due to the currently high rate of inflation.

The Current Dilemma

Economic decollectivisation in the rural areas has dismantled a collective welfare system that had previously provided a basic level of protection and care to the rural peasants. The refusal, or the inability, of the government to re-establish an alternative welfare programme in rural areas has led to reliance on voluntary initiatives, mutual-help and self-responsibility.

In 1992, the MCA issued a set of guidelines on the development of social security system in the rural areas. The MCA has clearly indicated that it would turn down any development for the rural areas based on the SOE model of urban occupational welfare. It has also rejected an approach where service recipients do not have to pay or contribute.[48]

Most of the proposals from the government have simply been general guidelines which local governments can implement according to their situation. As there is no intention to develop an unified model of welfare system in the rural areas, a disjointed and pluralistic pattern can be expected. With characteristic pragmatism, Chinese officials have emphasised that welfare development should only correspond to the level of economic development.

It seems likely that, for some time to come, the informal family system with varying support from the local community, will be the basic source of welfare assistance in rural areas. As welfare decisions are decentralised with little top-down initiatives from the central government, local variations are inevitable. In some better off areas, the Five Guarantees can provide a relatively high standard of care; in other rural areas, the level of care will remain low; and in still others, there may be no care at all.

The official responsibility for development of welfare services in rural areas rests in the hands of the MCA and its departments. At the operational level, a township government is involved but very often, it is the civil affairs cadre who is the only person available to carry out the work. In the midst of experimentations and debates on different models of social welfare for rural areas, perhaps the most honest appraisal has come from a civil affairs cadre:

> ... the social security system that we are attempting to establish in rural areas is not, in a general sense, a social security system, but a minimal level of self-protection with limited coverage. If we are to build a social security system with Chinese characteristics, I am afraid this will be the basic characteristic. To talk about the characteristics of social security in rural areas, this would be the fundamental characteristic.[49]

Notes

1. SSB, *China Statistical Yearbook* (Beijing: China Statistical Publishers, 1993), p. 330.
2. Ibid, p. 24.
3. Ibid, p. 333.
4. In 1978, there was only a total of 1.5 million rural enterprises, employing 28 million employees, with a production value of 49 billion yuan. Ibid., pp. 395–96.
5. The average cultivated area per capita in 1992 was 1.3 hectare which is only

one quarter of the world's average, and is only half of the figure in 1952. Y. Y. Mu, "Analysis on Village Population and Economy," *Economic Problems*, 8 (1992), pp. 54–57; *SCMP*, 2 July 1994, p. 8.

6. SSB, *China Rural Areas Statistical Yearbook* (Beijing: China Statistical Publishers, 1993), p. 207.

7. E. Vogel, *One Step Ahead in China* (Cambridge, Mass.: Harvard University Press, 1989), p. 273.

8. The Synthetical Study of Social Development Project Group, "A Synthetical Analysis of China's Social Development in the Structural Transition Period", *Sociological Studies*, 4 (20 July 1991), pp. 74–93.

9. J. Gray, "The State and the Rural Economy in the PRC", in *Developmental States in East Asia*, edited by G. White (London: Macmillan Press, 1988), pp. 193–234.

10. All-China Committee on Elderly Problems, *Collection of Academic Articles on Elderly Problems* (Beijing: Labour Personnel Publishers, 1987), p. 217.

11. For a history of the development of the commune system, see H. Q. Zhang and Y. H. Bai, *The Evolution of the Chinese Village Grassroots Construction* (Chengdu: Sichuan Peoples' Publishers, 1992), chapter 15; X. W. Chen, *China Rural Reforms: Retrospect and Prospect* (Tianjin: Tianjin People's Publishers, 1993), chapter two.

12. *CS*, 3 (1993), p. 8.

13. J. T. Li, *The Tradition and Situation of Elderly Care in Guangzhou Villages*, paper presented at the Elderly Care Seminar, organised by the Guangzhou Academy of Social Science and The Chinese University of Hong Kong, 1988.

14. Even though the coverage of the rural medical insurance was not as comprehensive as the scheme in SOE, it was estimated that only 15 per cent of the rural population was without medical insurance. G. Henderson, "Increased Inequality in Health Care", in *Chinese Society on the Eve of Tiananmen*, edited by D. Davis and E. Vogel (Cambridge, Mass.: Harvard University Press, 1990), p. 266.

15. China People's Broadcasting Station, Theory Department, *Reform and Improve the Social Security System of the Country* (Beijing: Economic Publishers, 1988), p. 157.

16. E. Ahmad and A. Hussain, "Social Security in China: A Historical Perspective", in *Social Security in Developing Countries*, edited by E. Ahmad, J. Dreze, J. Hills and A. Sen (Oxford: Clarendon Press, 1990), p. 266.

17. The economic cost of the collectivisation strategy included:

    ... poor managerial efficiency, low incentives to producers, a bias towards urban areas, rigidity in planning and management, and low rates of growth. The entrenched regional inequalities, a low social status for peasants which left them with minimal geographical mobility, and low levels of income, especially by comparison with urban areas.

A. Watson, "The Management of the Rural Economy", in *Economic Reform and Social Change in China*, edited by A. Watson (London: Routledge, 1992), p. 174.

18. Land is rented to individual households on the basis of equal amount per capita. Agricultural products are sold to the government partially (fixed quota) at a basic price fixed by the state, partly at a price slightly higher than the basic level, and partly at a negotiated price. After fulfilling the government production quota, the peasants can sell any surplus quantity in the free market with the price substantially higher than the basic procurement price.

19. K. M. Qiu, "Policy Development in Rural Areas Since 1978", in *Ten Years of Rural Reform in China*, edited by K. He and Y. Z. Wang (Beijing: People's University Press, 1990), pp. 933–37.

20. J. T. Li, op. cit.

21. J. Leung, "Social Welfare Provisions in Rural China: Mutual-help or Self-protection?" *Hong Kong Journal of Social Work*, 24 (1991), pp. 11–24.

22. C. Riskin, *China's Political Economy* (Oxford University Press, 1987), p. 303.

23. *SCMP*, 31 May 1993, p. 8; L. Jiang, X. Y. Lu and T. L. Yan, *1993–1994 China: Social Situation and Forecast* (Beijing: China Society Publishers, 1993), pp. 289–305.

24. *SCMP*, 26 June 1993, p. 1; *Far Eastern Economic Review*, 15 July 1993, p. 68.

25. *SCMP*, 10 August 1993, p. 17.

26. SSB, *China Statistical Yearbook*, op. cit., p. 329.

27. A township people's government consists of departments on mediation, culture and education, finance, production, military and defense, public security, civil affairs and family planning. The committee on civil affairs or social welfare is chaired by the director of the township people's government. Other members include cadres responsible for civil affairs, military, legal, and financial affairs, the CYL, and the Women's Federation.

28. The elections and organisation of the village committees are governed by the *Regulation on the Organisation of Village Committees in Rural Areas* promulgated in 1987. These elected representatives would then become official cadres. Each village committee has five working committees (mediation, security, public health, women, and social welfare). Similar to the residents' committees in the urban areas, their functions are also prescribed in the *1982 PRC Constitution*, Article 111.

29. A survey by the MCA on 17 provinces in 1989 identified many problems in the functioning of the Village Committees. In terms of the ability to carry out the assignments from the state, promoting productivity, improving services and management of public and social affairs, only 50 per cent were considered as satisfactory; and about 20 per cent were considered as loosely structured or even completely paralysed. *Social Security Bulletin*, 4 August 1989, p. 6. The party seems to have lost much of its influence in rural areas. A survey in 1989

showed that only 30 per cent of the party branches were performing well, some 50 to 55 per cent were fair, and 15 to 20 per cent were not functioning at all. *CCA*, 4 (1991), p. 10.

30. SSB, *China Statistical Yearbook*, op. cit., p. 808.

31. Ibid., p. 807.

32. *CS*, 13 October 1992, p. 10.

33. *CS*, 6 December 1991, p. 9.

34. In real terms, there is no retirement age for peasants, and most of them have to work till 65 to 70 years old. Both the *Constitution* (Article 49) and the *Marriage Law* (1980) state that "parents have the duty to rear and educate their minor children, and children who have come of age have the duty to support and assist their parents." Thus, the responsibility of caring for the elderly parents is registered in the law.

35. *Social Security Bulletin*, 29 December 1989, p. 1.

36. *CCA*, 2 (1992), p. 6.

37. *OW*, 21 June 1993, p. 9.

38. Henderson, op. cit., p. 269.

39. China People's Broadcasting Station, Theory Department, op. cit., p. 158.

40. To illustrate the importance of collective enterprises in financing the welfare programmes, an example of the revenue of the social welfare fund of a town in the NEZ of Shenzhen is depicted in the following:

> In 1987, the income of the fund amounted to 507,000 yuan. Contributions from the township enterprises and welfare enterprises (collective enterprises) were 30 per cent and 12.1 per cent respectively, whereas contributions from the township government and county civil affairs bureau were 23.2 per cent and 19 per cent respectively. Donations only amounted to 1.6 per cent. On the other hand, expenditure in 1987 was only 351,000 yuan which included 40.1 per cent for welfare purposes and 50.9 per cent for investments. Investments referred to the building of farms and homes for the elderly.

> X. Y. Chen, *Report on the Social Security Experiment: Shenzhen, Baoan Xian, Nong Kong Zhen*, Research Monograph (Guangzhou: Zhongshan University, Sociology Department, 1989).

41. N. F. Cui, *Explorations in the Work of Civil Affairs* (Beijing: People's Publishers, 1989), p. 129; *CCA*, 4 (1994), p. 6.

42. Peasants can deposit their savings into the trust funds which can then be used, in form of loans, to provide assistance to individuals in difficulties. Currently, there are 174,000 village mutual-help trust funds, with a total amount of 160 million yuan. L. Jiang et al., op. cit., p. 98.

43. Affluent areas are those counties with annual per capita income over 800 yuan which should have sufficient income to fund a contributory insurance scheme. This is based on the assumption that the annual per capita income of the

peasants is approximately 600 yuan. Therefore, an income of 700 to 800 yuan would imply a capacity for sufficient savings to participate in contributory insurance schemes. In 1990, there were 431 counties with annual per capita income over 800 yuan, representing 22.5 per cent of the total number of counties. Y. Zhu and J. Tang (eds.), *Model Selection in Retirement Insurance in Rural Areas in China* (Nanning: Guangxi People's Publishers, 1991), p. 19.

44. Ibid., pp. 244–53.
45. *CCA,* 3 (1994), p. 6.
46. Ibid., p. 28.
47. L. Jiang et. al., op cit., p. 98.
48. The guidelines are:
    (a) The insurance is financed mainly by individual contribution, supplemented by assistance from the collectives, and supported by state policies;
    (b) The extent of assistance from collectives can vary according to regional differences;
    (c) Self-reliance and family care should be promoted and prevented from further erosion;
    (d) The role of the state is not a service provider;
    (e) Regional variations are accepted;
    (f) The level of protection is set at a minimal level, supported by other forms of protection, such as personal savings and private insurance on the top;
    (g) The notion of retirement at the age of 60 should not be applied strictly in rural areas. *CCA,* 6 (1992), pp. 12–13.
49. T. M. Liu, "Discussion on Self-protection and Self-protection Awareness in Rural Areas", in *Explorations on Rural Social Security*, edited by the Ministry of Civil Affairs (Wuhan: Wuhan University Press, 1987), p. 357.

The Work of Civil Affairs

In our discussion up to now, we have made reference at various junctures to the MCA. It is time to examine the specific welfare responsibilities and functions of this important government department. As mentioned in previous chapters, the Chinese Government is only minimally involved in the direct administration (as distinct from the financing) of social welfare provisions and services. The services directly provided by the MCA and its operating departments are limited as compare with the size of their working targets. In principle, their working targets have over 300 million people, a figure which includes: 100 million people annually affected by natural disasters; 50 million disabled persons; 50 million veterans and their family members; and another 100 million or so persons who are poverty-stricken.

The Meaning of Civil Affairs

The term, civil affairs, is a translation of *minzheng*. The word *min* refers to ordinary civilians, and *zheng* means administration. Historically, this term first appeared in the Song dynasty when the work of civil affairs referred to almost any matter involving the civilian (non-military) population. This work included the registration of households; demarcation of district boundaries; collection of taxes, care of the elderly, the destitute, the disabled, and the widowed; and the resettling of homeless migrants.[1]

A specific government department to carry out the work of civil affairs was not established until the late Qing dynasty in 1906. This work was later placed under the auspices of a Ministry of Internal Affairs after the fall of the Imperial dynasty, and the Nationalist Government came to power in 1921. At this time, additional civil tasks were laid on including the administration of local elections, appointment of local government officials, charity work, prohibition of opium taking, registration of publications, registration of societies, and overseeing of industrial disputes.[2] In 1931, the

Chinese Soviet also established a Ministry of Internal Affairs in territories controlled by the Communist.

When the PRC came to power in 1949, the work of civil affairs continued to remain under a Ministry of Internal Affairs. The broad nature of tasks carried out is reflected in the comments of key Communist revolutionary leaders:

"Civil Affairs is the work of making people." (Mao Zedong)
"Civil Affairs is the organisation department of the masses, and people look for Civil Affairs Department when they have problems and difficulties." (Zhu De)
"The Ministry of Civil Affairs shares the burden of the state and solves the problems of the masses." (Chen Yi)

Under the Ministry of Internal Affairs, departments responsible for civil affairs were established at the provincial level, and in bureaux at the city and county level. In the First National Conference on the Work of Civil Affairs held in 1950, its priorities were defined to include the re-settlement of ex-servicemen and migrants; relief of the unemployed, and the construction of grassroots political organs. The slogan for relief work was: "Self-salvation through production, austerity, mutual-help, and employment; supplemented by necessary relief." Thus, a basic philosophy was already taking shape: individuals and collectives must take primary responsibility in resolving their own difficulties through hard work and self-reliance; the role of the government would be secondary and remedial.[3]

The Fourth National Conference on Civil Affairs in 1958 emphasised the role of collectives in relief work (no doubt influenced by the formation at this time of the communes). Indeed, in the following year, the communes took over some of the work of civil affairs; and in some locales, government cadres were removed and offices closed down. In 1969, in the midst of the chaos created by the Cultural Revolution, the Ministry of Internal Affairs was disbanded and most of its work terminated.

In 1978, the central State Council re-established an independent MCA. In 1983 (at the Eighth National Conference), three major responsibilities of MCA were emphasised; those of social security, administrative management, and construction of political organs. As a result of the crisis associated with the student uprising in Tiananmen Square in the summer of 1989, the work of civil affairs came to emphasise a stabilising role in resolving social conflicts.

The Chinese regard civil affairs activities as somewhat similar to the functions of social work in the West.[4] However, one important difference is noted — civil affairs serves to protect the socialist foundation of Chinese society, and to promote the improvement of a material and spiritual civilisation through the resolution and management of internal contradictions. It is interesting to hear some Chinese officials express the view that civil affairs in China before the Communist revolution, and social welfare in the West in the present day, both serve to protect a system of exploitation and the interests of the ruling class.[5]

The annual state expenditure on civil affairs has never been more than 2 per cent of total government expenditures.[6] In 1991, expenditures amounted to only 1.65 per cent, or about 6.254 billion yuan.[7]

Current MCA Responsibilities

The central government's Office of the Committee of State Organisation and Classification set out, in 1990, an official statement on the current responsibilities and tasks of the MCA and its departments at different levels of government. Functions and activities are identified in over twenty areas of civil affairs. (This rather lengthy list is reproduced in full in Appendix 2, which also shows a structural plan of the MCA.)

Over the years, civil affairs work does have the flavour of being "all things to all (civilian) people". In this chapter, we are primarily interested in the social welfare services provided by the MCA and it various departments.

Welfare Institutions

A prominent form of MCA welfare service is identified under the term, "Welfare Institutions", which broadly refers to agencies providing residential care to the mentally ill, the physically disabled, the childless elderly, and orphans. The basic policy has been to restrict service to persons classified as the "three nos"; that is, those who have no family support, working ability, or source of income.

Most of the residential institutions were started in an earlier era by Western missionaries who had set up orphanages, relief organisations, and homes for the elderly. Others were established by the Nationalist Government before 1949. During the years immediately following the Communist takeover, the government used these institutions mainly for the rehabilitation of beggars, migrants, criminals, and prostitutes. By the mid-1950s, the use of the residential quarters shifted to provide care to the types of clientele noted above.

In 1954, a total of 666 such types of institutions existed, taking care of 120,000 people.[8] Over the past two decades, there has been an enormous increase in institutional care. In 1992, some 43,319 institutions were providing care to nearly 696,182 residents.[9] A breakdown of these figures is shown in Table 7.1.

There are four main features to these institutions. First, some 95 per cent are operated by semi-governmental collectives at the neighbour-hood level. Secondly, they are comparatively small, with an average of 77 persons per institution for those operated by the Civil Affairs departments, and 18 persons per institution for those operated by the collectives. Thirdly, these institutions are, on average, only 78 per cent full. Fourthly, a majority of these institutions, particularly for those in the rural areas are homes for the elderly.

There is, perhaps, one other feature in these welfare institutions. With the availability of excess space, and because of a chronic shortage of operating funds, the institutions have opened their doors (since 1983) to those who are not qualified as a "three nos" person but have the resources to pay for the service.[10] This principle was endorsed at the Eighth National Convention on the Work of Civil Affairs held in 1983. Specifically, the policy stated:

> If conditions permit, welfare institutions can admit elderly or handicapped people whose families, for some reasons, cannot take care of them, provided that they or their families pay the required fees.[11]

As one example, the province of Guangdong has 36 welfare institu-tions, and a total of 771 fee-paying residents in 1990.[12] Furthermore, the concept of a "responsibility system" has been introduced into the manage-ment and funding of these welfare institutions — management must now be accountable for losses and profits. Subsequently, the implementation of this principle has taken many forms. One example is the contracting of the management responsibility of a psychiatric hospital in Daidong city to public tenders. Based on the contract, the new superintendent is required to fulfil specific performance indicators which include increased admissions, higher rate of patient recovery, and less subsidies from the government.[13] To further increase the revenue of government departments, it is a common practice for them to operate profitable business enterprises, such as transportation companies, restaurants, hotels, nightclubs, etc.

Table 7.1: Figures on Welfare Institutions in 1992

Sponsorship	Organisations	Capacity	No. of Residents
Civil Affairs	2,035	155,869	121,596
Convalescent	850	46,032	33,065
Urban social welfare homes	1,185	109,837	88,531
Collectives	41,284	741,917	574,586
Urban social welfare homes	14,440	279,673	215,261
Rural social welfare homes (elderly homes)	26,844	462,244	359,325
Total	43,319	897,786	696,182

Source: SSB, *China Statistical Yearbook* (Beijing: China Statistical Publishers, 1993), p. 807.

Yet another development, again stimulated by the need for increased revenue, is the charging of a fee for each baby adopted from an orphanage. The amount of this fee ranges from US$ 3,000 to 5,000 for each baby adopted overseas.[14] Recent years has seen a shift in the orientation of the welfare institutions from one that catered almost exclusively to the physical and maintenance needs of the residents to the provision of rehabilitation services.

Welfare Factories

A second form of welfare provided by the MCA is a programme involving "Welfare Factories". These are economic and industrial units, providing employment for the physically disabled. They appeared in the 1950s from the efforts of production groups at the neighbourhood level. Based on the principle of "self-salvation", a total of nearly 300,000 welfare factories were operating by 1959. In that year, the Fifth National Convention on the Work of Civil Affairs transferred the majority of these groups to the supervision of the government's industrial departments.

According to a state policy promulgated in 1980, if the number of disabled persons in an enterprise exceeds 35 per cent of its total working staff, the state would exempt it from income tax. If the proportion reaches 50 per cent, the exemption would extend to industrial and commercial taxes. Under the reform policies of the 1980s, welfare factories are supposed to be independent economic entities, responsible for their own profits and losses. The high priority on their development is marked by their rapid expansion. There were only 1,466 welfare factories in 1981 remaining under the supervision of the MCA; by 1992, the figure has swelled to 49,783. Production value also increased from 0.7 billion yuan in 1980 to 66.2 billion yuan in 1992, which produced a tidy net profit of 2.6 billion yuan.[15]

Similar to the case of welfare institutions, the majority of the welfare factories are operated by the collectives. In the year 1992, over 780,000 disabled persons were employed in welfare factories. The distribution of the disabled employees were approximately as follows: 15 per cent were blind, 36 per cent deaf and mute, 40 per cent physically disabled, and the remaining 9 per cent mentally disabled.[16]

However, not all is well with this imaginative programme. Facing intense competition from the private sectors, some of these welfare factories are losing money. It is estimated that in 1990, some 30 per cent of the state welfare factories and 21 per cent of the large collective welfare factories were losing money, as compared to 19 per cent and 14 per cent respectively in 1989.[17] The losses are due to a number of factors, including weak markets, together with the lack of capital, energy, raw materials, credit, and transportation support.[18] The profitability of these enterprises are declining, especially in those operated by the departments under Civil Affairs.

The PRC's general economic reforms of the 1980s promoting the responsibility system and market competition in industry have also made it difficult for welfare factories to compete with other economic enterprises. On the whole, state investment in these welfare factories is low, as compared to government investments in other SOE.[19] Furthermore, there are known cases of mismanagement and misuse of welfare factories (i.e., some have not provided job placements for the disabled).[20]

In order to upgrade the quality of their products, the MCA has recently provided loans to welfare factories to improve their technology. Within the Seventh Five-Year Plan (1985–1990), the MCA approved a total of over 700 proposals on technological improvement, with the total amount of investment reaching 740 million yuan.[21]

Relief Work

The third MCA programme of interest to us provides financial aid to

Table 7.2: Relief Assistance to the Poor

	1985	1988	1989	1991	1992
Number of people receiving aid from state and community (in million)	38.0	34.5	34.5	29.9	24.6
As the % of the poverty-stricken population	39.4	39.0	39.8	40.9	39.2
Total amount of fund for the poor from the community (in million yuan)	146.5	292.7	167.2	126.3	123.5

Source: SSB, *China Rural Areas Statistics Yearbook* (Beijing: China Statistical Publishers, 1993), p. 307.

poverty-stricken people. This is a public assistance scheme with extremely stringent criteria. There are three kinds of people eligible for public assistance: single elderly or disabled persons with no source of income; persons who were encouraged to early retirement during the period of economic readjustment between 1961 to 1965, and have difficulties in livelihood; and persons who fall into one of the 25 categories of special targets recognised by the government. (Included are those who had been victimised in political campaigns, released political prisoners, former Kuomintang officers, and old overseas Chinese who have returned to the homeland.)[22] There is no universal standard rate of assistance. The principle is for each local district to work out its own standards according to the needs of specific situations and, of course, to the resources available.

In the rural areas, the specific responsibilities of Civil Affairs is assisting the poor. The Chinese policy of assisting the poor involves two major approaches: they are the "basic assistance" and the "motivation assistance". Basic assistance includes the provision of market information, technique training, loans, and employment referrals. The assistance would enable the recipients to increase incomes by participating in economic production, or to develop some alternative economy. Reduction of, or exemption from, taxes together with a policy of preferential employment of poverty-stricken persons by rural collective enterprises are also means to help the poor. To be effective, relief work must motivate the poor to participate in productive work. Ideological education is believed to be necessary to develop the motivation to change, and to remove the fatalistic and dependency orientation of the peasants.

The importance of relief work is recognised by the government. Noteworthy was the launching of a programme by the Central Committee of the Communist Party and the State Council aimed at "wiping out poverty" in 1984. (The objective was to achieve a minimum level of warmth and food in poverty-stricken areas.) A reiteration of this programme occurred in March, 1990 (under directives issued by the State Council, Leading Group on the Economic Development of Poverty-stricken Areas), at a time when the Chinese economy experienced particular difficulty, especially in rural areas.[23] In 1991, 679 counties with an annual per capita income below 300 yuan were identified as areas requiring assistance from the central government. In 1994, the State Council has pledged to wipe out the problem of poverty by the year 2000.[24] This appears to be an unrealistic goal.

In recent years, the number of people receiving aid has been on the decrease, from 38 million in 1985, to 24.6 million in 1992. Slightly more than one-third of the poverty-stricken population has received aid from the local community and the state. About 29.5 per cent of the 7.2 million poverty-stricken households under the relief programme have been helped out of poverty in 1992.[25] Undoubtedly, the economic boom in recent years has increased incomes in many households.

The government has consistently shown unwillingness to take up the sole responsibility for financial relief. Decentralisation, as part of the economic reforms in the 1980s allows villages to retain their profits from economic enterprises. The government position is that each village should look after its own needs for assistance. For the future, the government hopes to establish relief insurance schemes at a level higher than the village so that the costs of relief programmes can be shared and spread out.

The provision of relief associated with problems caused by natural disasters is treated as a special case. In such situations, Civil Affairs departments are charged with the task of "grasping" the situation in the disaster area, disseminating and making effective use of relief funds and materials, and recording the experience in disaster relief. The basic principle, as laid down in 1983 directives, is:

> Rely on the masses and the collectives, tide over disasters through production, mutual help and support while receiving necessary aid and support from the state.[26]

Because of its geography and topography, China is a country that is susceptible to natural disasters such as flooding along its major river banks, and monsoons in the tropical southern coast. In an average year, natural disasters will affect about 200 million people, destroy three million houses, and kill between 5,000 to 10,000 persons.[27]

Table 7.3: State Expenditure on Social Welfare Relief (in billion yuan)

Year	Total	For ex-servicemen	Social relief	(Rural areas)	Relief in natural disaster
1952	0.295	0.123	0.066	(0.016)	0.106
1955	0.494	0.203	0.125	(0.058)	0.166
1960	0.794	0.146	0.215	(0.112)	0.433
1965	1.094	0.231	0.292	(0.165)	0.571
1970	0.653	0.267	—	—	—
1975	1.288	0.375	0.347	(0.175)	0.566
1980	2.031	0.792	0.536	(0.250)	0.703
1985	3.115	1.201	0.889	(0.265)	1.025
1990	5.504	1.680	—	—	—
1991	6.732	—	—	—	—
1993	6.645	—	—	—	—

Source: SSB, op. cit., p. 226.

The information in Table 7.3 show that increases in expenditure have taken place in all areas of relief work under the MCA. It is also evident that the item receiving more significant increases are relief of ex-servicemen, whereas expenditures on rural relief and natural disaster relief have received only moderate increases in recent years.

"Preferential treatment", refers to the assistance given to families of martyrs and servicemen, disabled servicemen, former army officers, and veterans of the Red Army. The services include financial assistance, housing arrangements, medical care, job placements, and convalescent homes for demobilised servicemen suffering from chronic diseases. The resettlement of ex-servicemen includes services to ensure that the demobilised servicemen and retired army officers are satisfactorily settled in the places where they were recruited. In 1991, government expenditures for this programme amounted to 1.68 billion yuan, serving a total of over 39 million people. In addition, there were 1,169 sanatoria, and 1,175 residential institutions for those ex-servicemen in need of special care.[28]

Resettlement of Homeless Migrants

In addition to the areas of work described above, Civil Affairs departments are also charged with the responsibility of taking care of migrants and beggars in the cities who mainly come from rural areas. Civil Affairs departments are responsible to receive migrants in centres, make investigation of their backgrounds, provide re-education, and then, send them back to their places of origin. For those who are homeless, or have become long-term migrants, the departments would resettle them locally in resettlement farms for re-education and labour production.

The relaxation of control over population mobility has led to a dramatic increase of rural migrants moving into cities looking for jobs. The problem is further aggravated by the decollectivisation movement in rural areas which has made a lot of rural labour redundant. For example, in Hainan province in southern China, the reception centre processed, and sent back, 48,000 migrants in 1990. The figures increased to 58,000 in 1991.[29] Such experiences suggest that the numbers of dislocated people on the move in China are presenting a major social problem that threatens to overwhelm the limited resources of the MCA and the government departments responsible for public security.

Welfare Costs and Funding

The total bill for all of the relief programmes is 6.6 billion yuan in 1993, and seems to be increasing inexorably. This is shown in Table 7.3.

The MCA is obviously constrained in its work by the lack of funds allocated from the government. Even though lotteries can be regarded as a form of "gambling" (which is ideologically incompatible with the puritan morality of socialism, and is therefore illegal), the MCA introduced lotteries in 1987 as a means to raise funds for welfare purposes. From 1987 to 1992, sales of lotteries amounted to 2.9 billion yuan. Of this amount, 1 billion yuan were devoted to welfare programmes in both urban and rural areas.[30]

Unlike the previous era under Mao, the use of public appeals for donations from rich individual entrepreneurs and large economic enterprises is a now common practice in China. For examples, The China Handicapped People Welfare Trust Fund, established in 1988, is financed mainly by donations from individuals, associations, and enterprises from both within China and overseas. Hong Kong people had donated over HK$ 700 million to assist the flood victims in 1992. Receiving financial aid from outside represents an unprecedented orientation, deviating from the orthodox ideology of self-reliance.

Welfare Reforms under MCA

In the late 1980s, a failing economy, weak market demands, and a national policy of austerity had threatened to undermine the work of the MCA. Under a policy which gives high priority to economic growth, the functions of Civil Affairs, viewed generally to be non-productive, inevitably becomes less-emphasised. Impending difficulties facing the MCA include: reduced financial allocation by the government for welfare programmes, increased difficulties in job placements for the handicapped and ex-servicemen, and an uncertain profitability in the welfare factories.

As a response to these challenges, the MCA has introduced reforms under the concept of "socialisation". The reforms are based on the belief that a traditional ameliorative approach to welfare does not encourage productivity and work incentives, and the responsibility for welfare is too narrowly based on the state. The new approach will shift basic responsibility for welfare from the government to other sectors of society. The intention is to mobilise individual, families, mass organisations, and collectives to make concerted efforts to meet welfare needs. The role of the MCA would be that of an advisor, enabler, demonstrator, promoter, and coordinator. This approach has been accepted as the direction for Civil Affairs departments in the Eighth Five-Year Plan (1991–1996).[31]

The PRC party line is that in the "Primary Stage of Socialism", economic conditions are not favourable for the government and the enterprises to assume total responsibility for financing welfare expenditure. Thus, other sources of income are required, such as: profits from economic production, fees from service users, donations from individuals and enterprises, and income from lotteries. *Welfare Plans* published in the late 1980s have emphasised the shared responsibility of family support and contribution from collectives and individuals.[32] Furthermore, instead of relying on the state and enterprises, contributory insurance schemes in both urban and rural areas should be based on a philosophy of "self-protection".

Most of the welfare institutions and welfare factories are already operated by non-governmental sectors (to be specific, semi-governmental sectors). The collectives and local neighbourhood associations (which have expanded welfare services in the past several years) will be asked to take on an even greater role, based on the slogan, "social welfare must be provided by the society." In the Chinese context, there are no voluntary agencies similar to those in the West, the concept of "society" here loosely means the semi-governmental collectives.

Following the cherished ideology of "mass line", a society orientation means that all relevant sectors will be mobilised, and contribute to the solution of defined welfare needs. This direction is taken not only because of practical considerations demanded by limited finances but also because Civil Affairs leaders have recognised that much of its work requires co-ordination and collaboration with other government departments and non-governmental organisations. More attention is now being given to the design of organisational structures, and the integration of services among welfare institutions at neighbourhood, district, and city levels. Previously, the efforts of the Civil Affairs departments were targeted on the "three nos". Now, partly because of financial considerations, services will be also aimed at those who can afford to pay. In this regard, special attention will be given to welfare institutions that are under-utilised.

The MCA has recognised the importance of legislation to support and to institutionalise welfare programmes. Thus, there has recently been a spate of legislations covering a number of welfare areas. Some examples are: *Law on the Protection of the Rights of the Disabled* (1990); *Law on the Procedures of Marriage Registration* (1986); *Regulations on the Organisation of the Village Committee* (1987); *Regulations on the Organisation of the Residents' Committee* (1989).

Summary

Much of the work of the MCA is remedial and ameliorative, with notable exceptions such as the welfare factories and activities by departmental cadres in local community development. The MCA is the one government department taking direct responsibility for dealing with the casualties of Chinese society. The Ministry and its departments are overloaded with a variety of miscellaneous administrative duties that come under the rubric of "civil affairs". Its policy has been to coordinate with other state depart-ments, and encourage the collectives and individuals to bear the respon-sibility for welfare services. As the work of civil affairs is highly decentralised, the effective implementation of its policies and programmes is determined by the support of, and cooperation from, local governments. Consequently, the level of welfare services in any given community is largely dependent on the discretion and priority of the local government and officials.

Unable to rely on centralised and long-term planning, the overall development of the Ministry is marked by incremental policies and the encouragement of experimentation by local groups to resolve their own problems. Faced, at times, with overwhelming demands and a limited budget, the MCA has in fact come up with some imaginative and innovative adaptations.

The work of civil affairs has not been formally included in the Five-Year Plan of the PRC (which says something about its priorities). In view of the economic difficulties and a continuing shortage of reliable funding sources, it is evident that only those services that can develop their own economic base or funding sources will expand in the near future. If the central government has its way, the already limited role of the state in direct welfare service provision will be even further reduced, and "a mixed economy of welfare" (in Western terminology) will be adopted, embracing a combination of individual and family, collective, and state responsibilities.

Notes

1. Z. H. Meng and M. H. Wang, *History of Chinese Civil Affairs* (Harbin: Heilongjiang Publishers, 1986), chapter three.
2. H. Y. Yuan and Q. S. Wang, *Introduction to Social Work* (Jinan: Huanghe Publishers, 1990), pp. 50–54.
3. *Social Security Bulletin*, 16 December 1988, p. 4.
4. H. Y. Yuan and Q. S. Wang, op. cit., p. 19.
5. M. H. Lu, *China Social Work* (Beijing: China Society Publishers, 1990), p. 87.
6. L. Wong, "Financing Social Welfare and Social Relief in Contemporary China — An Historical Review", *Hong Kong Journal of Social Work*, 24 (1990), pp. 25–40.
7. *CS*, 13 October 1992, p. 6.
8. *Social Security Bulletin*, 22 September 1989, p. 4.
9. SSB, *China Statistical Yearbook* (Beijing: China Statistical Publishers, 1993), p. 807.
10. *CS*, 22 February 1991, p. 8.
11. M. H. Lu, *Introduction to Civil Affairs* (Beijing: Civil Affairs Cadre Administration College, 1984), p. 181.
12. *Guangdong Civil Affairs*, 2 (1990), p. 16.
13. *Social Security Bulletin*, 27 May 1988, p. 8.
14. In 1993, over 2,000 orphans, mainly girls were adopted overseas. *MP*, 29 June 1994, p. 12.
15. *CS*, 13 October 1992, p. 10; SSB, op. cit., p. 810.
16. SSB, op. cit., p. 810.

17. *CCA*, 4 (1992), p. 12.

18. *CCA*, 2 (1994), pp. 11–13.

19. *CCA*, 4 (1992), p. 14.

20. *CS*, 20 November 1990, p. 6; 11 December 1990, p. 7.

21. *CS*, 11 December 1991, p. 10.

22. Y. G. Liu and Y. M. Su, *Introduction to Civil Affairs* (Changsha: Hunan University Publishers, 1987), pp. 176–83.

23. *PD*, 16 March 1990, p. 1.

24. *SCMP*, 2 March 1994, p. 10.

25. SSB, op. cit., p. 808.

26. MCA, *Civil Affairs Work in China* (Beijing: Ministry of Civil Affairs, 1986), p. 25.

27. *CCA*, 3 (1990), 7.

28. *CS*, 13 October 1992, p. 2.

29. *MP*, 10 February 1992, p. 8.

30. In 1992 alone, sales have amounted to 1 billion yuan, and 300 million yuan had been devoted for welfare purpose. L. Jiang, X. Y. Lu and T. L. Shan, *1993–1994 China: Social Situation Analysis and Forecast* (Beijing: China Social Science Publishers, 1994), p. 96.

31. *CS*, 30 April 1991, p. 1.

32. *The Marriage Law* (1980), the Seventh Five-Year Plan (1986–1990), the Five-Year Work Programme for People with Disabilities (1988–1992), the *Law on the Protection of the Rights of the Disabled* (1990) prescribes the obligations of family members to take care of their dependents.

Social Development: Attaining *Xiao Kang*

Over the past fifteen years, China's economy has experienced a remarkable growth. Between 1978 and 1991, the annual rate of growth averaged about 9 per cent, and the rate has been well above this into double digits in the past two or three years. Indeed, the International Monetary Fund, using purchasing power to calculate national income, placed China as the third largest economy in the world in 1992 after the United States and Japan.

Demographic Changes

The enormous size of the country's population has been a fundamental restraint in the development and modernisation of China. When he first came to power in 1949, Mao Zedong did not see this as a problem. On the contrary, he advocated a "Human-hand Theory", whereby the human labour of the masses could be turned into capital for the development of the society (more hands, more power). Subsequently, the population of China more than doubled in size.[1] As indicated in Table 8.1, growth occurred in three peak periods; between 1953 and 1957, and between 1962 and 1971 when birth rates averaged over 30 per 1,000 persons. And the third growth period occurs from 1986 to 1995, in which there are 25 million new born babies each year.[2] By 1993, China recorded a population of 1.185 billion.[3]

In time, the sheer size of the Chinese population and its restraining effects on social and economic development became an inevitable concern to CCP leaders. The enormity of the challenge may be better understood when placed in the following perspectives:

(a) The number of persons governed under one state is equivalent to the combined populations of Western Europe, North America and South America (which are governed under more than 50 independent states);

(b) Approximately 22 per cent of the world's total population must be fed from China's 7 per cent share of the world's total arable lands;

Table 8.1: Basic Demographic Data, Including Population, Birth Rate,
Death Rate and Natural Growth Rate

Year	Population	Birth rate*	Death rate*	Natural growth*
1949	541,670,000	36.0	20.0	16.0
1953 (1st census)	587,960,000	37.0	14.0	23.0
1964 (2nd census)	704,990,000	39.1	11.5	27.6
1982 (3rd census)	1,015,900,000	21.1	6.6	14.5
1987 (By-census)	1,093,000,000	23.3	6.7	16.6
1990 (4th census)	1,133,680,000	21.0	6.3	14.7
1993	1,185,000,000	18.1	6.6	11.5

* Birth rate, death rate and natural growth rate are figures per 1,000 population.
Sources: SSB, *China Statistical Yearbook* (Beijing: China Statistical Publishers, 1993),
p. 82; *BR*, 14–20 March 1994, p. 26.

(c) And, when we speak of provinces in China, we are referring to
some jurisdictions with more people than most independent
countries. For example, the most populated province in China is
Sichuan, with 109 million people.

Serious family planning campaigns were initiated in the early 1970s
which began to reduce the birth rate significantly.[4] The government announced the Single-child Policy in 1979, with the aim of stabilising the
population at 1.2 billion by the year 2000. However, the impetus for population growth created by former policies will actually result in a population numbering 1.29 billion by the end of this century, before expected
decreases will occur.[5] In fact, the demographic situation is rather un-
balanced. The birth rates in big coastal cities are under 10 per 1,000
population (9.2 for Beijing and 7.3 for Shanghai) whereas the rate is as high
as 22.8 in Xinjiang.[6] For two consecutive years, Shanghai has recorded
negative population growth.[7]

The age structure of the Chinese population is marked by several
features. The proportion of older persons (65 and above) is on the increase,
moving from nearly 5 per cent in 1982 to 5.6 per cent in 1990 (and
projected to reach 12.9 per cent in the year 2025). At the other end, the

Table 8.2: Demographic Structure by Age

Year	Distribution of age group (in percentage)			Median age
	0–14	15–64	65 & over	
1953	36.3	59.3	4.4	22.7
1964	40.7	55.7	3.6	20.2
1982	33.6	61.5	4.9	22.9
1987	28.8	65.7	5.5	24.2
1990	27.7	66.7	5.6	25.3
2025	20.7	66.4	12.9	—

Sources: Y. X. Yuan, *China Population* (Beijing: China Finance and Economics Publishers, 1991), p. 28; G. F. Zhou and X. Dang, *China Demographic Situation* (Beijing: China Demographic Publishers, 1992), p. 56.

proportion of the young people (aged between 0 to 14) is on the decrease, and projected to fall from 33.6 per cent to 27.7 per cent during this period. Correspondingly, the median age for the whole population has increased from 22.9 to 25.3. (See Table 8.2)

According to the State Statistical Bureau's last census figures (1990), the size of the Chinese family is getting smaller, especially in cities. In 1947, the average household size for the whole country was 5.34 persons.[8] This has gradually decreased to 3.96 persons in 1990 (4.41 persons in 1982). The size is expected to decrease even further in the future. The data in Table 8.3 show that contrary to the image of a large extended family popularly held in the West, the household composition in China is actually moving towards a nuclear type of family.[9] Another notable (some would say a very troublesome) feature is the rising male ratio, the 1990 census shows the sex ratio of new born babies was 111 boys for every 100 girls.[10]

Income Levels

Based on standard comparative measures, China is classified as an extremely poor country. With an official GNP per capita of US$ 393 in 1991, it would be ranked among the poorest countries in the world (at the same level as Chad, Bhutan, Laos, Ethiopia and Bangladesh).[11] However, these figures are very misleading.[12] As Perkins observed:

Table 8.3: Household Composition in the 1990 Census

Household type	Percentage
Nuclear (two generation)	65.7
Three-generational	17.1
Single couple	6.5
Single person	4.9
Four-generational and above	5.8

Source: L. Jiang, X. Y. Lu and T. L. Shan, *1992–1993 China: Social Situation Analysis and Forecast* (Beijing: China Social Science Publishers, 1993), p. 107.

Official exchange rates are a treacherous basis for converting GNP per capita calculated in terms of some domestic currency into US dollars under the best of circumstances, but China's official exchange rate bears no relation to what is required for comparisons of this sort.[13]

Another writer Hamer, referring to recent works by Western researchers, also came to the conclusion that the local purchasing power of the *Renminbi* (Chinese yuan) far exceeds its foreign exchange value. Indeed, the actual purchasing power of urban Chinese residents may exceed the exchange rate by a factor of four to eight. Hamer goes on to say:

The exact level is not as important as the fact that our assessment of urban development (in China) is seriously flawed because of our failure to understand the relative prosperity of urban households. Only by revising our estimates can we make sense, for example, of the fact that urban household diets and consumer durable ownership rates are comparable to those of Japan and Korea when their income levels per capita, using conventional foreign exchange rates, were far higher than China's is today.[14]

With consideration given to purchasing-power and the cost of living, a more recent estimation made by the World Bank on the adjusted GNP per capita in 1992 for China was US$ 2,040, and by the International Monetary Fund, US$ 1,450.[15] Chinese leaders do not object to the use of standard comparative measures (which favour China as a "have-not" country for international loans). At the same time, they do acknowledge that the basic problem of feeding and clothing its people has been solved.

Furthermore, it is expected that the nation will, in the near future, become "well-to-do", which is expressed in the Chinese term, *Xiao Kang*. (See Chapter 1) Applied to social and economic development, the condition

Table 8.4: Classification of Average Income of Urban Residents in 1990

Income level (in yuan)	Poor (below 600)	Well-fed (600–1680)	*Xiao Kang* (1680–2400)	Rich (above 2400)
Percentage	3.7	68.2	20.6	7.5
Average house-hold income (in yuan)	400	1,186	1,956	3,000
Population (in million)	11.17	205.9	62.2	22.64

Sources: Q. F. Zhu, "Social Development Indicators in Rural Areas and the Developmental Target in the Year 2000", *Agricultural Economic Research*, 10 (1991), pp. 9–15; "The City Xiao Kang Social Indicators System and an Integrated Assessment", *City Problems*, 3 (1992), pp. 6–11.

of *Xiao Kang*, loosely translated, would correspond with a middle income economic status in the West.[16] The figures in Table 8.4 show income levels according to the various categories used by the Chinese.

Another misleading cross-country measurement is in the area of household expenditures. According to official statistics, urban residents in China spend over 80 per cent of household money on food and clothing.[17] This expenditure pattern may be so but only because urban residents enjoy heavy subsidies from their work units for basic goods such as housing, medical care, transportation, and education expenses. Thus, a much greater proportion of their disposable income is available for expenditures in other areas such as food and clothing.

The proportion of household expenditure devoted to basic food (Engel coefficient) has been used as an indicator of poverty, and according to the United Nations' criteria, any country with a coefficient of over 59 per cent can be described as living in poverty. The percentages for China in 1990 were 54 per cent in urban areas and 54.7 per cent in rural areas, placing China on the margin.[18] In actuality, as noted in Table 8.4, the majority of the people are considered as "well-fed" or better.

Life Expectancy and Mortality Rates

In addition to economic improvements, the PRC has achieved impressive improvements in the area of health. Consider, for example, the following:

(a) Life expectancy at birth has doubled from 35 years old in 1949 to

69.5 in 1990 (67.6 for men and 70.9 for women). This tremendous achievement in the space of one generation is the outcome of a massive preventive public health programme which, among other beneficial results, dramatically lowered the number of infant deaths so that the record in China is now, on average, better than those countries with similar per capita GNP.[19]

(b) In rates of infant mortality, which may be the best single indicator of social development, the figure in 1991 was 31.4 per 1,000 births.[20]

(c) The crude death rate in general has declined steadily from 20 per 1,000 in 1949 to 6.6 in 1993.

Some comparative rates are given in Table 8.5 (in which "low-income" nations include India, Bangladesh, Vietnam, Ethiopia, Chad, and Sudan; and "middle-income" nations include Thailand, Turkey, Egypt, Mexico, Korea, and the Philippines.

Developmental Shortcomings

Notwithstanding the impressive record noted above, there are areas where China obviously lags behind other nations. We have already mentioned in an earlier chapter the poorly developed communication and transportation networks, which isolate significant parts of the country. The absence of a formal school system in many rural areas is another shortcoming.[21] And, among human rights advocates, an area of major concern is reflected in a Human Freedom Index published in a United Nations report that ranked

Table 8.5: Figures on Social Development Indicators of China As Compared to Low-income Nations and Middle-income Nations

	China	Low-income nations	Middle-income nations
Life expectancy	69.5 years	62 years	66 years
Mortality rate	7/1000	10/1000	8/1000
Literacy rate	69%	56%	75%
Infant mortality	30/1000	70/1000	51/1000

Source: World Bank, *World Development Report 1991* (Beijing: China Finance and Economics Publishers, 1991), pp. 204–205, 256–58.

China as 84th among 88 countries.[22] Among the forty indicators used in this ranking, China only scored a point for allowing its citizens the legal right to a nationality.

According to a survey on human well-being among 141 countries which covered 99 per cent of the world's population, China was put into the category of "moderate human sufferings" along with 33 other nations.[23] The United Nations Development Programme ranked China at 101st in human development.[24] On the other hand, a compilation by the Chinese Academy of Social Sciences in terms of 16 specific social development indicators in the areas of social structure, population quality, economic efficiency, quality of life, and social order showed that China was ranked 68th among 119 countries.[25]

In recent years, China has made efforts to build up social development indicators as a basis for setting specific objectives both for national development and for comparative development in different regions and provinces. The first set of indicators, comprising 10 general areas (and 130 specific items), include environment, health, population, economy, livelihood, labour, social security, technology and education, culture and sports, and public order.[26] Nationally, improvements are claimed in the areas of environment, technology and education, economy and livelihood. Deterioration is found in population growth, culture and sports, and public security. Among the provinces, the municipality of Beijing was ranked first, followed by Shanghai in these developments whereas the interior province of Guizhou was ranked last.

A second set of indicators was to evaluate the development of the rural and urban areas, and the nation as a whole. These indicators include GNP per capita, the proportion of tertiary industry output, living area per capita, daily protein and calorie intake, life expectancy, and secondary school admission rate. It is expected the level of development would achieve *Xiao Kang* for everyone by the year 2000. Although some variations in criteria are used to measure *Xiao Kang* in rural and urban areas to adjust for different conditions, the compilation shows that at 1990, the level in urban areas is two-thirds from the target, but the level in rural areas is only half way there.[27]

The *Xiao Kang* target level of the quality of life was laid down in the Eighth Five-Year Plan (1991–1995) and the Ten-Year Programme Plan of Development (1990–2000). The latter stipulates the goals of social development:

Standard of living will improve from sufficient food and clothing to a comfortable level. The means of subsistence will be plentiful and consumption pattern more reasonable. The housing conditions will be remarkably improved, cultural life further enriched and the people's health continuously improved. Social service facilities will be continuously developed.[28]

The developmental aim is to surpass the level of moderately developed countries in health, nutrition, average life expectancy, literacy, and other standard of living indices by the year 2000. Table 8.6 shows the comparison of the *Xiao Kang* level of development with middle-income nations, with the lower category of middle-income nations, and with year 2000 targets.[29]

Summary

The Chinese leadership has always insisted that social development has to proceed within the limits of economic development. With a booming economy that shows no evidence of slowing down, the PRC seems to have the capability to attain its expressed social development goals by the year 2000, if no major political or social crisis intervenes. Such a proposition, however, may not hold up. Some recent publications have already used the term "crisis" to describe disturbing trends now appearing in the reform process.[30]

Table 8.6: Comparison between the *Xiao Kang* Level of Development with Middle-income Nations

Items	Unit	Middle-income economy	Middle-income economy (lower category)	*Xiao Kang* level
GDP per capita	US$	1,930	1,380	1,090
Tertiary industry proporation	%	50	45	36
Living space per capita	room	1	0.67	1
Heat intake per day	calories	2,672	2,600	2,600
Protein intake per day	gm	70	65	75
Life expectancy	years	66	65	70
High school admission rate	%	54	49	57
Engel coefficient	%	40	45	48

Source: *China Statistical Information Bulletin*, 11 May 1992, p. 1.

While it is true that the economy has continued to grow at an annual rate of over 10 per cent, the accompanying rate of inflation has also remained very high, hitting over 20 per cent in some of the large cities. The most worrisome element is the increase in the budget deficit run up by the central government. This will amount to 66.9 billion yuan in 1994–1995, as compared to 20.5 billion yuan in 1993–1994;[31] and the size of the government's total debt (foreign and domestic) has reached a staggering 129.2 billion yuan in 1994.[32]

The state deficits can be traced to two main sources. First, government revenues have not kept pace with expenditures. This has occurred because the majority of the SOE, a primary source of government income, are not profitable. In fact, many of them are losing money and cannot even pay for the wages and welfare benefits (for examples, pensions and medical bills) of their employees. According to rules devised for the economic reform programme, an ailing SOE is required to declare bankruptcy or to layoff redundant workers. However, this policy is extremely difficult to put into practice because of the political risks involved whenever there are grievances and unrest among the working class. It is common knowledge that instances of industrial actions and rural violence have recently occurred. Instead of taking the political risk, the government has resorted to the use of tax exemptions, loans, and subsidies to pump cash into ailing SOE so they do not have to declare bankruptcy.[33]

The continued need for state subsidies adds to state budget deficits, and is a further reflection of the dilemma facing the government. As another example, immediately after price controls were relaxed over essential commodities political stability was again threatened, this time by soaring food prices. In response, the state felt compelled to re-instate price controls which in turn meant the continuation of state subsidies. In the government's 1994–1995 budget, subsidies to support price controls came to 37.7 billion yuan, up from 29.6 billion yuan in 1993–1994.[34]

The stresses and tensions noted in the foregoing reflect some inherent contradictions in the reform process. They also give rise to the question as to whether or not China's social development achievements are based on a sound economic foundation.

Notes

1. The population size was estimated to be 405 million in 1912, and slightly increased to 461 million in 1947. High death rate (between 25 and 33 per

1,000) and high birth rate (around 38 per 1,000) accounted for a moderate
annual increase of only 0.78 per cent in population between 1912 and 1949.
G. F. Zhou and X. Q. Dang, *China Demographic Situation* (Beijing: China
Demographic Publishers, 1992), pp. 2–3.

2. *BR*, 4–10 July 1988, p. 25; *MP*, 8 March 1994, p. 10.

3. *BR*, 14–20 March 1994, p. 26.

4. The campaigns which emphasised *wan*, *xi* and *shao* (late marriage, long birth
   intervals and fewer children) had rapidly reduced the birth rate from 33.4 per
   1,000 in 1970 to 17.8 per 1,000 in 1979, and the natural growth from 25.8 to
   11.6 per 1,000. It took 50 to 100 years in the Western countries to achieve a
   similar decrease in birth rate. X. Y. Tian, *China Elderly Population and Society*
   (Beijing: China Economics Publishers, 1991), p. 32.

5. *BR*, 13–19 April 1992, p. 6.

6. SSB, *China Statistical Yearbook* (Beijing: China Statistical Publishers, 1993),
   p. 83.

7. *SCMP*, 17 May 1994, p.8

8. Y. X. Yuan *China Population* (Beijing: China Finance and Economics Publishers, 1991), p. 67.

9. In terms of household size, the 1990 census showed that 67 per cent of the
   households were less than four persons. SSB, *China Statistical Yearbook*
   (Beijing: China Statistical Publishers, 1992), pp. 70–71.

10. *BR*, 2–9 May 1993, p. 10. Results of a 1992 survey showed that the national
    ratio had reached 118.5 boys born for every 100 girls. (The average global
    ratio is 105 boys for 100 girls.) *SCMP*, 3 September 1994, p. 10.

11. *MP*, 20 March 1994, p. 2.

12. Although Gross National Product (GNP) and Gross Domestic Product (GDP)
    have been popularly used in the world as comprehensive indicators to reflect
    socio-economic development, it has suffered drawbacks in applying to the
    Chinese setting. First, China has only established the GNP statistical system in
    1987, and a large proportion of the calculations before this date are estimations
    based on incomplete information. Secondly, it is generally believed that the
    figures do not reflect the standard of living in China as government subsidises
    heavily on a lot of essential commodities.

13. D. Perkins, "The Influence of Economic Reforms on China's Urbanization",
    in *Chinese Urban Reform*, edited by Y. W. Kwok, W. Parish, and A. Yeh
    (Armonk, N.Y.: M. E. Sharpe, 1990).

14. A. Hamer, "Four Hypotheses concerning Contemporary Chinese Urbaniza-
    tion", in Y. R. Kwok et al., op. cit., pp. 238–39.

15. *OW*, 7 June 1993, p. 4.

16. The *Xiao Kang* level has been operationalised by planners to be a target of
    economic growth and population control sufficient to produce a per capita
    income of US$ 800 and a level of grain consumption of 400 kg per capita

per annum by the year 2000. J. Y. Wang and T. Hull (eds.), *Population and Development Planning in China* (London: Allen and Unwin, 1991), p. xvi.

17. L. J. Chen, *Social Security Curriculum* (Beijing: Knowledge Publishers, 1990), p. 10.

18. Q. Liu, *Contemporary China Housing Economy* (Beijing: China Construction and Industrial Publishers, 1992), p. 15.

19. *SCMP*, 12 July 1994, p. 9.

20. *MP*, 20 January 1993, p. 8.

21. The World Bank described that China's investment in transportation was only 1.4 per cent of the GNP, and was only half that of South Korea, India and Brazil. *Hong Kong Economic Journal*, 12 May 1994, p. 26. In education, China invests only 3.7 per cent of its GNP in education, less than 120 other countries. *Guangming ribao*, 19 April 1989, p. 1.

22. *SCMP*, 24 September 1991, p. 10.

23. The survey, reported in the *SCMP*, was conducted by the Washington-based Population Crisis Committee. Indicators included life expectancy, daily calorie supply, access to clean water, infant immunisation, secondary school enrolment, per capita income, inflation rate, the number of telephones in the population, political freedom and civil rights. *SCMP*, 18 May 1992, p. 9.

24. *BR*, 14–20 June 1993, p. 9.

25. *Hong Kong Economic Journal*, 28 October 1993, p. 10.

26. *OW*, 11 January 1993, p. 10.

27. *China Statistical Information Bulletin*, 5 (1992), p. 1.

28. *BR*, 6–12 May 1991, p. 14.

29. The data in this Table are based on the assumption that the developmental indicators for the middle-income economies in 1990 would remain unchanged till the year 2000. According to the World Bank, middle income nations refer to those with annual GNP per capita between US$ 580 and 6,000 in 1989. The dividing line between the lower and upper categories of the middle income nations is US$ 2,335. World Bank, *World Development Report 1991* (Beijing: China Finance and Economics Publishers, 1991), p. x.

30. For examples, see D. Goodman and G. Segal, *China at Forty, Mid-life Crises* (Oxford: Clarendon Press, 1989); A. Nathan, *China's Crisis: Dilemmas of Reform and Prospects for Democracy* (New York: Columbia University Press, 1990); P. Lichtenstein, *China at the Brink* (New York: Praeger, 1991); G. White (ed.), *The Chinese State in the Era of Economic Reform: The Road to Crisis* (Macmillan, 1991); M. Dassu and T. Saich (eds.), *The Reform Decade in China, from Hope to Dismay* (London: Kegan Paul International, 1990); A. Watson (ed.), *Economic Reform and Social Change in China* (London: Routledge, 1992); A. L. Rosenbaum (ed.), *State and Society in China, the Consequences of Reform* (Boulder: Westview Press, 1992); G. White, *Riding*

the Tiger, The Politics of Economic Reform in Post-Mao China (London: Macmillan, 1993).

31. *SCMP*, 12 March 1994, p. 7.
32. *SCMP*, 10 March 1994, p. 1.
33. *SCMP*, 20 May 1994, p. 9; 21 May 1994, p. 2; 23 May 1994, p. 1. In the 1994–1995 state budget, a total of 14 billion yuan was allocated as tax exemptions to ailing SOE. *SCMP*, 10 March 1994, p. 1.
34. *SCMP*, 12 March 1994, p. 8.

Social Disparities and Disadvantaged Groups

Since 1978, China's economic reforms have indisputably brought about a general improvement in the well-being of the nation's population. However, the benefits are not evenly spread. Significant numbers of persons have been "left behind", and some have become more vulnerable to life contingencies due to changes in social welfare policies and practices. Furthermore, with the rapid liberalisation of the economic structure and a loosening of social controls, problems such as poverty, family breakdown, juvenile delinquency, housing shortages, and unemployment have re-emerged as matters of major concern.

During Mao's time, the mere mentioning of social problems in China was regarded as an attack on, or a denial of, the superiority of the socialist system. It was believed that social problems could no longer exist in a socialist society where private property was abolished, class conflict and exploitation were absent, and the common people were masters of the means of production. Under the communist system, it was expected that the transformation of the economic structure together with the provision of jobs for everyone would eliminate all forms of deprivation and social pathology.

With the recent relaxation of control over academic research and the mass media, Chinese publications are now beginning to reveal the extent of social disparities and inequalities in the PRC. The open recognition and discussion of these problems has also required a shift in the official party line.

At the 13th Party Congress in 1987, China described her development as at the "Primary Stage of Socialism". The concept confirms that China is a socialist country. Yet, being in a primary stage, China cannot be exempted from the occurrence of social problems. During this period, the major contradiction is the rising material and spiritual needs of the masses and the low economic productivity of the society. There remains the insistence that all social problems would be ultimately eliminated when the country has attained a more mature state of socialism.

Social Disparities

The Chinese leadership today openly acknowledges significant disparities and inequalities in the incomes and the living standards between and among various sectors of the Chinese society. The main areas of concern are in the continuing, and perhaps growing, discrepancies in the following sectors:

(a) Between rural and urban areas;

(b) Between geographic regions; and

(c) Between state and non-state enterprises.

There is of course overlap among the three categories but it is illuminating to examine each of them in turn.

Urban and Rural Differences

Urban residents enjoy a number of benefits provided by the state which are not available to rural people:

a. Higher Incomes

Under the Communist rule, the income of the urban residents has consistently been higher than those in the rural areas.[1] This is clear when we trace the ratio between the annual per capita income in the cities and in the rural areas over the past decades:[2] 3.47: 1 in 1957; 1.24: 1 in 1978; 1.83: 1 in 1983; 1.99: 1 in 1988; 2.14: 1 in 1989; 2.32: 1 in 1992; and 2.54: 1 in 1993. Income differentials between rural and urban areas narrowed significantly after the Household Responsibility System was established after 1983 as part of Deng's reforms, but are beginning to move again in the former direction. In 1993, the average per capita income available for living expenses for urban residents was 2,337 yuan (representing a real growth of 10.2 per cent over the 1992 figure), whereas the average per capita net income for peasants was 921 yuan (representing a real growth of 3.2 per cent over the 1992 figure).[3]

b. State Subsidies

As discussed in earlier chapters, efforts were made after the establishment of the PRC to control inflation and to suppress the prices of essential commodities in cities. Financial subsidies became the mechanism by which state revenue is used to subsidise commodity producers, service managers, and consumers to make up differences between high purchasing prices and low selling prices, as well as losses incurred by enterprises. The financial

Table 9.1: Financial Subsidies

Year	Total amount in million yuan	% of state revenue	Price subsidies in %	Subsidies for loss-suffering enterprises in %
1952	4	0.02	100.0	—
1957	7	0.2	100.0	—
1965	4,229	8.9	55.5	44.5
1978	15,403	13.7	60.9	39.1
1981	39,193	36.0	83.6	16.4
1984	43,800	29.2	84.5	15.5
1987	67,103	28.3	43.9	56.1
1991	87,722	25.7	42.3	57.7
1992	64,472	16.5	52.1	47.9
1993	70,900	14.6	41.7	58.3
1994(budget)	74,200	15.6	51.6	48.4

Sources: China Statistical Information and Consultancy Centre, *China Report (1949–1989)* (Hong Kong: Influxfund Co. Ltd. and Zie Yongder Co. Ltd., 1990), p. 413; *Far Eastern Economic Review*, 24 March 1994, p. 48.

subsidy serves to stabilise the price of daily necessities such as grain, oil, cotton, meat, eggs, poultry and vegetables. In the 1980s, state financial subsidies took up approximately 20 per cent of the state revenue. Of this amount, almost 60 per cent went to consumer goods, while the rest went to subsidise the losses of SOE.[4]

Each time the government has raised the purchase price of farm products so as to improve the income of the peasants, it has to pay a subsidy, often through work units to urban workers in order to minimise the impact of the price increase on the standard of living of urban residents. As a result of the state subsidies, grain and oil prices remained more or less unchanged from 1949 to 1991, with only a minor adjustment of price in 1966.[5] In particular, state subsidies have increased rapidly after the launching of the economic reforms. (See Table 9.1) In 1993, a total of 29.6 billion yuan was allocated by the central government to urban areas to compensate for price increases, representing 5.2 per cent of the total national expenditure. (The figure was increased to about 38.3 billion yuan in the 1994 national budget.)[6]

c. Occupational Welfare

According to a calculation in 1986, the annual social security expenses for each urban employee was 200 yuan, and only 11 yuan in rural areas — a ratio of 18 to 1.[7] Social security benefits include pensions and medical care. A more up-to-date estimation puts the difference even higher at 24 to 1.[8] The ratio is further widened to 30 to 1 if housing allowance, food subsidies and other public services are included.[9]

d. Employment Services

Urban residents receive government help in job assignments and referrals, job training, and even unemployment insurance. The government has no obligation to provide jobs for people in the rural areas; and rural peasants are not free to move into cities under the household registration regulations.

e. Public and Social Services

The educational level between rural and urban residents has wide discrepancies. While educational investments on facilities in cities can rely on government funds, investments in rural areas have to rely on resources of villagers themselves. Not surprisingly, illiteracy rates in rural areas are much higher. Some 24 per cent of the rural population are illiterate and semi-literate, and they make up almost 90 per cent of the national illiterate and semi-literate population.[10]

With the restriction of the Household Registration System, rural residents can only become state employees through the allocation system in schools. Since the educational system is biased against the rural areas, the rural villagers usually encounter great difficulty in becoming state employees.

In medical care, the ratios of a hospital bed to population size in 1991 are one bed to 211 persons in urban areas, and one to 688 persons in rural areas. As for medical doctors, the ratios are one doctor to 304 persons in urban areas, and one to 1,098 persons in the rural areas.[11]

Inequalities between Regions

The PRC is divided into 23 provinces, 3 municipalities, and 5 autonomous regions. They may be grouped into three general areas, namely the Eastern, Central, and Western regions.[12] As Table 9.2 shows, the income

Table 9.2: Per Capita Annual Income Differentials in Western, Eastern and Central Regions in 1987 (in yuan)

Regions	Urban and rural Resident	Urban resident	Rural resident
Western region	577.1	1,201.9	386.8
Central region	617.0	1,104.4	468.4
Eastern region	975.8	1,439.4	819.4
Ratio of West: Central: East	1: 1.1: 1.7	1: 0.9: 1.2	1: 1.2: 2.1

Sources: China Working Group on Income Distribution of Urban and Rural Residents, "The Characteristics of Individual Income Distribution in the Progress of Economic Reform", *Reform*, 5 (1991), pp. 80–88.

differentials are significant, particularly between the Eastern Region (which includes the NEZ) and the other two. Noteworthy is the fact that regional inequalities was significant even during the Maoist regime.[13]

The average income per capita in Shanghai in 1992 was 5,423 yuan whereas it was under 1,000 yuan in Anhui, Guizhou, Sichuan, Guangxi, and Henan.[14] Furthermore, 90 per cent of the nation's population where per-capita annual income is less than 400 yuan live in the Central and Western regions of the country.[15]

Differences between State and Non-state Enterprises

In the Maoist era, wage differences were a function of controlled scales set by central planning. Their differences tended to be small because of an egalitarian ideology.[16] With economic reforms, the income gap between different trades or occupations have widened. As a result of the return of the bonus system and the increased autonomy of SOE to set their wage scales, factory workers often are paid higher than government employees; and manual workers earn more than intellectuals and professionals. On average, the annual wages among the three economic sectors, SOE, COE, and Other Ownership in 1992 were 2,878 yuan, 2,109 yuan, and 3,966 yuan respectively.[17] A survey carried out by the All-China Federation of Trade Unions in 1991 comparing wages and welfare benefits of different economic sectors showed that employees in joint ventures (with foreign investors) were better off than those in the COE and the SOE.[18]

Another indication of rising inequalities is revealed by the distribution of savings deposits. The official data in 1992 showed that the high-income group represented less than 3 per cent of the total population, but their average per capita savings reached 5,400 yuan, which was 28 per cent of the total. Total savings of the peasants only accounted for 26 per cent of the national total.[19] A new middle class has emerged which includes owners of private enterprises, individual entrepreneurs, movie actors, writers, and joint venture managers.[20] The Gini coefficient, as a measurement of income inequalities, increased from 0.33 in 1979 to 0.4 in 1992.[21] The data clearly indicate that economic reforms have aggravated the problem of income inequalities.

Disadvantaged Populations

Inevitably, economic reforms and changes in the welfare system have brought benefits to some and threats, if not losses to others. Within the areas of inequities identified above, there are some obvious groups who are now more vulnerable to contingencies of life. Again, there will be overlap among the groups identified below, but it is informative to look briefly at each.

The Poor

Chinese officials tend to down play the existence of poverty in urban areas. Poverty refers to rural poverty, which means the problem of physical survival. The compilation by the Ministry of Agriculture in 1991 showed that 38 counties, with a total population of 19.6 million, had an annual per capita income of less than 200 yuan (2.2 per cent of the rural population). If the poverty line extends to 300 yuan, the population in poverty extends to 81 million (9.2 per cent of the rural population).[22] The common characteristics of these poverty-stricken areas include poor natural conditions for farming, under-developed industries, rapid rise in population (higher than the national average birth rate), low educational standard and technological knowledge among the people, and geographical isolation (low mobility).[23]

In urban areas, a survey carried out by the SSB in 1990 showed that 5 per cent of the sample households experienced financial difficulties. Their average annual income was 689 yuan (sample average was 1,387 yuan). Estimations based on the survey showed that 7 million employees are living in poverty, and if family members are included, the number of people living in poverty would reach 20 million.[24] The perceived reasons for poverty included inflation, large family size with small number of working persons, and having family members sick or disabled.

The Unemployed

China has denied the existence of unemployment. Officially, there are only figures on persons "waiting for employment", referring to registered job-seekers, aged between 15 and 55 in the cities. During Maoist times, the strategy of job creation and administrative procedures controlling the movement of the labour force were effective in keeping the "unemployment" rate low.

In 1979, the unemployment rate was 5.8 per cent, which was then reduced to only 1.8 per cent in 1985. But the unemployment rate has since been on the rise, reaching 2.6 per cent in 1993 (approximately 4.2 million people).[25] It is expected that the figure will rise to between 3 and 4 per cent.[26] Under the unemployment crisis, the situation is more critical among the disadvantaged populations such as the women, the young, the elderly and the disabled. According to Chinese forecasts there are several factors which will contribute to the severity of the problem in the 1990s.[27]

(a) Demographic predictions show that the number of economically active population will increase from 580 million in 1991 to 780 million by the year 2000. The average annual increase is 20 million people.

(b) The largest category of job transfer will come from agricultural workers turning to non-agricultural work in industrial and service sectors. It is estimated that there is currently a surplus labour force of 125 million (some put the figure to 200 million) in agricultural work, and is increasing at a rate of 10 million a year. The implementation of the Household Responsibility System in the rural areas has improved the efficiency of the agricultural production thereby reducing the labour requirement in agricultural work. Another source of job transfer comes from the demobilised soldiers. Each year, there are 500,000 demobilised soldiers require job placements.[28]

(c) Furthermore, it is roughly estimated that up to 20 per cent of the labour-force in SOE are redundant. In the process of economic rationalisation, some 20 million under-employed or surplus workers will be required to change jobs.

In 1978, before the introduction of economic reforms, almost three-quarters of the new jobs were created in the SOE, with the remainder in COE. Among the 7.4 million new jobs created in 1992, less than one-half were in SOE.[29] It is obvious that the non-SOE sectors will play an increasingly important role in the years to come.

The Dislocated

Closely related to the problem of unemployment is the problem of migrants and temporary residents who make up a floating population. China had apparently controlled the problem of rural migration in the late 1950s through the Household Registration System. However, with economic reforms and the loosening of control over mobility, a population of floaters has increased dramatically. It was estimated in 1992 that their numbers reached over 70 million; with over a million in some of the big cities such as Beijing, Shanghai, Tianjin and Guangzhou.[30]

Surplus labour leave the rural areas because of the better job opportunities, facilities and living conditions in cities. Most of these migrants are young people, coming from rural areas in the Central Region, such as Anhui, Wunan and Henan, moving into cities in the coastal regions.[31] In fact, the greater affluence among city-dwellers has increased the need for cheap manpower in construction, transportation and domestic services. The result of the "push" and "pull" forces creates a large unplanned and floating population that may represent over 10 per cent of population in a city, thus threatening to overload public services and facilities which include food supply, housing, medical care and transportation. In particular, rural migrants are claimed to create problems in public order and the implementation of the family planning policy.

The Disabled

According to a national survey in 1987, there is an estimated 51,640,000 disabled people in China, representing 4.9 per cent of the national population. The disabilities are associated with hearing or speaking problems, mentally handicap, physical functioning, visual problems, and mental disorders.[32]

According to the 1987 survey, disabled children under the age of 14 made up some 2.66 per cent of the national total in this age group. Among the disabled children population, mentally handicap is the biggest problem, affecting over two-thirds (66 per cent) of this group.[33] Less than six per cent of those with visual, hearing and speaking disabilities can be admitted to schools. Consequently, most of the disabled are illiterate.[34]

The major problem of the disabled is financial. Nearly 70 per cent of the disabled must rely on family support. Only 2.7 per cent receive government assistance, while the remainder have personal resources for self-support. A major service for the disabled in the PRC is the system of welfare factories, which in 1992 provided employment to 700,000 disabled people. (See Chapter 7) Despite this admirable record, only 50 per cent of those with working abilities were able to find jobs.[35]

According to the Five-Year Plan for the Disabled (1988–1992), the three rehabilitation programmes for the disabled receiving highest priority are: operations for children with infantile paralysis (300,000 people); persons with cataracts (500,000 people), and speech therapy (30,000 people).

The Elderly

The elderly population in China is defined as people aged 60 or over (the retirement age for male employees). At present, the elderly as a proportion of the total population in China is still relatively low when compared with those in developed countries such as Sweden, Japan, and the United Kingdom. However, there are some ominous portends for the immediate future:

(a) A large jump in both numbers and proportion are imminent.[36] Improved preventive health care has resulted in longer life. A dramatic decrease in birth rate in the 1980s will result in a much lower proportion of younger persons in the coming years. Projections indicate that the elderly will account for nearly one-fifth of the Chinese population by the year 2025.

(b) The population is large in sheer numbers. In 1990, the number of elderly had reached 100 million, and will more than double in size to 250 million by the year 2025. This will represent one-fifth of the world's total elderly population.

(c) The distribution of the elderly population is uneven, with numbers much higher in cities than in rural areas. In large municipalities such as Shanghai, Beijing and Tianjin, the aging population has reached over 10 per cent whereas in the mountainous areas, the figure is below five.[37] An interesting phenomenon is that the percentage of elderly population in cities is rising rapidly, and the rural

Table 9.3: Gender Differences among Pensioners (in percentage)

	City	Town	County
Male	83.64	76.04	6.12
Female	35.08	22.84	0.72
Total	57.96	47.82	3.26

Source: X. Y. Tian, *China Elderly Population* (Beijing: China Economics Publishers, 1991), p. 378.

areas also registered moderate rise, but the elderly population in towns are actually decreasing.[38] This is a result from migration of young people from counties into towns.

(d) With the implementation of the Single-child Policy, a "4-2-1" family structure: four grandparents, two parents and one child would emerge by the turn of the century, with concomitant economic and caring burden on the sole child.[39]

According to a national survey in 1987 of elderly people living in the rural areas, some 67.5 per cent were supported by their children, 26.2 per cent by working, and 5 per cent by their spouses. The remainder were supported either by relatives, the government, or collectives. The percentages of the elderly having pensions in cities and towns were 56.1 per cent and 47.5 per cent respectively.[40] Large differences were also found between male and female pension recipients, as shown in Table 9.3. Pensionable jobs are clearly a domain that is male dominated.

Only one out of five older persons (18.4 per cent) enjoy free medical care, fully subsidised by their previous work units. A further 10 per cent pay half of the cost, with the other half paid by the work units of their spouses. The remaining 71.7 per cent must pay for medical care themselves.[41]

As to the mode of care, 82.6 per cent of the elderly care for themselves, 11.1 per cent depended on their children, 3.8 per cent on their spouses, 0.5 per cent on friends and relatives, 0.2 per cent on maids, 0.1 per cent on neighbours, and 0.1 per cent on welfare organisations.[42]

Children and Youth

Young people in China refers to persons aged under 25. They comprise one of the most prominent groups affected by the policy of reform.[43] Their values are often uprooted, and they become confused with the meaning of life and their own future direction. There is much cynicism today about unconditional and unquestioned conformity to state regulations, and reluctance to accept the exhortations of authorities telling them what to believe.[44]

In 1992, the official dropout rate in primary schools was 2.2 per cent, and in secondary schools, 5.8 per cent. The rate is much higher in remote provinces.[45] Most of the dropouts are girls living in rural areas. A survey by the State Education Commission in 1990 showed that the major reason for their leaving school was economic. Girls are required to work at early age in order to contribute to family income.[46] To rural peasants, education is also a luxury which is not to be "wasted" on girls in family. Chinese authorities admit that the practice of child labour (Chinese laws have banned child labour) is a cause of the rise in school dropout rates.[47]

In Guangzhou, the Civil Affairs Bureau received a total of 3,225 runaway adolescents in 1992, and most of them left home because of financial and family problems at home.[48] According to a government estimate, 14.2 per cent of the migrants served by the Civil Affairs Bureaux in 10 cities were aged 7 to 16.[49] Regarding the problem of abandoned children, it was reported that the government in Wunan province had received a total of 16,121 abandoned babies between 1986–1990. Of this number, 91 per cent were female and 25 per cent were disabled.[50]

Between 1950 and 1959, the delinquency rate represented about 25 per cent of all crimes committed. This figure, however is on the increase: 60 per cent between 1965 and 1975, 71.42 per cent in 1983, and 75 per cent in 1991.[51] The average age of first-time offenders fell sharply from 16.7 in 1990 to 14 in 1991.[52] The increase in criminal activity among youth is attributed by authorities to the attractions of a materialistic life style and a money-oriented attitude.

Status of Chinese Women

Women, who made up of 49 per cent of the Chinese population in 1992, were described as "holding up half the sky." The *1982 Constitution* (Article 48) stipulates the rights of women:

> Women in the PRC enjoy equal rights with men in all spheres of life, political, economic, cultural and social, including family life. The state protects the rights and interests of women, applies the principle of equal work for men and women alike and trains and selects cadres from among women.

Politically, there is the official claim that women's participation is high.

There is some evidence to support this. In 1954, only 147 women were found among the deputies in the NPC, representing 12 per cent of the total. In 1993, when the Eighth NPC was convened, the number of women deputies had increased to 626, accounting for 21 per cent of the total.[53] In government offices, there were only 150,000 women cadres (8.5 per cent) in 1951; but this number has increased to over 10 million (32.4 per cent) in 1993.[54]

However, a closer look shows that the number of women representatives in the people's congresses at county and town levels are falling. It is acknowledged that few women have been elected to leading bodies. An official of the Organisational Department of the Communist Party, Central Committee explained:

> In the past, we set quotas for women in leading bodies and the vacancies for leading positions equalled the number of candidates. The number of women cadres was therefore stable. This method has some advantages — it can ensure the number of women leading members and is conducive to training women cadres and bringing the role of women into play. But, it also has some shortcomings. For instance, it affects the free choice of the electors. We no longer decide the number of women members in leading bodies.[55]

In economic enterprises, there were only 600,000 women employees (7.5 per cent of the non-agricultural employee population) in 1950. By 1992, the number of women employees reached 55.9 million (37.8 per cent).[56] In the 1990 census, 73 per cent of the women aged over 15 were economically active.[57]

With the economic reforms and the introduction of competition in enterprises in the 1980s, employment of women faces new difficulties. In the past, employment was centrally-controlled and assigned, and enterprises had little choice of workers. But, economic reforms have given enterprises a greater control over the organisation structure. Now, 60 per cent of the workers dismissed by SOE[58] and over 70 per cent of the "persons waiting for work" are female.[59] High costs of welfare, including fully paid maternity leave (six months for one-child mothers), breast-feeding hours, and physiology are given as the reasons for the reluctance of enterprises to hire, or to keep, women workers.

To deal with the surplus women workforce, the government has provided assistance in re-training and transfer of jobs to the service sectors, such as sewing, laundry work, and repairing. Those who cannot be immediately assigned a job are given long leave backed by benefits. They are encouraged to stay at home, take care of children and do house work. In several provinces, women workers are encouraged to take long leave up to seven years after the birth of a baby, and take early retirement at the age of 40.[60]

Women made up of over 70 per cent of the illiterate and 80 per cent of the school dropout population.[61] Even though 46.6 per cent of the students in primary schools are female, the figure drops to 43.1 per cent in secondary schools, 33.7 per cent in college, and 24.8 per cent in postgraduate studies.[62] A national survey in 1990 also showed that on average, men received two more years of education than women.[63]

A large scale survey carried out by the Chinese authorities in 21 provinces in 1990 (covering 40,000 men and women in both urban and rural areas) claims that women have achieved rapid progress in their status over the past four decades.[64] However, the development is uneven and dependent on the region and particular social and economic situation.[65] Moreover, women as victims of emerging social problems such as abduction, violence, prostitution, infanticide, arranged marriage, and pornography are becoming serious again.[66]

The problems facing women, such as the pressure to give birth to a son, unequal opportunities in employment and assignment of housing quarter in work units are apparently recognised by the government. But even with the enactment of the *Law on the Protection of Women's Rights* in 1991, the state is apparently hesitant to enforce rigorously equality in work place because this would apparently contradict the policy of granting greater discretion to enterprises. In preparing the United Nations Fourth World Conference on Women held in Beijing in 1995, China has published a *White Paper on the Situation of Chinese Women*.[67]

Status of Minority Populations

Apart from news that occasionally appears in the mass media, or occasional references by officials, very little is actually known about ethnic minority groups in China. One reason may be that many of the groups live in remote areas of China, and contact with outsiders has been minimal. Another may be that the relationship between the minorities and the majority Han Chinese involve political, if not religious issues such as, for example, the case of Tibet.

China has an official definition of an ethnic group, which is referred to as *minzu*, or literally a "nationality". There are three criteria. A group must:

have its own language; reside in a defined territory sharing with others blood and tradition; and possess a common sentiment and identity.[68] Based on these criteria, China has recognised a total of 56 "nationalities". The majority Han nationality, who in the past were referred to as "the Chinese", constitute 91.9 per cent of the total population in 1990.[69] The other 55 groups have a total of some 91.3 million people, who predominantly live along areas bordering foreign countries in the northeast, northwest, southeast, and south China. The main groups include: Mongolian, Zhuang, Hui, Miao, Uygur, Tujia, Yi, Manchu, and Tibetan. On the whole, the economic conditions of these regions are poor. Among the 181 poverty-stricken counties receiving direct state assistance (with per capita income under 200 yuan), 90 of them were inhibited by ethnic minorities.[70]

The official policy is equality of all nationalities, and respect for the minority cultures. Reference is made to the classical Marxist explanation that oppression of nationalities stems from class oppression and exploitation. Once class exploitation is eliminated, nationalities will disappear.

The party line is that class oppression has resulted in many minorities being backward in development. Minority nationalities must now use their own resources but the Han majority, being in an advanced stage of development, is duty-bound to provide assistance. Thus, thousands of cadres, teachers, engineers, and technicians have been sent to minority areas to assist the local people. This objective is to help minorities to be "cultured", which in the Chinese mind means education and modernisation; but to the minorities may mean control and subjugation.

Despite their vulnerability to political control by the majority group, the fact that they are officially recognised does provide some degree of autonomous administration and sharing of political power. For example, while the dominant Han Chinese are restricted to one child per family, national minorities are allowed up to three or four children. The national minority population has increased 63.4 per cent since 1978 whereas the Han population increased only 14.9 per cent in the same period. According to official estimation, the minority population will grow to 132 million by the year 2000.[71]

Summary

In the midst of a growing affluence in the Chinese society, there are significant groups of people who have not shared the benefits of economic reforms. Generally speaking, there are three such groups:

(a) The first comprise persons who have not been touched by economic reforms. The main examples are rural peasants living in the interior regions of China.

(b) A second group comprises persons who have been caught up in the economic and social reforms since 1978, but who have not particularly benefitted from the changes. Some examples are the elderly, the youth, and the disabled.

(c) The third group involves persons who have actually become more disadvantaged as a consequence of economic and social changes. Examples here would include the unemployed, the dislocated, women, and children.

Notes

1. C. Riskin, *China's Political Economy* (Oxford: Oxford University Press, 1991), pp. 237–48.
2. Q. F. Zhu, "Social Development Indicators in Rural Areas and the Developmental Target in the Year 2000", *Agricultural Economic Research*, 10 (1991), pp. 9–15; *BR*, 14–20 March 1994, p. 26.
3. *BR*, 14–20 March 1994, p. 26.
4. China Statistical Information and Consultancy Service Centre, *China Report 1949–1989* (Hong Kong: Influxfunds Co. Ltd. and Zie Yongder Co. Ltd., 1990), p. 421.
5. State Economic Systems Reform Committee, *China Economic Systems Reform Yearbook* (Beijing: Reform Publishers, 1992), p. 415.
6. *Far Eastern Economic Review*, 24 March 1994, p. 48.
7. *Social Security Bulletin*, 27 June 1989, p. 4.
8. The calculation is as follows: social security expenditure for 0.13 billion urban workers was 34.1 billion yuan, and the average was 170 yuan for an urban resident (urban population taken as 20 million). Expenditure on social security in rural areas was 5.7 billion yuan, and the average was 7 yuan for a rural resident (rural population taken as 840 million).
9. Z. Y. Gao, "The New Exploration into the Work of Civil Affairs", *Sociology and Social Research*, 4 (1988), pp. 12–17.
10. The Synthetical Study of Social Development Project Group, "A Synthetical Analysis of China's Social Development in the Structural Transition Period", *Sociological Studies*, 4 (July 1991), pp. 74–93.
11. SSB, *China Statistical Yearbook* (Beijing: China Statistical Publishers, 1993), p. 798.
12. Eastern Region refers to those coastal provinces such as Guangdong, Jiangsu, Beijing, and Liaoning. Western Region refers to those interior provinces such

as Guizhou, Gansu, and Yunnan. Central Region refers to those provinces such as Sichuan, Anhui, Shanxi, Hubei, and Henan.

13. Riskin, op. cit., p. 225.
14. SSB, op. cit., p. 40. In average wage per capita, it was 4,273 yuan in Shanghai whereas it was only 2,308 yuan in Jilin and 2,154 yuan in Jiangxi (national average was 2,711 yuan). SSB, op. cit., p. 134.
15. *BR*, 11–17 April 1994, p. 13.
16. Riskin, op. cit., p. 251.
17. Ibid, p. 132.
18. *China Labour Science*, 8 (1992), pp. 3–8.
19. The per capita savings of the peasants being only 295 yuan whereas it was 1,500 yuan for urban residents. *MP*, 12 February 1992, p. 10.
20. Y. Xin, "Views concerning the Problem on the Division between the Rich and the Poor", *Gansu Journal of Theory*, 1 (1994), pp. 46–50.
21. Y. D. Ke and Y. D. Yue, "Contemporary Contradictions and Policy of Income Distribution", *China Science Forum*, 4 (1993), pp. 14–18.
22. Ministry of Agriculture, *China Agricultural Statistical Material* (Beijing: Agricultural Publishers, 1992), pp. 378–79.
23. *Population and Economics*, 6 (1992), pp. 57–60.
24. *SCMP*, 20 October 1993, p. 9.
25. *SCMP*, 29 April 1994, p. 9.
26. Y. W. Shi, "Exploration into the Problems of Unemployment in China", *Journal of Huadong Teachers' College, Society and Philosophy*, 1 (1991), pp. 21–27.
27. J. J. Shen and Y. Pan, "The Challenge and Response to the Problem of Unemployment in the 1990s", *Journal of China Labour Movement Institute*, 3 (1991), pp. 25–29.
28. *SCMP*, 15 December 1993, p. 8.
29. SSB, op. cit., p. 119.
30. Y. N. Chen, "An Analysis on the Wave of Migrants", *City Reform and Development*, 2 (1993), pp. 43–45.
31. *Social Work Studies*, 1 (1994), pp. 51–52.
32. All-China Sampled Disabled People's Survey Office, *China Disabled People's Manual* (Beijing: Earthquake Publishers, 1988), p. 1.
33. About 80 per cent of the mentally handicapped people in the country are said to be victims of iodine deficiency. Every year, it is estimated that over one million mentally handicapped children are born. *SCMP*, 4 July 1994, p. 7.
34. In 1992, there was a total of 1,077 special schools for the blind, deaf, mute, and mentally retarded, with a total enrolment of 129,455 students. SSB, op. cit., p. 748.
35. *MP*, 27 September 1993, p. 13.

36. The annual increase in the elderly population was only about 2 per cent from 1953 to 1982, but from 1982 onwards, the increase reaches 3 per cent. By the end of the century, the elderly population would reach 0.13 billion, or 10.5 per cent of the national population. By 2025, the population would be 0.28 billion, 19.34 per cent of the national population. Z. Wu and P. Du, "Understanding the Trend of Elderly Problem in China", *China Demographic Science*, 3 (1992), pp. 1–5.

37. J. H. Yuan and Z. H. Zhang, *The Challenge to the Trend of Increasing Number of Elderly* (Shanghai: Fudan University Press, 1991), p. 149.

38. X. Y. Tian, *China Elderly Population* (Beijing: China Economics Publishers, 1991), p. 126.

39. D. Phillips (ed.), *Aging in East and Southeast Asia* (London: Edmond Arnold, 1992), pp. 8–9.

40. *BR*, 14–20 November 1988, p. 11.

41. Ibid.

42. Tian, op. cit., p. 183.

43. In a recent classification of the case nature of a hotline service for young people in Guangzhou, the breakdown of the content according to the problem identified were: 24 per cent relationship with opposite sex; 22 per cent employment; 17 per cent student-teacher relationship; 14 per cent with family relations; 7 per cent health problem with puberty; and 16 per cent others. *Youth Exploration*, 2 (1992), p. 16.

44. S. Rosen, "Prosperity, Privatisation, and China's Youth", *Problems of Communism* (March/ April 1985), pp. 1–20.

45. *MP*, 30 May 1993, p. 9.

46. K. M. Cheng, *China's Education Reforms* (Hong Kong: Commercial Press, 1992), p. 40.

47. *SCMP*, 30 April 1993, p. 10.

48. *Social Work Research*, 2 (1994), p. 29.

49. *CS*, 9 (1991), p. 10.

50. *CCA*, 1 (1992), p. 15.

51. *BR*, 13–19 January 1992, p. 6.

52. *SCMP*, 15 January 1992, p. 7.

53. *BR*, 6–12 June 1994, p. 15.

54. *OW*, 23 March 1992, p. 14.

55. *BR*, 7–13 March 1988, p. 26.

56. SSB, op. cit., p. 116.

57. W. Wang, "The Analysis on the Employment Characteristics of the Female Population in China", *China Manpower Resource and Development*, 4 (1992), pp. 18–21.

58. L. Jiang, X. Y. Lu and T. L. Shan, *1993–1994 China: Social Situation Analysis and Forecast* (Beijing: China Social Science Publishers, 1994), p. 256.

59. *OW*, 23 March 1992, p. 4.
60. Jiang, et al., op. cit., p. 257.
61. *BR*, 11–17 March 1991, p. 15. For people aged above 15 years old, 9.1 per cent of the women (3.6 per cent for men) were illiterate. SSB, op. cit., p. 871.
62. SSB, op. cit., p. 728.
63. C. F. Tao and R. P. Zhang, *A Review of the Women's Social Status in China* (Beijing: China Women Publishers, 1993), p. 42.
64. In an international study comparing the status of women in 99 countries, the ranking of Chinese women is regarded as "poor". Population Crisis Committee, *Population, Briefing Paper*, 20 (June 1988).
65. *BR*, 30 December–5 January 1992, p. 10.
66. *OW*, 3 May 1993, p. 10.
67. *BR*, 6–12 June 1994, pp. 9–23.
68. D. Y. Wu, "Cultural Change and Ethnic Identity among Minorities in China", in *Ethnicity and Ethnic Groups in China*, edited by C. Chiao and N. Tapp (Hong Kong: Chinese University Press, 1989), pp. 11–22.
69. SSB, op. cit., p. 69.
70. M. Liu, "The Characteristics of Ethnic Minorities", *Sociological Studies*, 1 (1994), pp. 30–34.
71. *China Daily*, 18 May 1993, p. 1.

A Confucian Welfare State or a Confused State of Welfare?

For three decades after coming to power in 1949, the PRC adopted a Soviet model of social welfare that centred on the workplace. Whether a factory in an urban area or a cooperative in the countryside, the collective work unit functioned as a "welfare society" within which an individual received employment and income protection, and enjoyed benefits and services in such basic areas as housing, food, education and health care. Although benefits differed between and among collectives, disparities within the same collective were limited. Rights to welfare were not based on legal entitlement; rather, it was the moral obligation of the collectives that ensured a paternalistic protection of its members.

Social and economic policies under Mao Zedong reflected the principle of egalitarianism. In attempting to incorporate income redistribution, financial benefits and social services as an inherent part of living in a cooperative, Mao's strategy was to build up what has been referred to as "Type I Welfare". The general approach was based on the belief that, apart from contingencies caused by natural disasters, the large majority of people would come under the care of collectives, leaving only a residual number of "three nos" who would require financial relief and the ameliorative and restorative services associated with "Type II Welfare".

At the macro-level, the state's role was to provide a stable societal order for the collectives to develop and to fulfil the functions of political education, economic production, and welfare protection. It was also the role of the state to ensure that every citizen belonged to a collective through the mechanism of the Household Registration System which limited rural-urban migration and a job assignment system which further controlled worker mobility. The collectives functioned as a mini-society, much like a traditional extended family.

Although attempts to sever income from employment (a cherished Marxist ideal) did not succeed, a compressed wage scale did serve to minimise differences between the highest and lowest levels, and subsidies in urban areas kept essential goods affordable. Benefits and services were de-commodified and considered as a social wage. Schools and medical facilities were established in rural areas where none had previously existed. This brought about a level of social welfare equal to, or above, that of other countries at a comparable stage of development. Moreover, for decades, China was free from problems such as inflation, absolute poverty, drug addiction, and unemployment. A dramatic fall in the death rate along with a corresponding increase in life expectancy must also be included among the notable achievements of the PRC under Mao's regime.

These achievements, however, came at a very high cost. Purportedly, the collectives were self-governing, self-managing and self-serving units. In actuality, they were controlled by a Communist Party organisation to ensure that the collectives would follow the party line. Under Mao, the average Chinese lived in a tightly controlled environment with limited mobility.

The country itself was isolated from the outside world which restricted access to capital and technical expertise required by a modern economy. As a result, the well-being of the people showed little improvement and the economy showed signs of regressing. A centralised command system that relied on a rigid bureaucracy to implement policies from the centre together with the edict of "red over expert" created much inefficiency. And, the resort to mass campaigns such as the Great Leap Forward and the Cultural Revolution resulted not only in social and economic turmoil but also in tragic losses of human life.

Under the banner of economic reforms pushed by Deng Xiaoping since 1978, a practical economic rationality replaced the idealistic principles of egalitarianism and redistribution. Ironically, the first major reform occurred in the rural areas which had provided key support for Mao during the revolution.

Poor peasants had been among the first beneficiaries of the Communist take-over in 1949 after the redistribution of land in the countryside. The establishment of rural communes then removed control over land from individual households to the collective. With the subsequent failure of the rural collectives, peasants readily complied with the Household Responsibility System introduced in the early 1980s, which again made it possible for an individual household to till its own piece of land.

The opening of China to foreign capital investments and technical expertise and the introduction of free market practices have brought new

life to a moribund economy, provided opportunities for individual initiatives, and helped to develop new rural industries. Indeed, private individual
businesses together with newly formed COE involving joint ventures with
foreign investors represent the fastest growing sectors in the economy. But
it is not that easy to move from a state-controlled system to an open market
economy.

Systemic problems have appeared such as runaway inflation and growing government deficits. Increasing demands of regional governments to
participate in economic reforms and increased regional power as the result
of economic development threaten the legitimacy and mandate of the
central government. Corruption among cadres at the local level is becoming a common occurrence. According to press reports, a total of
170,000 cases involving cadre corruption is reported for the year 1993,
bringing the accumulative total number of such cases since 1988 to 1.22
million.[1]

Despite signs of progress such as a rise in general living standards,
economic reforms are by-passing large segments of the population. More
than this, a relaxation of controls has resulted in a large floating population of unemployed seeking work, a growing rate of family breakdown, a
shortage of housing in the cities, an increase in crime and delinquency, and
the appearance of beggars in the streets. Some observers now speak about
an impending crisis confronting China due to inherent contradictions involved in a programme of economic reform that attempts to apply capitalist
practices on top of a socialist structure.

In its annual *Social Situation Analysis and Forecast*, the Chinese
Academy of Social Sciences has repeatedly warned the CCP leadership of
the potential for unrest and instability.[2] According to press reports, industrial actions by workers and rural violence on the part of peasants are
apparently already taking place.[3]

The Chinese leadership is caught up in two dilemmas. First, greater
freedom in the economic sector has inevitably raised the issue of political
reform among Chinese intellectuals and the emergent middle class. The
government has up to now been able to suppress demands for political
change but Deng Xiaoping and his supporters continue to walk on a tight-
rope between "conservative" left-wing elements who long for a return to a
Maoist type of regime, and "reactionary" elements who yearn for a more
democratic political system. To complicate matters, there is the impending
problem of leadership succession because of the imminent demise of the
elderly and ill patriarch, Deng Xiaoping. No one can foretell what will

happen when Deng dies, but there is always the possibility that a major leadership struggle will break out.

The other dilemma involves attempts to reform the social welfare system. The egalitarian social security network created during the Maoist period is now considered as a major impediment to market reform. Unchallenged as gifts of a benevolent state under Mao's regime, such things as job guarantee, price control, state subsidies, and narrow wage differentials are now perceived as mechanisms that stifle work incentive and impede economic progress. The economic boom in recent years has been led by non-SOE sectors while the performance of the SOE themselves has been dismal. The majority of the latter are money-losing enterprises and the costs of the employee welfare programmes are now targeted as the main reason. However, cutting back on welfare benefits enjoyed by the working class carries such enormous political risks that the Chinese leadership has been very hesitant to take any real action in dismantling the "iron rice bowl".

In response to the threats and pressures noted above, the Chinese Government seems to have placed all of its hopes on further economic growth that will bring improvement in the people's livelihood and living standards, and at the same time can provide the CCP with a continuing governing mandate.

Despite the rhetoric of "an unswerving commitment" to state socialism, the traditional ideal of *Xiao Kang* is now used as a yardstick for national development. It would appear that Chinese leaders believe an appeal to Chinese traditions will find a better reception than any plea for socialism.[4] Little mention is made today of the glories of socialist ideology as a motivating and unifying force. Instead, attention is placed on economic prosperity, national pride, and the improvement of the quality of life, and values such as filial piety, stability and harmony, individual discipline, and cultural heritage can be increasingly found in policy statements.

The government is clearly attempting to keep politics separate from economic reforms. Maintaining this duality seems to be part of a strategy that fits the label of "neo-authoritarianism", a doctrine based on the belief that the PRC requires a strong autocratic government to create the conditions for the emergence of a free market. This is consistent with Deng's approach of implementing economic reforms from the "top-down". To support the relevance of this strategy, frequent reference is made to the economic success of Hong Kong, Taiwan, Singapore and South Korea. These "Four Little Dragons" are prosperous, and have authoritarian governments.

The CCP will undoubtedly continue to exercise tight control over the political process. The conflicts and dislocations caused by the breakup of former state socialist regimes in Eastern Europe and the former Soviet Union provide a further argument for the need of a strong authoritarian government that can maintain an orderly society.

Main Features of Welfare Reform

It is clear that the development of social welfare in the PRC must occur within the framework of a host of conflicting demands. In trying to keep a balance between the need to achieve economic reforms on the one hand and to maintain political and social stability on the other, China's current social welfare approach shows the following features:

Minimal State

Because of growing budget deficits, and mindful of the fiscal problems experienced by welfare states in the West, Chinese leaders are trying to avoid any further government commitments in the provision of welfare. Although a complete withdrawal of state support for the "iron rice bowl" is politically unpalatable, the new slogan is "big society and small government". The role of the state would primarily be that of a regulator and enabler, promulgating laws, guidelines and regulations on welfare policy rather than a service provider and financier. While laws are not always made to be strictly enforced, Chinese leaders do use legislation as an instrument for providing guidelines and projecting the image of a caring and paternal government. Generally speaking, the CCP has never abandoned a state-guided national development policy in which it is the responsibility of the government to maintain a stable and harmonious environment.

The one exception in the government's retreat from welfare may lie in the function of the MCA. The role of MCA cadres serving both the urban and rural Residents' Committees will be pivotal in building up collective identity and a spirit of mutual care at the local level. As neighbourhood-based collectives begin to take up a greater responsibility for social services, there will be a need for better trained staff. This could lead to the development of special cadres to handle a social service portfolio which, in turn, would stimulate interest in social work training programmes such as exist in the West.

Decentralised and Localised Development

In line with the economic policy of allowing regional jurisdictions to have more autonomy, the central government actively encourages local innovations in welfare provisions even if it inevitably leads to different standards in different regions. In some of the economically better off provinces and cities, the local governments have already started to develop their own regulations on social security provisions for the needy, and on social service programmes for the elderly, the disabled, and problem families and children.

Non-governmental Organisations

While emphasising the policy of a minimal state, the government is actively encouraging the development of "semi-governmental organisations" such as neighbourhood organisations, charitable trust funds, and societies sponsored by government departments to share the welfare responsibility. Since it is very difficult for a non-governmental organisation to survive without government patronage, there seems little likelihood for a system of independent non-governmental organisations (such as voluntary welfare agencies in the West) to develop on any substantial scale.

Family and Individual Responsibility

In recommending the introduction of contributory retirement insurance schemes in both rural and urban areas, the government stresses a philosophy of self-protection, self-responsibility and mutual care. The important role of the family is stressed in any legislation concerning family care, and the protection of children or the disabled. As the size of families in the PRC will decrease as a consequence of the Single-child Policy, the informal relationship network or *guanxi*, which can include significant persons who are not blood-related will be an important vehicle for protection and welfare benefits.

Profit-making Social Services

Fee-charging programmes in the fields of medical care, housing, and schooling have been developing rapidly in the PRC. This trend is inevitable due to the expanding wants and needs of an emerging middle class on the one hand, and the lack of financial support from government on the other. In many of the homes for the elderly run by the Civil Affairs departments, the majority of residents are fee-paying. Another development found in both government departments as well as in neighbourhood organisations are businesses set up for the express purpose of producing money to finance welfare services.

Tax Reform

Chinese leaders are aware that tax reforms are required which can effectively increase state revenue and redistribute income. A personal income tax system was supposed to have been introduced in the 1980s, but this is still in the process of implementation.[5] There are plans to introduce shortly a capital gains tax and a sales tax. It remains to be seen whether or not these plans will put into actual practice. Again, there are political risks involved. Additionally, due to the poorly developed transportation and communication networks, there is an enormous task of establishing an effective mechanism for tax collection.

International Donations and Assistance

The idea of a self-reliant China that can remain aloof and independent of other nations has pretty much been abandoned. It is now a common practice for the Chinese Government, following a severe natural disaster, to appeal for international assistance and donations, particularly from Hong Kong. International organisations such as World Vision and Oxfam have been encouraged to operate regular relief projects in poverty-stricken areas.

To summarise, the picture presented in the foregoing indicates that social welfare in China will no longer be based on a centrally planned blueprint as was the case in Mao's time. On the contrary, social welfare policy will be characterised by piecemeal, short-term and pragmatic steps, often in the form of limited and localised solutions to tackle immediate needs. This is in line with the pragmatic developmental strategy of Deng Xiaoping — "groping for stones to cross the river." Both the quality and quantity of programmes and services will be determined by the economic vitality of an individual enterprise or a local neighbourhood.

The East Asian Model

With the collapse of communism in Eastern Europe and in the former Soviet Union, socialist regimes no longer provide a viable model for the modernisation of China. The fiscal problems and economic recessions experienced by welfare states in the West have also dampened Chinese enthusiasm to copy the West. An alternative model that now fascinates the Chinese leadership has emerged from the modernising experiences of East Asian countries which include Japan and the "Four Little Dragons". The successful economic performance of these countries have generated a number of publications which, among other things, are interested in common factors that can account for their success.[6]

In the area of social development, these countries have taken different approaches but they exhibit some striking similarities in their orientation to social welfare. For example, the respective governments have actively intervened in the areas of housing, medical care, public health, employment creation, vocational training and basic education (Type I Welfare). Investing in human capital is conceived as essential for supporting economic development.[7]

The achievement of these countries in social development has in fact been impressive. There has been substantial reduction in absolute poverty and income inequalities, as well as improvement in life expectancy, adult literacy, public health and education.[8] One writer goes so far as to describe these countries as "leaders in social development".[9]

Another common feature among the East Asian countries is that state intervention in remedial social welfare (Type II Welfare) is very limited and largely residual. Welfare policy tends to reinforce work discipline and ethic. These countries have very little provision for unemployment, and public assistance benefits for the poor are minimal and stringent. Pensions (if any) are based on contributions from individuals and employers. Labour movements and other types of interest group lobbies are discouraged and tightly regulated.

The East Asian countries put heavy emphasis on the role of the family, the community, and private charity in the provision of welfare.[10] Individual rights are downplayed; state welfare is not an automatic entitlement even though one may be a fully-fledged citizen in good standing.

Some observers have noted that the orientation of these countries towards social welfare reflects Confucian values concerning the role of the state, family and individual; indeed, one writer describes them as "Confucian welfare states".[11] It may be premature to lump all the East Asian countries into one group based on their Confucian past but there is evidence to suggest that their welfare experiences do not fit the pattern of welfare states in the West. It is not our intention here to make a comparative analysis of Eastern and Western experiences. We would however raise the question as to whether we could really understand Asian welfare through the use of Western paradigms. It may well be that a "paradigm shift" is necessary. Coming back to the case of the PRC for example, sinologists are familiar with the capacity shown by the Chinese over the millennia to find their own way to overcome their own problems. As John Fairbank observed:

> Once the modern revolution in Chinese thought got under way in the 1890s, it became evident that no foreign model could fit the Chinese situation, that many models would be used but none would be adequate, and that the creative Chinese people would have to work out their own salvation in their own way. Having had a unique past, they would have their own unique future.[12]

Notes

1. *SCMP*, 8 June 1994, p. 2.
2. L. Jiang, X. Y. Lu, and T. L. Shan, *1992–1993 China: Social Situation Analysis and Forecast* (Beijing: China Social Science Publishers, 1993); *1993–1994 China: Social Situation Analysis and Forecast* (Beijing: China Social Science Publishers, 1994).
3. *SCMP*, 25 January 1994, pp. 1, 8.
4. The official newspaper of the CCP, the *People's Daily* has recognised the value of Confucianism in modern society. It claimed that "traditional Confucianism was a key factor in the economic development of other East Asian nations," and "would avoid or minimise the abuses that have resulted from the excesses of modern Western society." Quoted from *SCMP*, 20 September 1994, p. 8.
5. In the revised regulations on personal income taxation in 1994, salaries over 800 yuan a month will be taxed. For foreigners working in China, salaries over 4,000 yuan a month will be taxed. In both cases, the highest tax rate is 45 per cent. *BR*, 25 April–1 May 1994, p. 6.
6. R. Appelbaum and J. Henderson, "Situating the State in the East Asian Development Process", in *States and Development in the Asian Pacific Rim*, edited by R. Appelbaum and J. Henderson (London: Sage Publications, 1992), pp. 1–26; E. Vogel, *The Four Little Dragons, The Spread of Industrialization in East Asia* (Cambridge, Mass.: Harvard University Press, 1991); The World Bank, *The East Asian Miracle* (Oxford: Oxford University Press, 1993).
7. A. Chowdhury and I. Islam, *The Newly Industrialising Economies of East Asia* (London: Routledge, 1993), p. 230.
8. The World Bank, op. cit., chapter one; ibid., pp. 9–10.
9. H. Hughes, "Catching Up: The Asian Newly Industrialising Economies in the 1990s", *Asian Development Review*, 7.2 (1989), pp. 128–44.
10. H. Jernigan and M. Jernigan, *Aging in Chinese Society* (New York: Harworth Press, 1992); D. Phillips (ed.), *Aging in East and South East Asia* (London:

Edward Arnold, 1992); S. Anderson, *Welfare Policy and Politics in Japan, Beyond the Developmental State* (New York: Paragon House, 1993); C. Jones, "The Pacific Challenge, Confucianism Welfare State", in *New Perspectives on the Welfare State in Europe*, edited by C. Jones (London: Routledge, 1993), pp. 198–217.

11. Jones, op. cit., pp. 198–217.
12. J. Fairbank, *China: A New History* (Cambridge, Mass.: Belknap Press of Harvard University Press, 1992), pp. xvi–xvii.

APPENDIX 1

The Administrative Divisions of the Levels of Government in 1990 with the Number of the Divisions in Brackets

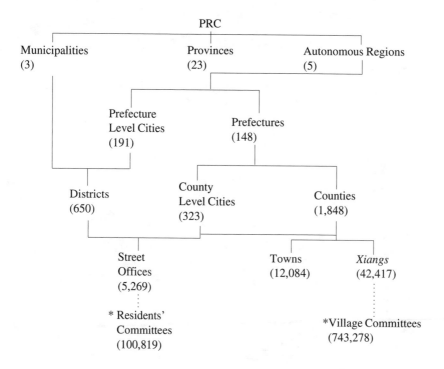

* Both residents' committees and village committees are officially regarded as mass organisations and not governmental offices. Therefore their relationships with street offices and *xiang* people's governments are represented in dotted lines.

Source: Ministry of Civil Affairs, *Simplified Administrative District Division* (Beijing: China Map Publishers, 1993), p. 1; W. F. Zhang, "Introduction to Administrative Division", in *The Theory and Practice of Civil Affairs*, edited by W. N. Liu and G. L. Liu (Beijing: CCP Central Party College, 1993), p. 345.

APPENDIX 2

A. The Responsibilities of the Ministry of Civil Affairs

Through the construction of the grassroots political organ, the village committees, and the residents' committee, the Ministry promotes economic development of cities and counties, encourages the institutionalisation of grassroots democracy. Through the management of social administrative affairs, the Ministry readjusts human relationships, resolves social contradictions, promotes the institutionalisation of social administration and management. Through the development of social security enterprises, the Ministry promotes the society orientation of public welfare; Through the preferential treatment to disabled ex-servicemen and to families of martyrs and of servicemen, the Ministry strengthens the unity of the army, and promotes the modernisation of the national defense. In the context of the new situation, the Ministry develops the mechanism of social stability function, and readjusts human relationships, resolves social contradictions, promotes stability and unity, and provides a healthy environment for the development of a modernised socialist construction. The principal duties include:

1. According to the plans of national economy and social development, the Ministry studies and formulates long-term and mid-term strategies for the development of civil affairs work and organisational structure. The Ministry also works out annual plans with a mechanism of supervision and monitoring.

2. The Ministry studies the working direction, laws, and regulations of: grassroots political organ, village committee, residents' committee, preferential treatment to and resettlement of ex-servicemen, relief to victims of natural disasters and the poverty-stricken people, social welfare, division of administrative regions, society and marriage registration, funeral service, reallocation of migrants.

The Ministry is responsible for the monitoring and supervision of their implementation.

3. The Ministry is responsible for providing guidance to those self-managed mass organisations in the daily work of the construction of the grassroots political organ.

4. The Ministry studies and decides the methods of giving preferential treatment to ex-servicemen and families of martyrs.

5. The Ministry is responsible for the resettlement of the ex-servicemen.

6. The Ministry is responsible for the relief of natural disaster, encourage self-salvation through production, monitors the use of relief material, and develops village cooperative insurance and assistance to the poverty-stricken people.

7. The Ministry is in charge of the relief work of poverty-stricken households and their regular assistance.

8. The Ministry studies and formulates plan to guide the development and management of community service and social welfare enterprises.

9. The Ministry studies and formulates laws and policies governing the employment of handicapped people and development of welfare production.

10. The Ministry is responsible for the administrative division and naming of provinces, cities, *xians* and districts.

11. The Ministry is responsible for mediating disputes concerning disputes in administrative territories.

12. The Ministry is responsible for the registration of societies.

13. The Ministry is responsible for the implementation of *Marriage Law* through marriage registration, management and reforms of marriage practices.

14. The Ministry is responsible for the management and reform of funeral service.

15. The Ministry is responsible for the relocation of migrants and beggars.

16. The Ministry is responsible for the management of the finances of civil affairs work, and monitoring the utilization and management of these finances.

17. The Ministry advises the work of the Federation of Disabled People.

B. The Organisational Structure of the Ministry of Civil Affairs

Ministry of Civil Affairs
– Administration
– Grassroots Political Organ Construction Department
– Services for Ex-servicemen Department
– Placement Department
– Relief Department
– Social Welfare Department
– Administrative Region Demarcation and Naming Department
– Society Registration Department
– Social Affairs Department
– Marriage Registration Department
– Policy and Law Department
– Personnel and Education Department
– Coordination and Planning Department
– International Cooperation Department

Source: Office of the State Organisational Structure Committee, *Organisation of the Chinese Government* (Beijing: China Economics Publishers, 1990), pp. 152–54.

English–Chinese Glossary

All-China Federation of Trade Unions 中華全國總工會

All-China Women's Federation 中華全國婦女聯合會

Book of Rites 禮記

Caring group 包護小組

Chinese Communist Party 中國共產黨

Chinese Communist Youth League 中國共產主義青年團

Collectively-owned enterprise 集體企業

Community service 社區服務

Five-guarantees scheme 五保戶

Floating population 流動人口

Hidden subsidies 暗補

Household Responsibility System 包產到戶

Individual entrepreneur 個體戶

Iron rice bowl 鐵飯碗

Joint venture 三資企業

Material civilisation 物質文明

Ministry of Civil Affairs 民政部

Ministry of Labour 勞動部

Ministry of Personnel 人事部

Preferential treatment 優待撫恤工作

Primary Stage of Socialism 社會主義初階

Residents' committee 居民委員會

Single-child Policy 獨子政策

Socialisation 社會化

Spiritual civilisation 精神文明

State Education Commission 國家教育委員會

State Statistical Bureau 國家統計局

State-owned enterprises 國營企業

Street office 街道辦事處

Three irons and one big 三鐵一大

Three nos 三無對象

Township 鄉鎮

Village committee 村民委員會

Waiting for employment 待業

Welfare factory 福利廠

Welfare institution 福利院

Workers' Congress 工人代表大會

Work unit 單位

Pinyin–Chinese Glossary

This book uses the Chinese phonetic alphabet (*Hanyu Pinyin*) system of spelling Chinese names, terms, and places. However, we have used names such as "Tibet", "Confucius", "Communist Party of China", "Communist Youth League", "Chiang Kai-shek", and others that have clearly been accepted in English language.

Baojia 保甲

Chan 禪

Chen Yi 陳毅

Changping cang 常平倉

Chiang Kai-shek 蔣介石

Da Tong 大同

Danwei 單位

Deng Xiaoping 鄧小平

Dingti 頂替

Diqu 地區

Dongshan 東山

Fengshui 風水

Fumu guan 父母官

Ganqing 感情

Guanxi 關係

Guojia 國家

Hangzhou 杭州

Hainan 海南

Hua Guofeng 華國鋒

Jiang Qing 江青

Jiaohua 敎化

Jinqin jiuye 近親就業

Jiuji 救濟

Kaifeng 開封

Kanke 看客

Lao you suo yang 老有所養

Li 禮

Lu Xun 魯迅

Minzheng 民政

Minzu 民族

Qing dynasty 清朝

Pudong 浦東

Renminbi 人民幣

Renqing 人情

Shan tang 善堂

Shang dynasty 商朝

Shantou 汕頭

She cang 社倉

Shehui fuli 社會福利

Shehui baozhang 社會保障

Sheng 省

Shenzhen 深圳

Song dynasty 宋朝

Tian 天

Tianzi 天子

Tongbao tongpei 統包統配

Wan, shao, xi 晚，少，稀

Xian 縣

Xiang 鄉

Xiao 孝

Xiao Kang 小康

Xiao shehui 小社會

Yi 義

Yi cang 義倉

Yin yang 陰陽

Zhen 鎮

Zhou dynasty 周朝

Zhu De 朱德

Zou houmen 走後門

Zhongyang 中央

Zhuhai 珠海

Selected Bibliography

The bibliography includes major works related to social welfare in China. The list is divided into five sections: society and political economy; official government reports; social welfare (English publications); social welfare (Chinese publications); and periodicals and newspapers.

1. Society and Political Economy

Chen, X. W. 陳錫文. *China Rural Reforms: Retrospect and Prospect* 中國農村改革回顧與展望. Tianjin: Tianjin People's Publishers, 1993.

Croll, E. *From Heaven to Earth: Images and Experiences of Development in China*. London: Routledge, 1993.

Dassu, M. and Saich, T., eds. *The Reform Decade in China: from Hope to Dismay*. London: Kegan Paul International, 1990.

Deng, X. P. *Deng Xiaoping, Speeches and Writings*. Oxford: Pergamon Press, 1984.

Dernberger, R., De Woskin, K., Goldstein, S., Murphey, R., and Whyte, M., eds. *The Chinese: Adapting the Past, Building the Future*. Ann Arbor, Michigan: Center for Chinese Studies, The University of Michigan, 1986.

Ding, Z. Y., Wang, X. F., and Shang, X. C. 丁禎彥、王興富、商孝才. *Introduction to Socialism with Chinese Characteristics* 中國特色社會主義概論. Nanning: Guangxi Education Publishers, 1988.

Dittmer, L. *China under Reform*. Boulder, Col.: Westview Press, 1994.

Edwards, R., Henkin, L., and Nathan, A. *Human Rights in Contemporary China*. New York: Columbia University Press, 1986.

Fairbank, J. K. *China: A New History*. Cambridge, Mass.: Belknap Press of Harvard University Press, 1992.

Fairbank, J., and MacFarquhar, R., eds. *The Cambridge History of China*, vol. 4. Cambridge: Cambridge University Press, 1987.

Friedman, E. *Chinese Village, Socialist State*. New Haven: Yale University Press, 1991.

Gao, P. Y. 高珮義. *A Comparative Study on Urbanisation between China and Foreign Countries* 中外城市比較研究. Tianjin: Nankai University Press, 1992.

Goodman, D. and Segal, G. *China at Forty: Mid-Life Crisis*. Oxford: Clarendon Press, 1989.

Gu, Z. L. 顧朝林. *Chinese City and Town System: History, Situation, and Prospects* 中國城鎮體系：歷史、現狀、展望. Beijing: Commercial Publishers, 1992.

He, K. and Y. Z. Wang 何康、王有照, eds. *Ten Years of Rural Reform in China* 中國農村改革十年. Beijing: People's University Press, 1990.

Ho, P. T. *The Ladder of Success in Imperial China*. New York: Columbia University Press, 1962.

Ho, P. Y. *Li, Qi, and Shu: An Introduction to Science and Civilization in China*. Hong Kong: Hong Kong University Press, 1985.

Ji, M. 齊墨. *Neo-Authoritarianism* 新權威主義. Taipei: Tangshan Publishers, 1991.

Jiang, L., Lu, X. Y., and Shan, T. L. 江流、陸學藝、單天倫. *1993-1994 China: Social Situation Analysis and Forecast* 1993–1994 中國：社會形勢分析與預測. Beijing: China Social Science Publishers, 1994.

Kelliher, D. *Peasant Power in China: The Era of Rural Reform 1979–1989*. New Haven: Yale University Press, 1992.

King, A. 金耀基. *Chinese Society and Culture* 中國社會文化. Hong Kong: Oxford University Press, 1992.

Kwok, Y. W., Parish, W., and Yeh, A., eds. *Chinese Urban Reform*. Armonk, N.Y.: M. E. Sharpe, 1990.

Laaksonen, O. *Management in China During and After Mao in Enterprises, Government and Party*. New York: Walter de Gruyter, 1988.

Lichtenstein, P. *China at the Brink*. New York: Praeger, 1991.

Liu, P., Li, Q. H., and Xia, A. P. 劉鵬、李慶華、夏愛平. *The Economic Thought of Deng Xiaoping* 鄧小平社會主義經濟思想論. Beijing: CCP Central Party College Publishers, 1992.

Liang, S. M. 梁漱溟. *The Essence of Chinese Culture* 中國文化要義. Taipei: Zheng Zhong Press, 1974.

Lieberthal, K. and Oksenberg, M. *Policy Making in China, Leaders, Structures and Processes*. Princeton, N.J.: Princeton University Press, 1989.

Liu, A. *How China is Ruled*. Englewood Cliff:, N.J.: Prentice Hall, 1986.

Lodge, G. and Vogel, E., eds. *Ideology and National Competitiveness*. Boston, Mass.: Harvard Business School Press, 1987.

Ma, H. 馬洪, *China's Economic Situation and Prospects* 中國經濟形勢與展望. Beijing: China Development Publishers, 1990.

Moore, C., ed. *The Chinese Mind*. Honolulu: University of Hawaii Press, 1986.

Munro, D. *The Concept of Man in Early China*. Stanford, Cal.: Stanford University Press, 1969.

————. *The Concept of Man in Contemporary China*. Ann Arbor, Mich.: University of Michigan Press, 1977.

Nathan, A. *China's Crisis: Dilemmas of Reform and Prospects for Democracy*. New York: Columbia University Press, 1990.

Needham, J. *Science and Civilisation in China*. Cambridge: Cambridge University Press, 1954.

Ogden, S. *China's Unresolved Issues: Politics, Development, and Culture*. Englewood, Cliffs, N.J.: Prentice Hall, 1992.

Oi, J. *State and Peasant in Contemporary China: The Political Economy of Village Government*. Berkeley: University of California Press, 1989.

Parish, W., ed. *Chinese Rural Development: The Great Transformation*. Armonk, N.Y.: M. E. Sharpe, 1985.

Perkins, D. and S. Yusuf. Rural Development in China. Baltimore: John Hopkins University Press, 1984.

Pye, L. *The Dynamics of Chinese Politics*. Cambridge, Mass.: Oelgeschlager, Gunn and Hain Publishers, 1981.

————. *The Spirit of Chinese Politics*. Cambridge, Mass.: The MIT Press, 1992.

Riskin, C. *China's Political Economy*. Oxford: Oxford University Press, 1987.

Rosenbaum, A. L., ed. *State and Society in China: the Consequences of Reform*. Boulder: Westview Press, 1992.

Salisbury, H. E. *The New Emperors: China in the Era of Mao and Deng*. Boston: Little, Brown, 1992.

Schram, S. *The Thought of Mao Tse-tung*. Cambridge: Cambridge University Press, 1989.

Selden, M. *The Political Economy of Chinese Development.* Armonk, N.Y.: M. E. Sharpe, 1993.

Selden, M. and Lippit, V., eds. *The Transition to Socialism in China.* Armonk, N.Y.: M. E. Sharpe, 1982.

Solomon, R. H. *Mao's Revolution and the Chinese Political Culture.* Berkeley: University of California Press, 1971.

Spence, J. *To Change China.* Boston: Little, Brown and Co., 1969.

———. *The Search for Modern China.* New York: W. W. Norton and Company, 1990.

Starr, J. *Ideology and Culture: An Introduction to the Dialectic of Contemporary Chinese Politics.* New York: Harper and Row, 1973.

Su, Y. T. 蘇玉棠, ed. *Local Governmental Organisation Reform Research* 地方機構改革研究. Beijing: CCP Central Party College Publishers, 1992.

Thompson, L. G. *Chinese Religion: An introduction. Belmount, Cal.: Wadsworth Publishing Co., 1989.*

Vogel, E. *One Step Ahead in China.* Cambridge: Harvard University Press, 1989.

Walder, A. *Communist Neo-traditionalism: Work and Authority in Chinese Society.* Berkeley: University of California Press, 1986.

Wang, G. W. *The Chineseness of China.* Hong Kong: Oxford University Press, 1991.

Wang, J. *Contemporary Chinese Politics: An Introduction.* Englewood Cliffs, N.J.: Prentice Hall, 1992.

Wang, J. Y., and Hull, T. *Population and Development Planning in China.* Sydney: Allen and Unwin, 1991.

Whyte, M. K. *Small Groups and Political Rituals in China.* Berkeley, Cal.: University of California Press, 1974.

White, G., ed. *The Chinese State in the Era of Economic Reform: The Road to Crisis.* London: Macmillan, 1991.

———. *Riding the Tiger: the Politics of Economic Reform in Post-Mao China.* London: Macmillan, 1993.

World Bank. *China: Socialist Economic Development*, vol. 1. Washington, DC: World Bank, 1983.

Yuan, Y. X. 袁永熙. *China Population* 中國人口. Beijing: China Finance and Economics Publishers, 1991.

Yue, Q. P. 岳慶平. *The Structure of the State and the Chinese* 家國結構與中國人. Hong Kong: Chung Hwa Book Co. Ltd., 1989.

Zhou, G. F. and Dang, X. Q. 周光復，黨小青. *China Demographic Situation* 中國人口國情. Beijing: China Demographic Publishers, 1992.

2. Official Government Reports

China Labour Yearbook Editorial Committee 中國勞動年鑒編輯委員會. *China Labour Yearbook 1989–1991* 中國勞動年鑒. Beijing: China Labour Publishers, 1992.

China Statistical Information and Consultancy Service Centre. *China Report (1949–1989)*. Hong Kong: Influxfunds Co. Ltd. and Zie Yongder Co. Ltd., 1990.

Office of the State Organisational Structure Committee 國家機構編制委員會辦公室. *Organisation of the Chinese Government* 中國政府機構. Beijing: China Economics Publishers, 1990.

Ministry of Agriculture 農業部. *China Agricultural Statistical Material* 中國農業統計資料. Beijing: Agricultural Publishers, 1992.

The People's Publishers 人民出版社, ed. *Supplementary Readings on the 14th Party Congress Report* 十四大報告輔導讀本. Beijing: People's Publishers, 1992.

State Economic Systems Reform Committee 國家經濟體制改革委員會. *China Economic Systems Reform Yearbook* 中國經濟體制改革年鑒. Beijing: Reform Publishers, 1992.

State Statistical Bureau 國家統計局. *China Statistical Yearbook* 中國統計年鑒. Beijing: China Statistical Publishers, 1993.

————. *China Rural Areas Statistical Yearbook* 中國農業統計年鑒. Beijing: China Statistical Publishers, 1993, p. 207.

3. Social Welfare (English Publications)

Ahmad, E. and Hussain, A. "Social Security in China: A Historical Perspective". In *Social Security in Developing Countries*. Edited by E. Ahmad, J. Dreze, J. Hills and A. Sen. Oxford: Clarendon Press, 1990, pp. 247–304.

Ascher, I. *China's Social Policy*. London: Anglo-Chinese Educational Institute, 1972.

Bacon, M. H. "Social Work in China". *Social Work* 20.1 (January 1975): 68–69.

Chan, C. "Inequalities in the Provisions of Social and Occupational Welfare in Urban China". *Hong Kong Journal of Social Work*, XXIV (1990): 1–10.

————. *The Myth of Neighbourhood Mutual Help*. Hong Kong: Hong Kong University Press, 1993.

————. "Defending Women's Rights in the Socialist People's Republic of China: Services of the Guangzhou Women's Federation". *Social Development Issues* 16.1 (1994): 98–106.

————. and Chow, N. *More Welfare After Economic Reform? Welfare Development in the PRC*. Hong Kong: Centre of Urban Planning and Environmental Management, University of Hong Kong, 1993.

Chow, N. "Western and Chinese Ideas of Social Welfare". *International Social Work* 30 (1987): 31–41.

————. *The Administration and Financing of Social Security in China*. Hong Kong: Centre of Asian Studies, University of Hong Kong, 1988.

————. "Modernization and Social Security Reforms in China". *Asian Perspective* 13.2 (Fall-Winter 1989): 55–68.

————. "Does Filial Piety Exist Under Chinese Communism". *Journal of Aging and Social Policy* 3.1 (1991): 209–25.

————. *Social Security Reform in China: An Attempt to Build up a Socialist Social Security System with Chinese Characteristics*. Monograph Series, Social Welfare in China, No. 4. Hong Kong: Department of Social Work and Social Administration, University of Hong Kong, 1994.

Croll, E. *The Politics of Marriages in Contemporary China*. London: Cambridge University Press, 1981).

————. *Chinese Women Since Mao*. London: Zed Books, 1983.

————. *Women and Rural Development in China*. International Labour Office, 1985.

————. *China's One-child Family Policy*. London: Macmillian, 1985.

Davis, D. "Unequal Chances, Unequal Outcomes: Pension Reform and Urban Inequality". *The China Quarterly* 114 (June 1988): 223–43.

————. "Chinese Social Welfare: Policies and Outcomes". *The China Quarterly* 119 (September 1989): 577–97.

Davis, D., ed. *Chinese Families in the Post-Mao Era*. Berkeley: University of California Press, 1993.

Davis, D., and Vogel, E., eds. *Chinese Society on the Eve of Tiananmen*. Cambridge: Harvard University Press, 1990.

Davis-Friedmann, D. *Long Lives: Chinese Elderly and the Communist Revolution*. Stanford: Stanford University Press, 1991.

Dixon, J. *The Chinese Welfare System 1949–1979*. New York: Praeger Publishers, 1981.

Dixon, J., ed. "China". In *Social Welfare in Asia*. London: Croom Helm Ltd., 1985, pp. 21–65.

Epstein, I., *Juvenile Delinquency and Reformatory Education in Chinese Society*. Berkeley: University of California Press, 1984.

Honig, E. and Hershatter, G. *Personal Voices: Chinese Women in the 1980's*. Stanford, Cal.: Stanford University Press, 1988.

Hooper, B. "The Youth Problem: Deviations from the Socialist Road". In *China: Dilemmas of Modernisation*. Edited by G. Young. London: Croom Helm, 1985, pp. 189–236.

Horn, J. *Away with All Pests*. New York: Monthly Review Press, 1969.

Kallgren, J. *Strategies for Support of the Rural Elderly in China: A Research and Policy Agenda*, Seminar Series No. 3. Hong Kong: Institute of Asia-Pacific Studies, The Chinese University of Hong Kong, 1992.

Ko, E. L. "Mobilization of Community Energy in China — A Case Illustration: Wah Nam Sai Street". *Community Development Journal* 23.3 (July 1988): 170–75.

Kwong, P. and Cai, G. X. "Ageing in China: Trends, Problems and Strategies". In *Ageing in East and South-East Asia*. Edited by D. Phillips. London: Edward Arnold, 1992, pp. 105–27.

Leung, J. "The Community-based Welfare System in China". *Community Development Journal* 25.3 (July 1990): 196–205.

―――. "Social Welfare Provisions in Rural China: Mutual-help or Self-protection?" *Hong Kong Journal of Social Work* 24 (1991): 11–24.

―――. *Family Mediation with Chinese Characteristics: A Hybrid of Formal and Informal Service in China*, Monograph Series, Social Welfare in China No. 1. Hong Kong: Department of Social Work and Social Administration, University of Hong Kong, 1991.

―――. *The Transformation of Occupational Welfare in the PRC: From a Political Asset to an Economic Burden*, Monograph Series, Social Welfare in China No.

3. Hong Kong: Department of Social Work and Social Administration, University of Hong Kong, 1992.

——— . "Authoritarianism in Chinese Societies: Implications for Social Work", in *Conference on Social Work Education in Chinese Societies: Existing Patterns and Future Development*, edited by Asia and Pacific Association for Social Work Education. Asia and Pacific Association for Social Work Education, 1994, pp. 30–36.

——— . "Development of Social Work Education in China: Issues and Prospects". *Asia Pacific Journal of Social Work* 4.2 (July 1994): 83–95.

——— . "Dismantling the Iron Rice Bowl: Welfare Reforms in the PRC". *Journal of Social Policy* 23.3 (1994): 341–61.

Lin, T. Y. and Eisenberg, L., eds. *Mental Health for One Billion People*. Vancouver: University of British Columbia, 1985.

Liu, A. "Opinions and Attitudes of Youth in the PRC". *Asian Survey* 24.9 (1984): 975–95.

Ministry of Civil Affairs. *Civil Affairs Work in China*. Beijing: Ministry of Civil Affairs, 1986.

Mok, B. H. "In the Service of Socialism: Social Welfare in China". *Social Work* (July/August 1983): 269–72.

——— . "Grassroots Organising in China: The Residents' Committee as a Linking Mechanism". *Community Development Journal* 23.3 (July 1988): 164–69.

Nann, R. and Leung, J. *Introducing Social Work and Social Work Education in the PRC*. Hong Kong: Department of Social Work and Social Administration, University of Hong Kong, 1990.

Olsen, P. "A Model of Elderly Care in PRC". *International Aging and Human Development* 24.4 (1987): 279–300.

Parish, W. and Whyte, M. *Village and Family in Contemporary China*. Chicago: University of Chicago Press, 1978.

——— . *Urban Life in Contemporary China*. Chicago: University of Chicago Press, 1984.

Pearson, V. "Making a Virtue of Necessity: Hospital as Community Care for the Mentally Ill in China". *International Social Work* 32 (1989): 163–78.

——— . "The Community and Culture: A Chinese Model of Community Care of the Mentally Ill". *The International Journal of Social Psychiatry* 38.3 (1992): 163–78.

Pearson, V. and Leung, J., eds. *Welfare in China: A Collection of Vignettes 1986–1989*. Monograph Series, Social Welfare in China No. 2. Hong Kong: Department of Social Work and Social Administration, University of Hong Kong, 1992.

Pearson, V. and Phillips, M. "Psychiatric Social Work and Socialism: Problems and Potential in China". *Social Work* 39.3 (May 1994): 280–87.

Rosen, S. "Prosperity, Privatisation, and China's Youth". *Problems of Communism* (March/April 1985): 1–20.

———. "The Impact of Reform Policies on Youth Attitudes". In *Chinese Society on the Eve of Tiananmen*. Edited by D. Davis and Vogel, E. Cambridge, Mass.: Harvard University Press, 1990, pp. 283–305.

———. "Youth and Social Change in the PRC". In *Two Societies in Opposition: The Republic of China and the People's Republic of China After Forty Years*. Edited by R. Myers. Stanford, Cal.: Hoover Institution Press, 1991, pp. 288–315.

Sankar, A. "Gerontological Research in China: The Role of Anthropological Inquiry". *Journal of Cross-Cultural Gerontology* 4 (1989): 199–224.

Sher, A. E. *Aging in Post-Mao China*. Boulder, Col.: Westview Press, 1984.

Sidel, R. *Women and Child Care in China*. New York: Hill and Wong, 1972.

———. *Families of Fengsheng: Urban Life in China*. Hammondsworth, Middlesex: Penguin Books, 1974.

Sidel, V. and Sidel, R. *Serve the People*. New York: Josiah Macy Jr. Foundation, 1973.

Stacey, J. *Patriarchy and Socialist Revolution in China*. Berkeley: University of California Press, 1983.

Tracy, M. *Social Policies for the Elderly in the Third World*. New York: Greenwood Press, 1991.

Tseng, W. S., and Wu, D., eds. *Chinese Culture and Mental Health*. London: Academic Press, 1985.

Watson, A., ed. *Economic Reform and Social Change in China*. London: Routledge, 1992.

Whyte, M. "The Politics of Life Chances in the People's Republic of China". In *Power and Policy in the PRC*. Edited by Y. M. Shaw. Boulders, Col.: Westview Press, 1985, pp. 244–65.

————. "Social Trends in China: The Triumph of Inequality?" In *Modernizing China*. Edited by A. D. Barnett and Clough, R. Boulder, Col.: Westview, 1986, pp. 103–24.

————. *From Arranged Marriages to Love Matches in Urban China*, University Seminar Series No. 5. Hong Kong Institute of Asia-Pacific Studies, The Chinese University of Hong Kong, 1992.

Wolf, M. *Revolution Postponed: Women in Contemporary China*. Stanford: University of Stanford Press, 1985.

Zhu, C. H. *Community Service in Urban China: A Case Study of a Street Office in Guangzhou*. M.Soc.Sc. dissertation, University of Hong Kong, 1993.

Zhu, C. Y., and Xu, Q. "Family Care of the Elderly in China: Changes and Problems". In *Family Care of the Elderly, Social and Cultural Changes*. Edited by J. Kosberg. Newbury Park: Sage Publications, 1992, pp. 67–81.

4. Social Welfare (Chinese Publications)

All-China Committee on Elderly Problems 中國老齡問題全國委員會. *Collection of Academic Articles on Elderly Problems* 全國老年學術討論全文集. Beijing: Labour Personnel Publishers, 1987.

All-China Sampled Disabled People's Survey Office 全國殘疾人抽樣調查辦公室. *China Disabled People's Manual* 中國殘疾人手冊. Beijing: Earthquake Publishers, 1988.

The Asia Pacific Association for Social Work Education and Sociology Department of Peking University of China 亞洲及太平洋區社會工作教育工作協會, ed. *Status-quo, Challenge and Prospect — Collected Works of the Seminar of the Asia Pacific Association for Social Work Education* 現狀、挑戰、前景、亞太區社會工作教育研討會論文集. Beijing: Peking University Press, 1991.

The Asia and Pacific Association for Social Work Education 亞洲及太平洋、區社會工作教育工作協會, ed. *Proceedings of the Conference on Social Work Education in Chinese Societies: Existing Patterns and Future Development* 華人社會的社會工作教育：現況及發展會議論文集. Hong Kong: Asia and Pacific Association for Social Work Education, 1994.

Chen, L. J. 陳良瑾. *Social Security Curriculum* 社會保障課程. Beijing: Knowledge Publishers, 1990.

China People's Broadcasting Station, Theory Department 中國人民廣播電台理論部. *Reform and Improve the Social Security System of the Country* 改革及完善我國的社會保障制度. Beijing: Economic Publishers, 1988.

Contemporary China Workers' Wage, Welfare and Social Insurance Editorial Committee 當代中國的職工工資、福利和社會保險編輯委員會. *Contemporary China's Wage and Social Insurance* 當代中國的職工工資、福利和社會保險. Beijing: China Social Science Publishers, 1987.

Cui, N. F. 崔乃夫, *Explorations in the Work of Civil Affairs* 民政工作的探索. Beijing: People's Press, 1988.

Deng, Y. T. 鄧雲特. *History of Disaster Relief in China* 中國救荒史. Beijing: Commercial Publishers, 1993.

Hong Kong Council of Social Service 香港社會服務聯會. *Proceedings of the Conference Into the Nineties, Social Welfare Development in the Mainland and Hong Kong* 中國內地及香港邁進九十年代社會福利發展研討會. Hong Kong: Hong Kong Council of Social Service, 1991.

Gong, J. L., Wu, S., and Li, Q. 龔建禮，吳思，李琪. *Textbook on Labour Laws* 勞動法教程. Beijing: Beijing Institute of Economics Publishers, 1989.

Jin, S. Q. 金雙秋. *China Civil Affairs History* 中國民政史. Changsha: Hunan University Publishers, 1989.

Liu, Q. 劉岐. *Contemporary China Housing Economy* 當代中國住宅經濟. Beijing: China Construction and Industrial Publishers, 1992.

Liu, Y. G. and Su, Y. M. 廖益光、蘇佑明. *Introduction to Civil Affairs* 民政工作概論. Changsha: Hunan University Publishers, 1987.

Li, W. H. and Zhou, Y. 李文海，周源. *Disasters and Famines 1840–1819* 災荒與飢饉 1840–1819. Beijing: Higher Educational Publishers, 1991.

Lu, M. H. 盧謀華. *Introduction to Civil Affairs* 民政概論. Beijing: Civil Affairs Cadre Administration College, 1984.

———. *China Social Work* 中國社會工作. Beijing: China Society Publishers, 1990.

Ma, J. 馬結. *Introduction to the Work of Education and Assistance* 幫教工作導論. Tianjin: Mass Publishers, 1986.

Meng, Z. H. and Wang, M. H. 孟照華，王明寰. *History of Chinese Civil Affairs* 中國民政史稿. Harbin: Heilongjiang Publishers, 1986.

Ministry of Civil Affairs 民政部, ed. *To Improve the Work of the Residents' Committees in the New Era* 做好新時期的居民委員會工作. Beijing: Legal Publishers, 1987.

———. *Explorations on Rural Social Security* 農村社會保障探索. Wuhan: Wuhan University Press, 1987.

Ministry of Labour and Personnel 勞動人事部. *Unemployment Insurance Manual* 待業保險工作手冊. Beijing: Labour and Personnel Publishers, 1988.

Tao, C. F. and Zhang, R. P. 陶春芳，蔣永萍. *A Review of the Women's Social Status in China* 中國婦女社會地位概觀. Beijing: China Women Publishers, 1993.

Tian, X. Y. 田雪原. *China Elderly Population and Society* 中國老年人口與社會. Beijing: China Economic Publishers, 1991.

———. *China Elderly Population* 中國老年人口. Beijing: China Economics Publishers, 1991.

Wang, G. Y. and Zhao, L. F. 王剛義，趙林峰. *Research on Community Service in China* 中國社區服務研究. Changchun: Jinin University Press, 1990.

Wang, M. K. 王夢奎. *China's Social Security System Reform* 中國社會保險制度改革. Beijing: Social Science Publishers, 1992.

World Bank, Asian Division 世界銀行，亞洲司，中國部. *Social Security Reforms in Chinese Socialist Economy* 中國社會主義經濟中的社會保障制度改革 (16 October 1989).

Yin, B. W., Xu, W. H., and Cao, H. C. 尹伯威，徐文虎，曹恒春. *China Social Insurance System Reform* 中國社會保險制度改革. Shanghai: Fudan University Publishers, 1992.

Yuan, S. Q. 袁守啓. *Comparing the System of Labour, Wages, and Social Insurance between China and Foreign Countries* 中國與外國勞動工資社會保險制度比較. Beijing: China Broadcasting and Television Publishers, 1992.

Yuan, H. Y. and Wang, Q. S. 袁華音，王青山. *Introduction to Social Work* 社會工作概論. Jinan: Huanghe Publishers, 1990.

Yuan, J. H. and Zhang, Z. H. 袁緝輝，張鐘洪. *The Challenge to the Trend of Increasing Number of Elderly* 老齡化對中國的挑戰. Shanghai: Fudan University Press, 1991.

Yun, P. and Wang, W. H. 雲鵬，王文華. *China Finance, Wage, Insurance and Welfare Encyclopedia* 中國財稅工資保險福利大全. Shenyang: Liaoning People's Publishers, 1991.

Zhang, S., and Gu, Z. 章俗，谷超. *History of Chinese Civil Affairs* 中國民政史話. Harbin: Heilongjiang Educational Publishers, 1992.

Zhu, Y., and J. Tang 朱勇，唐鈞, eds. *Model Selection in Retirement Insurance in Rural Areas in China* 中國農村社會養老模式選擇. Nanning: Guangxi People's Publishers, 1991.

Zi, M. 梓木. *Regulations on the Organisation of Urban Residents' Committees in*

China 中華人民共和國城市居民委員會組織法講話. Beijing: China Democratic Legal Publishers, 1990.

5. Periodicals and Newspapers

Agricultural Economic Research 農業經濟研究 (北京)

Beijing Review (Beijing)

China Civil Affairs 中國民政 (北京)

China Daily (Beijing)

China Demographic Science 中國人口科學 (北京)

China Labour News 中國勞動報 (北京)

China Labour Science 中國勞動科學 (北京)

China Manpower Resource and Development 中國人力資源開發 (北京)

The China Quarterly (London)

China Situation and Capacity 中國國情國力 (北京)

China Social Science 中國社會科學 (北京)

China Society 中國社會 (北京)

China Statistical Information News 中國統計信息報 (北京)

City Problem 城市問題 (北京)

Economic Daily 經濟日報 (北京)

Economic Problems 經濟問題 (太原)

Economic Science 經濟科學 (北京)

Far Eastern Economic Review (Hong Kong)

Gansu Journal of Theory 甘肅理論學刊 (蘭州)

Guangming ribao 光明日報 (北京)

Guangdong Civil Affairs 廣東民政 (廣州)

Hong Kong Economic Journal 信報 (香港)

Hong Kong Journal of Social Work (Hong Kong)

Jiang Hai Academic Journal 江海學報 (南京)

Journal of Beijing University 北京大學學刊 (北京)

Journal of China Labour Movement Institute 中國工運學院學報 (上海)

Journal of Huadong Teachers' College 華東師範大學學報 (上海)

Management World 管理世界 (北京)

Ming Pao 明報 (香港)

Ming Pao Monthly 明報月刊 (香港)

Outlook Weekly 瞭望 (北京)

People's Daily 人民日報 (北京)

Population and Economics 人口與經濟 (北京)

Reform 改革縱橫 (武漢)

Social Science 社會科學 (上海)

Social Security Bulletin 社會保障報 (北京)

Social Work Research 社會工作調查 (北京)

Social Work Studies 社會工作 (北京)

Society 社會 (上海)

Sociology and Social Research 社會學與社會調查 (北京)

Sociological Studies 社會學研究 (北京)

South China Morning Post (Hong Kong)

Youth Exploration 青年探索 (廣州)

Index